MW00754818

SAVAGE FEAST

ALSO BY BORIS FISHMAN

Don't Let My Baby Do Rodeo

A Replacement Life

To Joyce—
With so much thanks
for sharing in such a
lovely evening

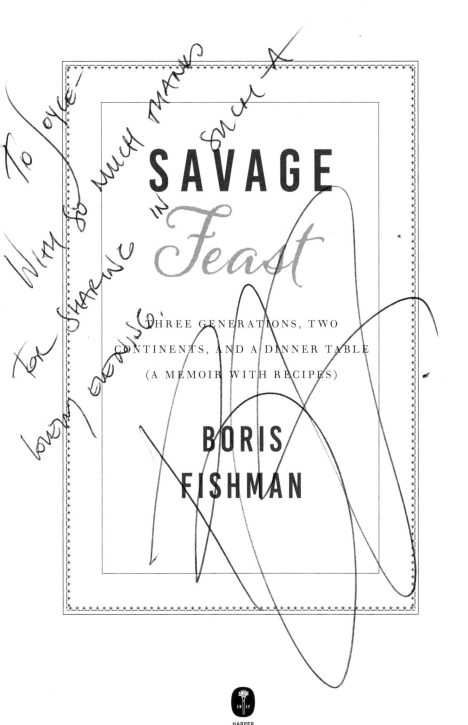

SAVAGE
Feast

THREE GENERATIONS, TWO
CONTINENTS, AND A DINNER TABLE
(A MEMOIR WITH RECIPES)

BORIS
FISHMAN

HARPER
An Imprint of HarperCollins*Publishers*

HarperCollins books may be purchased for educational, business, or sales promotional use. For information, please email the Special Markets Department at SPsales@harpercollins.com.

FIRST EDITION

Designed by Fritz Metsch

Library of Congress Cataloging-in-Publication Data has been applied for.

ISBN 978-0-06-286789-6

19 20 21 22 23   LSC   10 9 8 7 6 5 4 3 2 1

To Jessica Cole, who helps me translate

From time to time, [the Americans] are invaded by foreigners of questionable antecedents who, eager to do anything but honest work, capitalize on American naïveté by writing about the food and drink that, in another clime, sustained their useless lives.

—ANGELO PELLEGRINI,
The Unprejudiced Palate

The average American enjoys inexhaustible abundance. Nevertheless, he complains. . . . He is right, of course, in his efforts continuously to improve his circumstances. . . . [But] if he is willing to learn how to live well on what is immediately available to him, his best bet is to look to the immigrant for advice.

—ANGELO PELLEGRINI,
The Unprejudiced Palate

CONTENTS

SAVAGE FEAST

2008

I can argue my mother out of almost anything. Except the several days on the calendar when she needs everyone in the family at the same table. *Our family is so small*—World War II, the Holocaust, the Soviet Union. On Passover, Rosh Hashanah, birthdays, anniversaries, and Thanksgiving, we have to please come together.

We always meet at my grandfather's apartment in Brooklyn. "I don't want to ruin your weekend," the altruist says when we ask whether he might come to my parents' home in New Jersey instead. Imagine if he had an attack of some kind—my parents' joy-encrusted life would come to a halt and they'd have to take him to the local hospital (as opposed to an attack in Brooklyn, where reaching him would take two hours). My grandfather can't say that suburban New Jersey—with its deadly, arcadian quiet; where he can do nothing more than read the newspaper, rest, and talk with his family; where he wanders the too many rooms like an unoccupied child—is insipid. That would offend. And going to New Jersey would allow time for more subjects than concern him about his progeny. "I get up with you, and I go to bed with you," he likes to say, meaning we never leave his thoughts. And that is where he likes to keep us.

He really believes he'll have an attack. He awaits illness like an informant who knows the assassin will eventually come. So he pursues it instead—almost romantically. Many of the ex-Soviet boys and girls who came to America when I did (age nine) are now doctors; many of them have offices in south Brooklyn, where he lives; many have my grandfather as their fattest file. He frequents multiple neurologists to compare their diagnoses, and takes the pills each prescribes—just in case—creating complications and requiring the intervention of ever more doctors. His blood-pressure-measuring device is an appendage of his arm. When I walk into his apartment, he extends this bionic limb and its readout—101 over 54, a little low but not terrible, even a little athletic—by way of greeting. He can't very well leave all this for a weekend in New Jersey. More than twenty years after my parents moved there from south Brooklyn—"I didn't come to America to keep living among Russians," my father had said—my grandfather still doesn't understand why his daughter and her husband don't live near enough to be summoned easily every time he feels aches in his toe, his upper back, his you-know-where.

So we funnel toward him, my parents from the west—down the New Jersey Turnpike, across Staten Island—and I from the north, the F line across the East River and a dogleg toward the ocean. For me, leaving one place for another, even a trip as brief as Manhattan's Lower East Side to Midwood, his neighborhood in south Brooklyn, strikes some new well of anticipation. Not least because by the time the subway car rises aboveground at Ditmas Avenue, forty-five minutes after I've left Manhattan, there's almost no one left on it who hasn't at some point in their lives—maybe that very morning—had beef tongue for breakfast. Uzbeks and Georgians and Moldovans and Ukrainians and Belarusians and Russians, bonded only by the language and culture of their former overlords, a little ex-Soviet Andorra inside the Pyrenees of New York.

It's been like this since we got to the States. To take the backseat of my parents' Oldsmobile for the drive from New Jersey to Brooklyn (the Lincoln Tunnel, the river heavy above; the Brooklyn Bridge, the other river sparkling beneath) in our first years in America, in the 1990s, was to open up possibilities. On the other side, finally, things would be purposeful and true, my uncertainty alchemized into understanding. Like starting a fresh notebook. And flying somewhere was rare and momentous enough to dress in your best.

The nearest subway stop to my grandfather's lets out onto the nail salon/car service/body shop sequence without which no south Brooklyn block is complete. And temptation: an Ecuadorian luncheonette belching out clouds of roast pork, garlic, and goat stew; a Georgian place where they're frying *chebureki*; the Uzbek lamb emporium—on spits, buried in dumplings, braised in soup. I ate before leaving. Nothing in life—and mine is a disciplined, even self-denying life—feels less bearable than even a faint whisper of hunger. You really do have to be a Persephone to withstand the blandishments of Hades's kitchen, meant to seduce her into staying underground. And even she succumbed. In any case, the culinary ambush by the subway makes me hungry all over again. But I have to close my eyes and stride past—a table awaits at my grandfather's.

It didn't go well last time I visited. It hasn't gone well for years. My parents ask what I am going to do if writing doesn't work out. My grandfather asks what my friends make. My mother mentions— just FYI—that Alana, my American girlfriend, took a full twenty- four hours to return her call the previous week. Seeing no fish at the end of her hardworking line—I've learned how to deflect—she asks how things are going between us. *This* bait I can never resist, and fit my cheek onto her hook. Things are not well with me and Alana. I certainly want to discuss it with someone, and no one in- quires with my mother's curiosity and attention. All I have to do is start talking.

It rarely takes long for me to regret it. Her responses suggest so little comprehension that I wonder whether she pretends not to get what I'm saying so the conversation has to keep going. I try to cut it off—hard to do, because by now my father and grandfather are contributing their insights. I ask quietly to change the subject several times, but by the fourth or fifth request I'm screaming. Screaming! Only then does the table grind to a rueful silence. Heads shake, eyes stare into plates, pinkies move crumbs around. I'm so ill-tempered, someone says, looking away. So short with people who only want to help. Was I not the one who asked for help in the first place?

But as I walk toward my grandfather's apartment, I'm looking forward to seeing these people. Because I've spent my years in America trying to cut so much of them out of myself—their cynicism; their aversion to risk; their faith in force as the proper solution; their terror of not being near each other at all times; their dread, always scanning for reasons to fear one thing or another, like a guard-tower searchlight—we are foreigners with each other. (They've spent these years taking advantage of the great American privilege of getting to stay exactly as they are—people I love voluntarily reenacting, as "free people," the things about their former homeland that made their lives, as Jews and as Soviet citizens, so miserable.) My dialysis hasn't always succeeded. Partly because, to be a good son, I've tried to somehow take advantage of everything America has to offer without changing as a person, as is their wish. But also because I lived in their country not until nine, when we left the USSR, but twenty-four, when I moved out. Beyond then, too. It's not something you can cut out simply by moving the body.

But in other ways, I have broken away so hard that my parents sometimes feel to me the way an American person's grandparents must feel; I've swallowed two generations in the time a native python eats one. But lately it feels like the indigestion isn't temporary; there are parts of America that won't go down. The dominion of money; the Anglo-Saxon handling of human relations; the suspicion toward smart people; the indifference toward art. My family does not mind the dominion of money—that's why they came here. The distrust instilled in them by the Soviet Union has made it fairly easy to transition to the Anglo-Saxon way of relating as well. It would upset them to learn that many Americans resent intellectuals, and that most of the country couldn't care less about novels—these things were sacrosanct in the Soviet Union—but they're saved by the iron lung in which they live; they don't know this is the case. But when I walk into my grandfather's apartment, I feel at home with these people in a way I can't manage to in almost any American home. Even with my American girlfriend. That's the issue between me and her—we can't overcome the cultural rift. We can't succeed because I am too much like my parents. It's a sad irony of these family encounters that for some diabolical reason they end up being dominated not by this fact, but by our divisions, misunderstandings, and resentment.

But—and this is another reason I'm looking forward to seeing them all—the rancor that follows every argument dissipates within minutes. No one in this family can hold on to a grudge. To no one is the dark pleasure of being wronged worth more than connection and love. Perhaps it's more that no pride can compete with the terror of a dissolved family bond.

When I get in, my mother will hang off my neck, my father will kiss my cheek, and my grandfather will slap me high five in a playful bit of Americana that—other than his ability to sign his name in English and the dozen words he's learned to bargain with the Chinese fishmonger—is the only English he knows after twenty years. Then my grandfather will show me his blood-pressure readout, my father will make a crack about my grandfather's hypochondria, my grandfather will flare his nostrils—their shtick—and my mother will throw her hands at the ceiling in an umpteenth plea to turn down the roaring television. Home. Then she will vanish into the galley kitchen to help Oksana, my grandfather's home aide, finish the cooking that's sending out such a narcotic aroma all the way into the stairwell.

That aroma is as much the reason why I am striding down Avenue P with such anticipation. Oksana, who appeared in our lives just as our previous kitchen magician, my grandmother, left them, is an extraordinary cook, her food so ambrosially satisfying to some elemental receptor that I might as well be a reptile when I sit down at her table. My tongue has shot out and immured half the things on it before the others have drunk the first toast. (Not that they're eating less slowly.) And this is only the appetizers.

I'm semiconscious as I shove rabbit braised in sour cream into my mouth before the sheaf of peppers marinated in honey and garlic I just put there has gone down. I'm vaguely aware of what's happening. From another part of my brain, I hear the faint call: *Slow down. You will feel ill. You will hate yourself.* I can make myself work at my writing for many more hours than I want to. I can make myself rise when all I want is to lie on the floor. I can make myself charm almost anyone, especially if it means they can give me something I want. But I can't make myself stop eating so quickly. I can't make myself stop eating even though I am full. It's too good. And I am too hungry.

When it's over, I feel ill. I hate myself. Like a self-loathing addict, I swear—*swear*—that next time will be different. In truth, this ill humor is as responsible for the argument about to occur as anything my parents or grandfather will ask. Regret mixed with disappointment, self-pity, and sadness: The meal is over. Suddenly, none of the comfort and recognition I had been looking forward to feeling feels possible. I drag myself through as much of the afternoon as I can, then beg off to begin the long, bloated journey home. It offers none of the hope of the original trip. Food conceals the emptiness between us—and between us and the world around us—but, once gone, doubles it.

Oksana's spectacular skill isn't the only reason I can't control myself at the table. We have been hungry for as long as we have existed. My grandmother lived on potato peels as she wandered the Belarus swamps with anti-Nazi guerrillas during World War II. When she saw her first loaf of bread after returning to Minsk, our native city—black rye, a small loaf because flour was scarce—she tore at it like an animal. The woman who was with her rushed to restrain her, but it was too late—she vomited everything onto the floor. Her first postwar job was at a bread factory—she wanted to be near bread all the time. When I was a boy, her favorite meal was a finger-thick slice of the white loaf, spun into a meringue-like swirl at its top, we called *polenitsa* *(paw-leh-NEETS-ah)*, another finger of butter spread on it; the apple we called Bely Naliv (White Transparent—the pink-veined white interior was almost translucent, and sharp with a tart sweetness); and instant coffee with too much boiled milk.

She married a man skilled at navigating the black market—Soviet scarcity took over where wartime scarcity let up—so that her table always "groaned" with food, and the house always had four or five loaves of bread, which (instead of being reused for stuffing or bread crumbs, as by many Soviet housewives) went into the trash as soon as it lost its "first freshness." Then my grandfather was dispatched to the bread store to test the loaves with the little spoon hanging from the wall. The price of bread had not changed in thirty years: fourteen cents for a loaf of Borodinsky. My grandfather wasn't for spoons, nor the in-house granny who milled by the loaves in order to press, punch, handle, and weigh them on your behalf; he hand-tested, and on his own. Once, a saleswoman shouted at him to "quit pawing the bread with your grubby Jewish fingers," loudly enough for the whole store. He turned, the loaf like a grenade in his hands, and said, also loudly enough, "I would stick this up your _____, you sour _____, but the line for it is too long." Then he flung the loaf across the counter. But not at the saleswoman; my grandfather had manners.

My grandmother wouldn't allow my mother to stop eating. And she stared at my mouth, following its movements, as I chewed what she made. She could go weeks without speaking to my mother over one thing or another, but I was without sin. Unless, that is, I wished to leave on the plate my fourth caviar sandwich or a corner of the seared slab of pork belly in its corona of garlicky mashed potatoes. "But why?" she would ask, her lovely face filling with anguish.

So I pressed on. But sometimes, with the pre-conscious wisdom, or freedom, of a child, I would feel that all this was bad rather than good, and find a way out. Once, when she left the kitchen, I tiptoed to the window and scooped my oatmeal out onto the bushes below. Another time, I lifted the seat of my stool (for some reason, our early-eighties Soviet footstools had compartments under the seats), and forked in the rest of my eggs. I slammed the seat shut and was dragging my fork across my empty plate when she returned.

But it wasn't enough. In my grandmother's Soviet kitchen, I felt so at home that I could try, now and then, to push away some of what she wanted to give me. By the time I was an adult in New York, I'd been trying to disown her hunger for years. But in this new home, I felt so not at home that my—her—Russian habits wouldn't let go of me. I couldn't figure out how to let go of them.

I'm dark-complexioned enough that people in first class—since 9/11, anyway—always look a second too long. I used to make myself shave before flights, but even if my ancestral darkness wasn't bristling from my jaw, I would try, as I walked the aisle, to drop from my eyes the look of sullen intensity that was my default in New York. I wouldn't go so far as to smile solicitously—that seemed like the kind of deflection a true foreign ill-doer would resort to. I would keep my eyes on the lumbering flier before me—just another passenger, patiently enduring.

Then I would walk the gantlet of economy, now up to six staring faces per row. (I fantasized about first class for different reasons than legroom—fewer seats to reassure.) Most people want a higher-up row to get out of the airplane sooner; I did so I had fewer rows to placate. In the Soviet Union, my parents and grandparents had managed this complex matter of what others would think. In America, my elders constrained by their accents and fear, the job became mine: I stood to gain the most from the things Americans had power to give me, or not take away.

When I reached my seat, though, my attempts at passing had to come to an end. Out came the large Ziploc with the tinfoil bundles, big as bombs. The length of the flight didn't matter. A flying day meant not knowing when the next good meal would arrive, and that meant a large pack of tinfoil bundles. I was mortified to reveal myself as the foreigner after all, but that foreigner would not allow me to pay more to eat less well at the airport concessions. Or up in the air: nine dollars for the Beef Up, or Perk Up, or Pump Up boxes, with their baffling combinations of the wholesome and processed, which reminded me of Russian people who consummated gluttonous meals with fruit because, look, they were health-conscious eaters.

No, I brought my own food. I brought pieces of lightly fried whiting. Chicken schnitzels in an egg batter. Tomatoes, which I ate like apples. Fried cauliflower. Pickled garlic. Marinated peppers, though these could be leaky. Sliced lox. Salami. If plain old sandwiches, then with spiced kebabs where your turkey would be. Soft fruit bruises easily, but what better inter-meal snacks than peaches and plums? (You needed inter-meal snacks, just in case.)

It wasn't only the money. A dime would have been too dear for the thing my seatmate was holding. How did Sbarro manage to make her pizza, black suns of pepperoni moated by a permafrost of white cheese, so smell-free? That arid iceberg, asiago, and turkey salad, watered by a cry-worthy ejaculation of chemical balsamic— its scentlessness I could understand. But pizza? That obese crust, made well, could have made the entire plane groan with longing.

One of the few things that seem to make Americans even more uncomfortable than being very close to each other for six hours in cramped quarters is when the next person over keeps pulling tinfoil bundles smelling sharply of garlic out of his rucksack. (I was kicked out of a bed once for radiating too much garlic under the covers. It was my father's fault, I tried to explain—in America he had converted to saltless cooking, and now garlic was his one-to-one substitute; I had just had dinner with my parents. "Down-stairs," she commanded.) With the extra peripheral vision that is a kind of evolutionary adaptation for refugees, persecuted people, and immigrants, I would sense, on the plane, sideways glances of savage, disturbed curiosity. Sometimes I swiveled and committed the unpardonable sin of gazing directly at my neighbor, whereupon her eyes broadened, her forehead rose, and the rictus of a stunned smile overtook her agony.

Sometimes we ate raw onions like apples, too, I wanted to tell her. Sometimes, the tinfoil held shredded chicken petrified in aspic. A fish head to suck on! I was filled with shame and hateful glee: everything I was feeling turned out at the person next to me.

I was the one with an uncut cow's tongue uncoiling in the re-frigerator of his undergraduate quad, my roommates' Gatorades and half-finished pad Thai keeping a nervous distance. I sliced it thinly, and down it went with horseradish and cold vodka like the worry of a long day sloughing off, those little dots of fat between the cold meat like garlic roasted to paste.

I am the one who fried liver. Who brought his own lunch in an old Tupperware to his cubicle in the Condé Nast Building; who accidentally warmed it too long, and now the scent of buckwheat, stewed chicken, and carrots hung like radiation over the floor, few of whose inhabitants brought lunch from home, fewer of whom were careless enough to heat it for too long if they did, and none of whom brought a scent bomb in the first place. Fifteen floors below, the storks who staffed the fashion magazines grazed on greens in the Frank Gehry cafeteria.

I was the one who ate mashed potatoes and frankfurters for

breakfast. Who ate a sandwich for breakfast. Strange? But Americans ate cereal for dinner. Americans ate *cereal*, period, that oddment. They had a whole thing called "breakfast for dinner." And the only reason they were right and I was wrong was that it was their country.

The problem with my desire to pass for native was that everything in the tinfoil was so fucking good. When the world thinks of Soviet food, it thinks of all the wrong things. Though it was due to incompetence rather than ideology, we were local, seasonal, and organic long before Chez Panisse opened its doors. You just had to have it in a home instead of a restaurant, like British cooking after the war, as Orwell wrote. For me, the food also had cooked into it the memory of my grandmother's famine; my grandfather's black-marketeering to get us the "deficit" goods that, in his view, we deserved no less than the political VIPs; all the family arguments that paused while we filled our mouths and our eyes rolled back in our heads. Food was so valuable that it was a kind of currency—and it was how you showed love. If, as a person on the cusp of thirty, I wished to find sanity, I had to figure out how to temper this hunger without losing hold of what fed it, how to retain a connection to my past without being consumed by its poison.

There's nothing surprising about the idea that trauma—the aftereffects of being dehumanized and slaughtered, of lives made of terror even in peacetime—travels from one generation to another, not least because, if undealt with, it mutates, so that you grapple with not only your grandmother's torment but what that torment did to your mother. All the same, it rattles you to learn, after devouring your own food year after year—a free country, sunlight outside, friends waiting, homework done—about the way your grandmother fell upon her first loaf all those years ago, *like an animal*. Nothing's changed. Not even the way her proxies, themselves once victims of her pushing, push food at you even after you manage to summon,

from somewhere, a modicum of brief self-control at the table on
Avenue P. You scorn them for not managing to let go of three and
six decades of grim lessons from *that* place, but have you managed
much more despite leaving as a child? At least you're trying.

In Chekhov's letters—he was alone among the nineteenth-
century Russian literary greats in having been born into the peasant class, with its servility and self-abnegation (his grandfather was
a serf, Russia's version of the feudally bonded)—you read: To be
a writer, "you need . . . *a sense of personal freedom*. . . . Try writing a story about how a young man, the son of a serf . . . brought
up venerating rank, kissing the hands of priests, worshiping the
ideas of others, thankful for every crust of bread . . . hypocritical
toward God and man with no cause beyond an awareness of his
own insignificance—write about how this young man squeezes the
slave out of himself drop by drop." You have to admit that you don't
know how to write that story.

He wrote the letter at twenty-nine—your age in 2008 as you
cross West Ninth Street and your grandfather's apartment building finally appears before you, the ornamental patterning of its
straw-colored brick giving way to the usual south Brooklyn vestibule of cracked mirrors and peeling paint in almost-matched colors. You know what's upstairs: polenta with sheep's milk feta and
wild mushrooms, pickled watermelon, eggplant "caviar," rib tips
with pickled cabbage, sorrel borshch, Oksana's wafer torte with
condensed milk and rum extract.

Once again, you have sworn to yourself: You will go slowly. You
will eat half—no, a quarter!—of what's shoved before you. You will
leave feeling chaste, clean, ascetic, reduced. There is perhaps as little reason to count on this as there has been for the past hundred
visits. As little reason as to hope that *this* will be the day when
your conversation with your family will finally end in understanding instead of the opposite. Hope dies last, though. Was it not also
Chekhov who wrote "The Siren," a seven-page ode to food in the

Russian mouth—"Good Lord! and what about duck? If you take a duckling, one that has had a taste of the ice during the first frost, and roast it, and be sure to put the potatoes, cut small, of course, in the dripping-pan too, so that they get browned to a turn and soaked with duck fat and . . ."

You come from a people who eat.

PART I

CHAPTER 1

1988

What to cook in a Nazi cast-iron pot in a furnace in Minsk after the war

What to cook to get your not-even-son-in-law the grade that he needs

What to cook when meeting your son's wealthy girlfriend

✢

The door of the sleeper sailed open, breaking the *tu-tum-tu-tum* of the wheels on the track, the medical blue of the overhead light panels dispelling the secretive blue of night on a train. Two uniformed men filled the doorway. My grandmother—the next compartment held my mother, father, and grandfather—lowered her swollen legs to the floor. In her sleeveless nightgown and the pink net in which she preserved her hairstyle at night, she looked too intimate next to the uniformed men. "*Dokumenty*," they said, the word just like the Russian.

If you want a shortcut to the Eastern European experience, you must have yourself woken from the sarcophagus of a sleeper's ceiling berth by border guards in the night. You must have every light lit. You must be spoken to in a language you understand slightly, or not at all, depending on the kind of estrangement you want. Trains: To a European person, an Eastern European person, a Jewish Eastern European person, they call up cattle cars and extinction as readily as a megaphone in a pickup summons revolution to a Latin American. Emigration, evacuation, extermination, exile—in Russia, a train has carried the quarry. The platform, the engine's weary exhalation, a whistle's hoot and blare, "the grey wet quay, over a wilderness of rails and points, round the corners of abandoned trucks," as Graham Greene put it—if we are to speak of the things that divide the Russian mind from the American, we could begin here.

One of the guards peered at the identity cards. My grand-mother winked at me: *Everything will be fine.* I didn't know what to think—I hadn't been told where we were going, though all the tears on the farewell platform didn't bode well. I was nine, too young for my own card, so I shared the photo on my mother's. The guard brought the card to my grandmother's face, the edge nearly grazing her cheek. What his doing that reminded her of, I couldn't imagine.

"*Kde matka?*" the guard said. The first word was like the Russian—*gde*: "where"—but the second was a coarse variant of our "mother." At home, we used only "mama"—its stiffening into the Czech *matka* somehow enclosed all the badness of the preced-ing twenty-four hours: my mother weeping on the train track in Minsk; the drunks slouching up and down the platform in Warsaw; being on this train instead of in third grade, which had started ten days before; the gold necklace concealed under my shirt; the emp-tying out of our apartment.

I started crying: quiet, polite tears, a good boy. My grandmother moved next to me and took my hair in her hand, the skin doughy and flimsy at once. Only then did she point the guards next door. They left, keeping the card. We heard the next compartment slam open, the muffled sound of familiar voices. Rummaging in her purse, my grandmother brought out a soft caramel candy and nod-ded to say it was okay, though it was night. I uncrisped the waxed wrapper and laid it on my tongue, waiting for it to melt a little before chewing. We rocked a little with the train, which hurtled through the night without concern for our trouble. After a while, the voices receded. My father appeared in the doorway, his eyes small and sleepy. "It's okay," he said. "The identity card has to stay with the mother."

Everyone was too shaken to go back to sleep. The illicit hour, the close call, the candy—I was filled with a sense of adventure. My grandmother boiled water for tea. The five of us, two adults per berth and me on my grandmother's knees, drank it from West German tea cups, cobalt with gold trim, that she and my mother had babied into our luggage. They were among the things we were told might sell well in Vienna and Rome, our transit points en route to America, but until then they were ours, and we sucked at their hot rims through the caramels on our tongues.

We'd never touched the West German teacups at home. Never sucked on candy with tea at four in the morning. Never encountered men in uniform on the other side of the door and come out of it fine. My elders had been spurred out of the fixity of their lives—what life was more fixed than an ordinary person's in Soviet Minsk?—by two forces greater than the stability they'd painstakingly built up despite being Jews: my arrival in their lives, and the unlocking of the Soviet border. So, in the train, their dread mixed with giddiness, the compartment shaking with laughter as my grandfather made lewd comments about the guards and my grandmother hissed reprimands at him because *I was right there.*

When the tea was done, glances were exchanged. The glances said: Did our celebration have to end so quickly? Were we not something like free people? In the skewering, overly intimate tone my father sometimes used with his parents-in-law—to defuse the tension that had always existed between them, to pretend they were on better terms than they were, to poke fun at the way my grandmother's iron hand always saved the best for the child—he pointed at the oilcloth bag with the food and said, "Will the store put something out on the shelves?" My grandmother stared at him with heavy eyes. Now they were really bound to each other forever. She followed his gaze to the window. If you squinted, you could make out an indigo stripe blurring all the black at the far edge of the horizon. So call it breakfast.

Out came rolls of salt-cured salami, a basket of hard-boiled eggs, a block of hard cheese, towel-wrapped cucumbers, tins of sprats, sardines, cod liver, and salmon. And a loaf of dark sourdough Borodinsky rye, sweetened with molasses, made with coriander seeds, finished with caraway. Borodinsky was our national bread—and we had eight hundred breads. The widow of a Russian general who had perished at the Battle of Borodino in 1812, the story went, had set up a convent whose nuns invented Borodinsky as a mourning bread, hence the dark, slightly charred top and the coriander seeds, to resemble grapeshot. We didn't know that it was made from American wheat; Soviet wheat was too poor and fed only cattle. As always, we needed the Americans for the original innovation, but our version surpassed the original. A Soviet bureaucrat had explained it to a newspaper: American bread was "unusual," he said. "There's a lot of air in it." Here was a Soviet bureaucrat telling the truth! In the hand, Borodinsky was as dense as a goose-down pillow, but in the mouth it was like soft flesh, giving.

My grandmother tapped my shoulder—she was holding a peeled hard-boiled egg with a snowcap of mayonnaise. Over it, she dusted some salt, disposing of the last bit over her shoulder as per superstition. Using our kitchen knife, baubles suspended in the Bakelite of its curved handle—it had come, too—she hacked the end off the loaf but held it away and sawed down a softer slice; an adult would chew on the crust. I knew we had taken food with us, but this appearance of it exactly as it would have looked in the kitchen at home felt like magic. I departed the Soviet Union as I'd lived in it: my ears "cracking," as the Russian had it, because I was chewing so hard.

We had been supposed to leave in 1979, right after I was born. Jews had been leaving the Soviet Union in fluctuating but significant numbers since the mid-seventies. By now, the story of why—the persecution of Soviet Jews by their government and fellow citizens—is perhaps well known. The Russian Empire gained most of its Jewish subjects only when it annexed parts of Poland in the eighteenth century. Jews were foreign and, as with minorities in many other places, kept this way through geographical isolation and professional restriction. Things got marginally better after late imperial reforms, and this somewhat improved coexistence carried into Bolshevik rule. At first, the new regime genuinely pursued a more egalitarian order—there were so many Jews in Communist ranks because they believed in the ideal—so that Russians (and Belarusians and Tatars and Poles and others) not only lived alongside Jews peacefully in Minsk in the 1920s and '30s, but sometimes knew Yiddish, the Jews' language.

All that changed with the war—it was as if Hitler had lost the war but won Stalin on the Jewish question. Paranoid and more concerned with centralization, fealty, and ideological homogeneity than ever, Stalin was planning a nationwide Jewish pogrom when he died. When a state begins to sponsor prejudice of this kind, its people listen, and Jewish life during the Soviet period was one of discrimination at best and physical danger at worst. (The steam baths my father and I visited every week stood on a street named for a seventeenth-century Ukrainian *genocidaire* of Jews, among others.) Things stayed this way until the 1970s, when a rising number of Soviet Jews managed to get out, thanks to nearly two decades of effort by Soviet refuseniks and American activists, and to the fact that the Soviet Union needed things. By the late 1970s, it had depleted its treasury to get ahead of the States in missile technology; meanwhile, the 1979 wheat harvest was disastrous. The USSR needed grain, and it needed the U.S. Congress to authorize an arms-reduction treaty. So that even though 1978 had been an especially oppressive year for the refuseniks—Natan Sharansky, perhaps the best known, was finally tried after more than a year in detention—in 1979, the doors opened.

The Soviet Union hardly wanted its Jews, but their departure presented two problems. First, brain drain: Many were the scientists and engineers who kept the USSR on pace with America. Then: How to grandstand to the world about the quality of Soviet life if people wanted to leave? Above all, the Soviet Union would not hand a victory to America. The Minsk Jews with apartments in desired locations—Lenin Prospect, Victory Square—got let go more easily. The rest the authorities discouraged however they could: They levied massive fees for renouncing citizenship and for the free educations the prospective emigrants had received. The higher the degree, the more money. My mother would owe four *years* of her salary. My grandfather chuckled at my father: "Good thing you didn't listen when we pushed you to go for more school." My father nodded evasively. "Good thing," my grandfather kept on, "I know how to make sure there's five grand stashed away when you need it." My father didn't argue. "Some people fly, and some people crawl," my grandfather tried. My father only shrugged.

Families were denied exit unless the entire extended family— which sometimes included ethnic Russians, who usually had no desire to go—agreed to leave. So that those wishing to depart would think again about where they were going, the KGB murdered several Soviet émigrés in Chicago, New York, and San Francisco, among them a woman we knew; she had just written home marveling at all the lovely old ladies walking around San Francisco with flowers in their hatbands. The television showed nothing but Skid Row in Los Angeles, defaced subway cars in New York, gangs of blacks on the streets, police nightsticks over stonelike Indian faces, and bodies rolled into drunk tanks like chattel.

Diplomatically, the face-saving solution went like this: Soviet Jews had religious brethren in Israel, the land of the Jews. For the humanitarian purposes of family reunification, the state, magnanimously, would release them. Soviet Jews almost never had brethren in Israel; Israel's postwar population arrived from elsewhere in Eastern Europe, Western Europe, the Middle East, and North Africa. But that didn't matter. A Soviet Jew wishing to leave got word to someone who got word to Israel, where an office invented an Aunt So-and-so in the city of Be'er Sheva who'd suddenly been afflicted by an inability to go on without her Soviet relatives. Sometimes things got mixed up and it was "Aunt Be'er Sheva" or "Uncle Haifa" whose name appeared on the invitation, but neither we nor our Soviet jailers knew the difference. There was no equally worked-out channel for getting our names and biographical details to the Israelis, however, so friends who had already gotten permission to leave sewed a little paper with the information into the elastic of a pair of underwear.

Ultimately, our friends wouldn't go on to Israel; when they arrived in Vienna, the first document-processing point, they would declare their desire to emigrate to the United States instead. Israel pressured America to close the door to maneuvers like these, but without success: Everyone—the Americans, Jews and not; the Dutch, who represented Israeli interests in Moscow; the Austrians; even the religious refuseniks stuck in the Soviet Union who wished to go nowhere but Israel—supported freedom in this choice for Soviet Jews.

The maneuver worked, in our case—soon the letter arrived from the Soviet visa office, summoning my father and grandfather, as the heads of their families, for the interview that would decide whether we'd be allowed to emigrate. But the situation had changed since we applied. In December 1979, the Soviet Union had invaded Afghanistan. Jimmy Carter grounded the arms reduction treaty, refused to send grain, and boycotted the 1980 Moscow Summer Olympics. The Soviets had nothing to gain from letting their Jews continue to go, and, just like that, the doors started closing. (That was always what we called them—"the doors.") By the time

my father and grandfather were called, they had been hearing
about far more rejections than approvals. If permission to leave
was denied, you became an official refusenik. (The term comes
from having been refused permission to leave rather than a personal refusal to remain in the USSR.) But if you didn't show up for
your appointment, maybe the application would be thrown away,
or stamped FAILURE TO APPEAR, which, at everyone's workplaces, the
right gifts for one's superior could transform into REALIZED THEIR
MISTAKE and a quiet return to previous positions.

When my father and grandfather heard their names called, they
looked at each other for a long time, trying to decide. If they slipped
through, they'd get out to America. If not . . . there was no way to
know. No matter what they could smooth over at work, their declaration of intention to emigrate assured them of a future of zero as-
surances. Their names were called again, people swiveling to look.

They didn't go in. The other thing this assured was that, instead
of getting started in America as a toddler, I would spend my forma-
tive years in the Soviet Union instead.

1945-1975

I was born into a minor scandal. The first involved my father's
mother, Faina (fah-YEE-nah). Instead of crowding the maternity
ward with everyone else, she went . . . cross-country skiing. It was a
perfect day for it, the cold February sun glittering off the snowpack,
taller than a man after four months of winter. (With us, half the
year was winter.) It was scorching and freezing at once.

My mother's parents regarded this as an act of unpardonable self-
indulgence. In their eyes, Faina was the Egoist. Instead of spending
all her time making money to pass on to her offspring, she sang in
a choir, performed calisthenics, and looked after herself. She wore
teal, periwinkle, magenta, and lemon—never black. She refused to
utter the word "death." Did not believe in bad moods. In a Soviet
version of Zen, she lowered herself into sleep by intoning the names

of the major body parts: *The shoulder is resting. The forearm is resting. The elbow is resting.* In the choir, she would sing only from the front row. The front row was for the best voices and, while Faina's was certainly . . . resounding, and without a doubt . . . enthusiastic, the truth was that her hearing wasn't the greatest. Faina heard out the choirmaster's delicate plea, then informed him that she would continue to sing from the front.

Evacuated to the Soviet interior during the war, she had endured obliterating hunger and had watched her sister die of typhus. She wanted to live. My mother's parents had endured no less, but their conclusion was different: they would live for their children. After my birth, they alternated between wishing Faina would come to her senses and offer more help and resentfully wanting her nowhere near. And yet, in a way, Faina was the one responsible for my appearance.

Shortly after World War II, she had been set to marry a veteran. He was a *serdechnik*—a "heart man"—so he went to a sanatorium near the Black Sea; the mineral treatments were supposed to help. As on so many Soviet occasions, they did the opposite, elevating his heart rate until it gave out. This man had lost so much family in the war that it fell to his second cousin Boris to retrieve his body for burial. Boris did not want to go to the Black Sea. He had been fighting since 1939—a border skirmish with Japan; a winter war with Finland; then the global slaughterhouse of World War II— and had managed to survive with nothing worse than shredded hearing and galloping blood pressure until he was shot in the arm in the war's final days. He came back to Minsk an artillery sergeant with a sling and a German cast-iron cooking pot. Everyone in his unit had gotten one—the Germans were evil, but they knew how to make things.

At home, Boris learned that both of his parents had been killed, no trace of the bodies. But a younger brother was alive in Kazakhstan, in Central Asia, more than two thousand miles away, where

he had married a Russian woman. The Russian woman had a wid-
owed younger sister. Millions of men having died in the war, almost any would do, so it was there that Boris wanted to go. But,
reluctantly, he took the train for the Black Sea instead; awkwardly,
he had to go down with Faina, his cousin's young wife. Boris—
stout, of medium height, mortified by all the hair on his body—
was shy around women. But the Black Sea wasn't much closer than
Central Asia; they talked the whole way. There was a sturdiness to
the young woman, a flushed radiance. By the time they reached the
Black Sea, Boris wasn't sure about Kazakhstan anymore.

After they married, they lived in a single room attached to
the furniture factory where Boris got work as a carpenter. The
heat came from a wood-fired furnace. That was where the German cooking pot spent most of its time. Their free hours revolved
around the procurement of things to cook in it. The store called
Fruits and Vegetables never had fruit, and only three vegetables—
cabbage, potatoes, and beets—so their garden supplied everything
else. They bartered with the neighbor, who owned a cow, for butter
and milk. The store called Bread had bread. The meat plant down
the road had beef. Mushrooms they picked in the woods behind the
furniture factory. All of it was what would later be referred to as
organic—alternatives had not occurred to anyone—and both seasonal and local, as refrigeration was rare.

In the iron pot, Faina made meatballs from ground beef and
pork, braised with caramelized carrots and onions, served alongside buckwheat dolloped with butter. The stew called *solyanka*—
cabbage and slippery jacks braised at low heat; the combination,
earthy, smoky, and nutty—was like eating the woods. Even breakfast came from the pot: Boris sometimes took their two sons (the
younger one was my father, born in 1953) to the furniture cafeteria
for pancakes—puffing through all their little pores and slathered
with sweet buttermilk—but for herself, Faina loved to reheat left-
over borshch.

SOLYANKA (BRAISED CABBAGE WITH SHIITAKE MUSHROOMS) (V)

Time: 2 hours   Serves: 6–8

Solyanka (so-lee-AN-ka) *is more commonly known as a soup, but this recipe makes a side dish so hearty, it'll easily work as a vegetarian main. Slippery jacks, the mushrooms my grandmother used in Minsk, aren't commonly available in America, but shiitakes are, and they make a very suitable substitute. For a more venturesome re-creation of that woodsy, just-picked taste—mushroom hunting is a religion in my part of the world—seek out a mix of shiitake, king trumpets, and hen-of-the-woods (maitake) mushrooms.*

2 pounds shiitake mushrooms, stemmed

2 tablespoons kosher salt, plus additional to taste

6 bay leaves

¼ cup vegetable oil

1 large or 2 medium onions, chopped

6 garlic cloves, divided (3 diced and 3 put through a garlic press)

1 large or 2 medium-size carrots, grated

1 small to medium-size head green cabbage (2 pounds), cored and roughly chopped

½ cup tomato paste

2 teaspoons sugar

1½ teaspoons allspice

2 teaspoons ground coriander

2 teaspoons caraway seeds

1. Pile the mushrooms into a big pot and cover with water. Add the 2 tablespoons salt and 3 of the bay leaves. Bring to a boil and boil for 15 minutes. Drain and set aside.

2. While the mushrooms are boiling, in a large, deep sauté pan, heat the oil over medium heat. Add the onion and cook until golden brown. Salt to taste. Add the diced garlic and cook, stirring, for 30 seconds. Add the carrots and cook until nice and soft. Add the cabbage and remaining 3 bay leaves and cook, stirring occasionally, until wilted. Salt to taste.

3. Mix the tomato paste with 2½ cups water and a big pinch of salt. Add to the wilted cabbage along with the sugar, spices, and pressed garlic. Bring to a boil. Lower the heat and let gently simmer for 45 minutes with the lid slightly ajar.

4. Add the drained mushrooms and cook for another 10 minutes. Salt to taste.

Let cool, and serve.

Cooking was a kind of torment for Faina—she could not do two things at a time, so while the gas was on, she stood by it like a flag lashed to its mast, staring, stirring, and tweaking. She made rolled crepes with ground beef and caramelized onion; chopped liver from freshly killed chickens; *forshmak* (minced herring, caramelized onion, hard-boiled egg, grated apple); and raisin-studded muffins dusted with confectioners' sugar. Her buckwheat was buttery, but her strudel was chaste—diced apple, apricot, raisin, and plum did all the flavoring.

My father's best friend was his father. Often, Boris picked the boy up from kindergarten and they went to the old Polish cemetery—Belarus now being Soviet rather than Polish, it had been turned into a park, but you could still see the old stones peering out, like half-drowned swimmers. There, Boris brought out a newspaper bundle with a beef patty, a large red tomato, and several pieces of black bread, and father and son chewed together in silence. Once, Boris pulled out a gift of a small vest and straw hat. My father wore it to school every day. His classmates jeered, but he didn't care. He was used to it. They made fun of him all the time because he was Jewish. "The boy is Jewish," his teacher's report-card assessment always began.

Sometimes Boris was imponderable. Once, a teenager in the play yard kept taunting my father—"kike, kike!"—so he ran home and told Boris. Boris got out a metal rod and had the older boy, now weeping, pinned under his knee—he would have killed him—when a passerby shouted, distracting Boris, and the boy squirmed out and ran off. My father watched, stunned. Boris didn't look at him, only tousled his hair before coughing into his sleeve and going inside. Because of his war injuries, his blood pressure was always too high. There was no medicine for it, so he endured terrible headaches and hours in bed with a cold compress over his forehead.

My father couldn't wait for their weekly trips to the steam

baths—unlike Boris, who was so embarrassed by the fur on his body that he wouldn't go to the doctor because it meant removing his shirt. He pruned the hair with scissors. My father didn't ask why Boris had so much hair when almost everyone in the steam baths did not; whether that meant he'd have it, too. There was so much love between them, but not the kind where you could ask too many questions.

After tenth grade, Boris and Faina told my father that he had all the education he needed—he should get work. Through a friend, he got a spot as a barber. Barbers wore white smocks, preferable to stained overalls down in the mine shaft, but my father couldn't do it. You had to stand there and do the same thing over and over, and banter about the same false, vacant subjects. He could go back to school, but what was the point? You couldn't get a job without a connection, and even then, being Jewish kept you from going very far.

One afternoon in December 1972, my father, now nineteen, was crunching through the snow with an old friend who had to return something to his cousin. My father said he'd wait downstairs—he didn't like meeting new people, especially in such a well-appointed building in the center of the city. But it was below freezing, and the friend got him upstairs. There, my father couldn't help staring. The apartment was enormous. The parquet floor gleamed. A massive wall unit tinkled with crystal. The shelves groaned with books, the cupboards with multiple sets of dishes. The walls were painted with abstract lines of color, then the fashion.

The young woman who greeted them had huge black eyes, the whites around the pupils so white they were blue, and two pigtails like cables. How warmly she was dressed. She, in turn, saw a young man with a handsome mustache, folded into a flimsy, short jacket. She wanted to give him a warm one. She didn't know he wouldn't have wanted it. He didn't like wearing too many layers— they made him itch.

Several days later, my father, Yakov, called to ask the young woman, Anna, if he could return on his own. He caught a ride on a street-washing truck, flowers in hand. She loved flowers, so he brought them every time he came—pansies if the season was right, because in Russian pansies are called "Anna's eyes." In this home, there was momentum, initiative, energy. The family had relatives in Moscow, where Anna had been sent several times for a taste of life in the capital. Unlike Yakov's parents, who didn't have friends—on holidays, a handful of relatives came and sat at the table in silence—hers interacted with everyone from pickpockets to ministers. Their salon chairs—he was a barber and she a manicurist—hosted African students, Czech functionaries, Armenians with thick beards. At home, the refrigerator was full, and so were the closets. The only reason the family didn't have a car was that Anna's father, Arkady (ar-KAY-dee), found it easier to maneuver among his contacts by taxi. Every day was built around these barter journeys—deficit food, doctors on call, doors for Anna to walk through when she needed it. Sometimes the currency was simply a "well-covered" table.

Anna's mother, Sofia, could knock out *tsimmes*, a carrot casserole that in her execution was savory rather than sweet; *tseppeliny*, potato pancakes humped with ground pork, named after the German dirigibles that crossed the sky during World War I; *babka*, a potato casserole studded with chicken-skin cracklings. Sofia brined her herring—after hacking off the head and tweezering the bones like a jeweler—with not only peppercorns and onions but coriander and cinnamon. She made cherry, plum, and raspberry jams so thick, a spoon would stand up in the jars. One of the house specialties involved a thick slab of *polenitsa* bread slathered with "the noise," the foam sent up by the jam as it boiled away.

Maintaining this existence required unflagging exertion. One day, Yakov proposed a walk, but Anna had to go to the dry cleaners, then visit the back door of a private food depot, then a woman who dealt in vacation vouchers. Yakov felt queasy about a life made from secret favors, but maybe being in this place was good for him. He felt pushed in a way he never had at home, where he had been provided for and kept safe, but nothing more. And if he made more of himself, maybe Anna's parents might look upon him less disapprovingly. He applied to a technical college specializing in telecommunications, studied hard for the entrance exams and passed, earning a junior position at a telephone exchange pending graduation.

"Now that you're in," Arkady said over dinner one night—the four of them always ate together; Arkady wasn't impressed by the telephone exchange, but you had to start somewhere—"you need a 'warm' person inside. You understand what I'm saying?" My father nodded vaguely. "Someone who likes a well-covered table. And wants to help as a way to say thank you." Arkady mimed a hand giving the top mark on a grade sheet. "You find him, I'll feed him."

Everything inside Yakov objected, but he decided to try. Eventually he spotted someone who seemed pliant in the right way—the safety instructor. He stumbled through the invitation, but men like the safety instructor knew their way around such conversations, and helped by accepting quickly. That left the question of what to cook.

Sofia decided against Jewish dishes. She made cabbage rolls stuffed with ground pork and rice, braised in a quilt of crumbled rye bread and sour cherry jam; and *karbonat*, a garlic-spiked pork tenderloin. Pork tenderloin was a deficit item—the right thing for the safety inspector to notice. Sofia stewed the hell out of it in a zinc-gray pot embossed with factory and model identifications that made it feel like a part of some engine. The lid closed over the rim with a distinct, plaintive peal that tolled all through the house and said, *Soon you will be licking your fingers.* Sofia served the *karbonat* with crispy potatoes and scallions. The assembled drained one bottle of cognac, then another. Like American hurricanes, Soviet grades went from 1 to 5, with 3 passing. The safety inspector gave my father a 5.

STUFFED CABBAGE BRAISED IN RYE
BREAD AND SOUR CHERRY JAM

Time: 2 hours   Serves: 6

Why would anyone braise cabbage rolls in bread and jam? Well, we didn't have tomato paste and raw sugar in the Soviet Union, and this was my grandmother's way of lending a sour-sweet depth to a standard. The pork and jam are sweet; the Borodinsky (or similar sourdough rye) is earthy; and the cabbage, cool and vegetal, cuts through both. (The cooking time below will leave the cabbage al dente, so that you'll end up with a dish at once pillowy and toothsome.) This recipe uses brown rice, as its nuttiness goes well with the other ingredients, but feel free to substitute your rice of choice.

½ cup brown rice
Kosher salt
1 medium head green cabbage
1½ pounds ground pork (or
    ground meat of your choice)
½ large onion, chopped
2–3 cloves garlic, minced

Black pepper
½ loaf Borodinsky or other
    sourdough rye bread (5–6
    slices)
1 13-ounce jar sour cherry jam
Vegetable oil, for the pan(s)

1. You'll want your rice half-cooked before it goes inside the cabbage rolls. Bring ¾ cup of salted water to a boil, add the rice, lower the heat to a simmer, and cover. You're boiling the rice in half the water it needs to cook fully, so keep an eye on it. The water should have boiled out in 15–20 minutes, or about half the time you'd need to cook it fully.

2. While the rice is going, fill a tall pot with enough water to cover the head of cabbage. Salt it well—1 tablespoon of salt per 12 cups of water. Bring the water to a boil. Meanwhile, cut the stem out of the cabbage head. When the water is boiling, drop the head in, flat part down. The cabbage will bob around, the top peeking out, but as long as there's enough water, that should be fine.

3. Within a minute or two, the outer cabbage leaf will be ready to come off. Use tongs to carefully peel it away from the *kachan*—that's Russian for "cabbage head"—and remove from the water. Pat dry with paper towels. Repeat until you have 20 leaves.

4. Using a small knife, slice off the part of each leaf rib that isn't level with the rest of the leaf. You're not cutting the rib *out* in a triangular cut; the rib stays in, and you're just shaving it down so the leaf is entirely flat, and easier to fold.

5. Mix thoroughly the pork, onion, garlic, and now somewhat cooled half-cooked rice. Season with salt and pepper.

6. Using your hands or a spoon, deposit a clump of the pork mixture at the broadest edge of a cabbage leaf. Fold that edge over the meat, then flap over the right and left sides, then roll over again until you've run out of leaf—a cabbage burrito. Set aside and repeat for the remaining pork mixture and leaves. You could also divide the mixture among the leaves before folding any, to make sure you have enough.

7. Tear the bread so that the pieces are no larger than a thumbnail and mix with the jam. Combine with 2 cups of water, and salt lightly.

8. Choose a covered pan deep enough to hold the cabbage rolls in two layers, or use two pans to fit them in one layer. Coat the bottom of the pan(s) with a tiny bit of oil over medium-low heat and place in the cabbage rolls. Pour the jam mixture around and between the rolls. The top of the uppermost layer of rolls should be peeking out of the liquid.

9. Cover, turn the heat down to low, and let braise for 30 minutes. Uncover and cook for another 30 minutes so some of the liquid can boil off.

✦

My father needed a boost, but only a boost: He graduated with strong grades all around. At the telephone exchange, they noted his accreditation and told him to wait. But no word came—as it never would. They didn't put Jews in the senior positions. The only way to live like a normal person, he saw again, to get people to forget you were Jewish, was to live the way his girlfriend's parents lived. But how to do it? Forget the oiliness of it—how could you know who your friends were, and who used you for pork? Anna's father didn't trouble himself with the question. Maybe it was too painful; maybe Anna's parents once wished to live differently, too.

At the dinner table, the talk turned to what other profession Yakov could try. Arkady, who was just fine with the telephone exchange not working out, was a barber—he could find the young man a "chair."

"I've tried it," Yakov said. "It isn't for me. Thank you all the same."

Silence took over the table. The talking resumed, but it was half-hearted. That night, Anna phoned Yakov, her voice tremulous. "Please apologize," she begged. "If you don't, they won't let me see you."

Yakov was stubborn, but not about things like that; he went and apologized. Everything returned to the way it was—these people didn't hold grudges; grudges were impractical. And barbering wasn't mentioned again. But at the next dinner—*he wants to work in tele-phones, let him work in telephones*—he was told to take gifts to the hiring personnel at the exchange; it would dislodge the impasse. To smile at the people who buried his file! No, he couldn't do it, he said. It was Anna's mother, Sofia, who spoke now. "Who do you think you are?" she hissed. "Enough! There will be nothing between you."

On the walk home, Yakov's mind squalled. He wouldn't have agreed for his daughter to stoop to someone like him, either. But who were *they*? Yes, they were ambitious. About lamb's-wool coats, rare liquor, and gold spoons. The best fun in the world was a bottle of cognac, a concert on television, and a rich meal they fell upon as if it were meant to save them from something. By now, Yakov loved Anna, and knew that she loved him, too, but he didn't think he could count on her—she didn't know how to disobey them.

He considered calling her but wondered if she would try to speak as if nothing had happened. This was something in Anna he didn't love: She was capable of falsehood. An irony—she was the most sincere person he'd ever met. It was her parents, slowly coming alive inside her. He called anyway—and hung up when her mother answered the phone. Then called back and announced himself—and was told that Anna was gone.

For winter recess, her parents had sent her to Moscow and forbidden her to call Yakov. She pleaded with them—Yakov's father was ill once again—but was told to leave it; they'd check on him. Anna spent the week in terrible agitation, short with her aunt and uncle, unable to sleep, indifferent to the magic of Moscow. But she didn't touch the phone.

How did Yakov find out that Anna would return to Minsk on the overnight Arrow? When she stepped onto the platform, there he was, in a warm fur hat, but with shoes so thin they could have been slippers, and a coat no thicker. He held a chaste bouquet wrapped in newspaper. It was the dead heart of winter, but flowers grew year-round in the Caucasus; at the market, the Georgians wedged each carnation into a tall glass with a candle to keep it from freezing.

By way of greeting, he said, "My papa is no longer with us." Boris's kidneys, diseased from his other ailments and with no dialysis to help, had succumbed to a flu. Faina fed Boris sugared slices of lemon—this was the only fruit she could find, and for some reason she thought the citrus would help. As usual, Boris was too embarrassed to go to the doctor, and by the time he finally did, it was too late. It had never occurred to Yakov to ask Anna's parents for help from any of the doctors in their barter network. They would have helped—health was health—but he was supposed to be out of her life and didn't even think of it. Anna had never gotten to meet his father. Yakov, ashamed of the meagerness of his home, had never proposed a visit; it wasn't proper for girls to visit boys at their homes anyway. Anna began to weep.

"I would like you to meet my mother," Yakov said quietly.

He didn't discuss feelings often; she felt she should encourage him. "I've wanted to meet her since we met," she said.

The following week, Anna told her parents she was staying late at the university. Lying to them made her feel ill—she had never done it before. It took forty minutes to reach the small apartment in the tall building blocks on the outskirts. It seemed like an impossibly long time to go from one place to another in the same city. Yakov was silent most of the way; he didn't even put his arm around her. Anna asked if he was all right, but he only smiled tightly. She wondered if this was all a mistake.

That afternoon, shuttling between shifts as a part-time accountant at two schools, Faina had stopped at a fish market and bought one newssheet's worth of sardines. The saleswoman in the peaked cap stacked them like little torpedoes, one eye periscoping out from each, and wrapped the bundle at both ends like a candy. Faina had bought the sardines because they were cheap. She splurged on the tomatoes, from Bulgaria.

At home, she covered the bottom of the cast-iron German pot—scratched here and there but still worthy thirty years later, only that now she cooked on a stovetop—with a little vegetable oil and scattered in two diced onions. While these sizzled, she sliced thick rings of tomato—tomatoes this firm did not end up under her knife very often. Once the onions had browned, she added the tomatoes, watching it all froth the right way. The silver arrows of the sardines went in last.

When the young couple entered, Faina offered the girl a perfunctory greeting. Anna would have assumed it was because Faina was in mourning, but her boyfriend's mother was dressed for an exuberant birth: a bright green blouse tucked into an apple-red skirt, big dangling earrings, and fake pearls that took up half her chest. The real reason Faina was short with her was that she couldn't stray from the gas.

Anna didn't have to look around many corners to see it was a homely place—there weren't that many corners around which to look. There was only one room large enough for a bed, which meant that Yakov slept . . . on that foldout cot. There was no chandelier in the dining room, only a lamp with an old-fashioned fabric lampshade with fringes.

After Faina shut off the heat, she set down a pitcher of fruit compote, an oval plate with slices of black bread she had charred on the stovetop (toasted bread was unheard of, but Faina liked hers that way, and so the young woman should, too), and then the cast-iron pot with its "nose-ripping" scent. The sardines had kept their shape. The tomatoes were blistered and sugary. The onion had melted almost to paste.

They ate largely in silence, Faina asking Anna no questions. Anna felt the last of her hopefulness draining away. She was used to the clamor of her parents' kitchen, someone on the way in, someone out, fish frying to a golden crust, crystal thimbles clinking away. Belatedly, she became aware that the others were staring; lost in thought, she was mindlessly working through sardine after sardine, her utensils forgotten. Everyone laughed.

Anna's shoulders relaxed, and she tried a compliment: *What a beautiful lamp.* Faina nodded: The pattern had been woven by a woman with whom she sang in a choir. A choir! Anna had never met someone who sang in a choir. Was that so? *Hear this, then—* and Faina broke into song. Then she described every woman who sang with her. If she had difficulty inquiring about Anna, she had none speaking about herself. She told Yakov to get his accordion.

His what? Why hadn't he ever told her? He shrugged—it never came up. He proposed a song that was popular that year, about one of the forests outside Minsk ("I understand your eternal sorrow, dense wood"), but Faina rejected that as too downbeat. "Let's do 'The Azov Sea,'" she said. She had gone to the Sea of Azov, near Crimea, on vacation; after a concert, she made the singer write down all the lyrics. Mother and son looked at each other, nodded, and:

> *Wide is your yonder so blue*
> *as a seagull flits by the white crest of a wave.*
> *The clearest dawns blaze above you,*
> *like the youth of our land.*

The young woman clapped and clapped. Then they buried their faces in what was left of the pot. To mustaches and flowers, Anna added sardines. My mother's insistence on marrying my father soon after that evening was the first thing about which she ever stood up to her parents.

SARDINES BRAISED IN
CARAMELIZED ONIONS AND TOMATOES

Time: 1 hour, 15 minutes   Serves: 4–6

Half the time for this recipe goes to cleaning the fish. It's a lot simpler and more fun than it sounds. The trick is to use scissors instead of a knife.

1 pound sardines (15–20 sardines)	5 vine-ripened or 3 juicy beefsteak tomatoes, cut into pieces the size of a fingernail
2 tablespoons vegetable oil	
1 large onion, chopped	Kosher salt and black pepper, to
1 large carrot, grated	taste

1. Rinse the sardines under cold water. Pat dry. Using scissors, cut away all the fins and tails. Then snip off the heads. This will create access to the body cavity; like the surgeon you always wanted to be, cut the fish open lengthwise far enough to get at the guts. (One side of the sardine will be noticeably thinner than the other. That should be the side facing up for the incision.) From here, you'll want to clear out all the innards—look for white and yellow slime—which would give the sardine a bitter taste. Remove the bone structure as well.

2. Heat the oil in a large pan over medium heat. Add the onion and cook until golden brown. Then add the grated carrot and cook until softened.

3. Add the tomatoes, season to taste with salt and pepper, and lower the heat to medium-low. After the tomatoes have broken down and some of their liquid has evaporated (but some is left), add the sardines, stir gently to mix in, turn the heat to the lowest setting, cover, and let braise for 20 minutes.

4. Check for seasoning and add more salt and pepper if necessary—but mix it in gently: Whole sardines show up better on Instagram.

Serve over your grain of choice or with a couple of rough hunks of bread.

✦

CHAPTER 2

1979-1988

What to cook after you've finally slaughtered your pigs

What to cook if you're feeding an army of hungry boys helping you with your harvest

What to cook if you're vacationing, "savage leisure" style, on the Soviet Riviera

✦

Faina's disappearance to the ski tracks on the day I was born was the last of my mother's concerns: She thought she was giving birth to a child pickled in moonshine.

After she graduated university with accreditation to teach chemistry, my grandfather secured her a sweet spot: at the school of continuing studies attached to the city's department of trade and commerce. If the head of a food store's dry-goods section had been chosen to move to prepared foods, this person needed to learn chemistry. Textiles, shoes—chemistry figured into all of it. Food store managers, however, had no interest in chemistry. Their interest was in trading deficit food items for the grades they needed.

My mother was an idealist. Her heart rattled when she sang the Soviet anthem. She wore the Young Pioneer kerchief with pride. Her perfect school record, and her father's connections, ensured her admission, her religion notwithstanding, to the Young Communist League, the pipeline for the Party. She was ready to have less so others had more. Chemistry wasn't exactly the course on Marxist-Leninist principles, but all the same, teaching was an occupation of great ideological consequence, and she ascended to it with honor.

But she was also her father's daughter. When she received her first invitation to a table laid with the finest underground products available to the supermarket elite, she said yes. Somehow, this led to no hand-wringing. Her father went around the law because he was galled to be expected to get by with less, not because he was a dissident. From this perspective, a daughter reared to burn with fealty to Communist principle had better chances of advancement than the opposite, and so she was reared. (Also to ignore the contradictions ignored by her parents.) "My children love Stalin most of all, and me only second," Boris Pasternak's wife used to say, and that was exactly how she wanted it. (*Doctor Zhivago* had made Pasternak an enemy of the state.) Above all, Anna had been taught how to get along and ahead.

At the getting-to-know-you table with her first "students," my mother had such a good time that she stumbled home squealing with laughter. My father had never seen her this way. He had to help her undress for the shower. His wife's giddiness switched to horror a week later when she learned that she had been pregnant for nearly a month. She endured the child's gestation in terror: She was going to give birth to a two-headed victim of her indiscretion. (Soviet medicine did not possess the means to reassure her.) When I came out in one piece, the family decided to thank fate by saving me from the further harm of being Jewish in the USSR, and joining the Jews streaming out of the country. Alas.

My grandfather had been only partly right about what gifts to superiors could fix after he and my father left the visa office empty-handed. My grandparents' beauty salon colleagues couldn't have cared less if my grandparents rubbed shit over pictures of Lenin. Same for my father, a lowly housepainter. (Finally, he had found a profession that entailed dealing with a wall instead of a person.) But my mother was demoted to a night school attached to a tractor factory on the outskirts. Its employees, many of whose educations had been interrupted by the war, were required to earn high school equivalency; that curriculum included chemistry. Some were illiterate.

My mother was responsible for recruiting her own classroom. With my father for support and protection, she rode the distant bus lines to ring doorbells and persuade mechanics and welders to come learn about sodium chloride. ("The various alcohols you derive from . . . nonstandard sources—that's chemistry in action.") Incredibly, some hauled themselves in. Maybe it was the chance to stare at an attractive young woman for an hour, though some did try to understand how chlorophyll converts carbon dioxide and water into glucose and oxygen. (Rust, fermentation, combustion—these came more easily.)

The attractive young woman was earnest about the work. "The periodic table is so important," she insisted. "You must know it so well that if I wake you up in the middle of the night and ask you to recite it, you won't scratch your head for a minute."

A man whistled, meaning "and how about you ask me to fly."

The young teacher admonished him. "You must! What would you do if I woke you and asked you the elements?"

"I'd say, 'Get in the bed!'" he answered, and the class roared. My mother shook her head, but she laughed, too.

I spent my Soviet years differently—with a silver spoon in my mouth. Literally. Almost all Soviet cutlery was made of cheap metals, so I got a special silver spoon that no one else was allowed to touch. It was useful, too, because it made a clean, loud clink against the first tooth when it appeared.

Ordinary Soviet people saw tropical fruit like bananas and tangerines only at "voting" time, when boxes upon boxes suddenly materialized from God knows where. (They also appeared for the holidays, and were hung like ornaments on holiday trees, too precious to eat.) My grandfather, however, was in bananas and tangerines all the time. Only I was allowed to touch them.

On the first day of preschool, my father climbed a giant oak. From the upper branches, he could see directly into the classroom. My mother waited for news down below.

"Now he is holding the teacher's hand."

"Now he is lying down for his nap."

They must have taken the day off.

My grandfather had ingratiated me with the school by getting hold of thirty small Persian rugs of which some consulate was disposing, and it was on these regally plush items that my classmates and I bedded down. I wasn't much of a sleeper, though, even at night. My grandmother loved me past reason, but she must have found this lack of discipline galling. "If you don't fall asleep," she would warn me from the side of the bed, "the inspector will come."

Overhearing her, my grandfather would rush into the bedroom: "What inspector? What are you talking about? You'll frighten the child! He'll become mentally ill!"

"Mentally ill?" she would give back. "You're the one who thinks you're going to have a heart attack every minute!"

"With everything I have to look after? Maybe I will!"

"Go have another glass somewhere! Go."

And then I was really awake.

I preferred the bedtime stories my father invented: "Once upon a time, there was a boy. He came home from work, ate some food, then sat down to read a book. But the cover was ripped, and inside, the words were washed out—"

"Wait, wait," I would interrupt. "Ripped how? Ripped, or curled back, or . . . ?"

My father would laugh. The housepainting work wore him down, and I had to touch his cheek to keep him from falling asleep as he invented the story.

In the summers, I was sent to fatten up in the woods. The property belonged to a cow and pig farmer who rented rooms in the countryside cottage he shared with his wife, and in several other constructions not used by the pigs. The wild and trackless forest from which his property had been hacked could outclass any Bavarian wood of fairy-tale density. (That's why people wrote songs about them.) Russian has a word for "forest," and then a separate word—*pushcha*—for forests like these. Because, as a teacher, my mother had summers off and was the next most pampered family member, she was forced to accompany me.

My mother hated the woods. As a child, she'd wept for hours after her parents left her at summer camp and sped away to the city. My grandparents disliked the countryside even more—it was the refuge of drunks and people without ambition, the fresh air its only redemption. Like them, my mother wanted the noise and pageantry of the city. Minsk was Houston—the fourth-largest city, with a similar population, two million, and something of its standing: solid but regional. Most of it—a thousand-year-old settlement—destroyed in the war, it was rebuilt in the monumental socialist style. The streets were as wide as a soccer field is long. But because of the fresh slate, it was also a relatively modern place. Things were clean and new; the circus was good, and so was the opera; supply chains were smoother, so people didn't have to go to Moscow to get certain things. We lived on a quiet side street just outside the center, near a botanical garden that made my mother tear up—she had wanted to become a florist. (In an early instance of the decades-long ventriloquism to come, I absorbed her secret longing—it wasn't a profession her parents would approve of—and developed a massive devotion to the solitary lilac tree that flanked our apartment building.) Nearby was a park with lots of warnings (CITIZENS: OBSERVE CLEANLINESS . . . CITIZENS: OBSERVE SILENCE), a playground of swings to make a boy think he could fly, and the steam baths I went to with my father, just as he had with his.

The summer I was three, the Jewish family with whom my mother and I shared the main summer cottage at the pig farmer's had a son, too, with a fellow Jewish boy's very black hair, and, though he was seven, we were closer in size than the numbers suggested. The reason for this became clear quickly: For breakfast I ate salmon roe on buttered bread; he had weak oatmeal and hot tea. Once, we saw his mother mixing a dollop of baked-salmon salad into farmer cheese so that her son had a red-looking meal, too, but my mother ruined it by trying to share the roe. One day, the boy put down his cheese sandwich and said, loudly enough for the whole kitchen, "Mama, why do they eat differently from us?" The room fell silent. "Please eat," his mother demanded in a mortified voice. "I'll explain."

It was a tricky thing to explain to a boy: His father was an engineer, his mother a urologist; I came from a barber, a manicurist, a housepainter, and a docked chemistry teacher. But his mother did not seem resentful. Once, she cornered my mother with a urologist's insider tip: It was now possible to give Jewish boys "cosmetic circumcisions"—all the health benefits, but hardly visible, "so they won't laugh at your boy in the steam baths because he's Jewish."

The farmer's pigs had it best. There was a summer camp next door. These Young Pioneers may have been firm in their resistance to imperialism, but they were children and therefore fickle in diet, and the man had somehow managed to get their castoffs for free. The pigs ate buttery potatoes with fried fish, millet with preserves, polenta with eggs sunny-side up, and hot tea. This also meant they grew fast, so that he had to slaughter them all the time. Gallantly, he waited till nightfall, when all the renters were in, but there was nothing to do while he waited, so he was profoundly drunk by the time he tried to find the pig's heart with his knife.

For hours, the cottage colony listened to the death squeals of one pig after another. One morning, my mother timidly inquired

whether the man might consider other means of destruction. He
was being paid for woodsy quiet, after all. He heard her out, then
announced, delphically, "There will be you—and there will be
them." But from then on, he drove his pigs to the woods. He was
still drunk, though, and it turned out to be hard to load a pig into
the trunk of a sedan. Once he finally managed, he swerved down a
woodland road until he reached a spot that was never far enough as
he hunted for the heart, and missed, over and over.

After the carnage was finished, he feasted. From a pig he kept,
he carved a giant square of well-marbled meat from the lower part
of the shoulder—the brisket, or most of a boned-out picnic ham—
which he fried up in butter until it glistened like gold. This he
placed on garlic-rubbed black bread from a special loaf nearly the
size of the brisket. Then he poured himself an eight-ounce glass of
vodka. These items he carried from the shared kitchen to a little
brick shed on the edge of the property that he never rented out—it
was cooler there, and his wife didn't bother him. As he walked,
the renter population gathered at the windows in dismay and reproach: *Just look at that degenerate.* I felt guilty in my dissent: The
scent from the plate in his hands was so far-reaching and fine that
it seemed to merit forgiveness of all, or at least a postponement of
judgment. Once the degenerate had reached the shed, he lowered
himself onto the cot that was the only thing in it and ate down
the brisket with vodka. Then he collapsed and slept for twenty-four
hours.

Only my father, who came up on the weekends, joined me in
thinking there wasn't anything wrong with the man. In fact, my
father wanted his life. For some reason, the original brick of the
farmer's sleeping shed had been encased in concrete that had then
been painted white, so my father the housepainter offered to repaint
the white into a brick pattern, at least. The farmer readily agreed,
and an unexpressed camaraderie existed between them after that.

Sometimes my father brought the pot in which my parents' matrimonial sardines had been made so we could sneak in a campfire picnic. (Faina had not parted with it eagerly. When she and I played cards, she ignored every wordless, raised-eyebrow admonishment from a passing adult to *make sure to lose to the child*, and demolished me every time. But even she wasn't impervious to generosity as defined by Regular People.) The pot—bulbous, scuffed, heavy, and forty—made me think of a slightly inactive uncle, laid up from arthritis or drink but taking in everything keenly all the same. It was not going to be a large family. My mother's parents had overruled my father's desire for another child because it was time to get back to work and earning sweet rubles. My mother acquiesced.

I couldn't tell you, as a five-year-old, why I preferred to eat out in the woods with my father "when there was a normal kitchen right there," but, as an adult, I've wondered how much of it may have had to do with the fact that it gave me a father as serene—as opposed to contained—as I'd ever seen him. Around that campfire, it was an understanding of nature that fed you, not the clandestine connections that did in the city.

After we ate, I slept the sleep of the young, dead, and well fed—my mouth open and my arms crossed at my chest, the way my father did sometimes.

He had been a retiring person since childhood—more like his father than Faina. When boys taunted him about being Jewish, he walked away. At recess, he played by himself. He liked silence and disliked crowds—he distrusted the falsehood that usually went with them. When, every October, young "volunteers" were conscripted to help with the countryside harvest, my grandfather bribed the necessary people to save my teenage mother from two weeks bent over potato fields. It was my father's favorite time of the year.

Few of the young faces on the early train to the village shared his enthusiasm. They were supposed to be the Soviet Union's first bourgeois generation; if their parents had found a way to believe, they were past the question. They wished to work in offices, shop for the clothes that were newly available, listen to Beatles bootlegs, sit late and gossip in one another's apartments, and fall in love without caution. (A literary figure of the time, allocated a precious new apartment, said, "Now . . . we must pray to God there won't be a revolution" to take it all away.) They didn't wish to break their asses helping with the harvest because the old village men were asleep with the bottle and the young ones had escaped to the city.

At the rural train platform, as everyone stamped their feet and waited for a truck to the village, my father stood aside. He didn't wear a hat, nor gloves, and his jacket was too thin. He balled his fists in his pockets and gazed across the silent web of the rails, the air so still he imagined noise—a branch cracking, a bird beating its wings.

Grandma Daria, to whose hut he was assigned one such October, along with several boys, had a furnace the size of a bed. Out of it came crispy quartered potatoes, dusted with dill before being slathered with sour cream; bowlegged, hand-lumped pork sausages; "eye-melets"—eggs sunny-side up—sizzling and spitting after a quick fry-up in the pork fat. Rough hunks of bread filled out the plate, as did chipped enamel mugs of boiling-hot black tea with honey. The potatoes were freshly dug up; the sour cream came from the cows in the field, morosely observing the encroachment of winter; the eggs from the chickens prancing around the yard; the sausages from the season's first hog slaughter (a little early, but there were guests); the honey from the village bees; the bread from its rye. Only the black tea came from the store—again, guests. Sometimes Grandma Daria had just the hot water with honey.

Thus fortified, the boys headed off on a back-crushing jumble over a rutted road to the fields. Some of the girls ran field kitchens—

milk-softened pork, potato pancakes, cabbage still speckled with dirt, washed down with a mead-like fermented beverage called *kvass* or that morning's milk. The air felt scored like crystal. The river was some other kind of blue. The grass rustled endlessly in the wind—here no one mowed.

By the end of their shifts, Grandma Daria's boys felt mind-numbing hunger. In went hunks of pork belly braised with carrots, onions, and scallions from the garden. In went roasted beets. In went rye bread pinned by slabs of hard cheese. The boys' cheeks burned—from the wind, from the furnace. The coiled cots into which they collapsed could have been clouds. Grandma Daria rose in the night and covered them with rough blankets stuffed with billows of cotton; she didn't want to burn precious firewood.

On Sunday, their day off, the boys heard Grandma Daria whispering in their ears: "Sonny, it's the last week to pick plums—I'm not tall enough and I can't carry Timofey's ladder all by myself." Or: "Someone has to move the hay. I'm an old woman . . ." And so, before heading off to the steam baths, where they washed off the week, the boys, many of whom had never thought to help their mothers at home (and whom the mothers hadn't bothered to ask), picked the plums and moved the hay. Two plums into the box and one in the mouth. My father proudly handed Grandma Daria box after box of plums and was stunned when she emptied half into the pig trough—she couldn't afford the sugar to turn them all into preserves.

In the end, even the other boys didn't want it to be over—for two weeks they smoked, flirted, and drank, away from the eyes of their parents. And they learned how to do things. That country, with its chronic breakdowns and shortages, made resourceful improvisers out of the clumsiest hands. A quarter of a century later, at family gatherings in San Francisco and Omaha and Chicago and New Jersey and Brooklyn, we children had to marvel at the hands of our fathers: small, rough with work—sometimes cracked with it—the thumbs squat and broad. Whether molecular biologists, programmers, or taxi drivers, they could dismantle radios, singe potatoes in firepits, swim to the other side of the lake—oh, how these tense men untensed at the sight of a rural body of water—get a chandelier to hang from the ceiling, and strum a guitar. They still wore the mustaches and trimmed beards of their youth, and they were beyond the reach of American fashion. To us, their Americanized children, these men were rigid, frightened, and withdrawn. But you had to love their hands.

With the pig farmer's antics finally deemed too much to bear, we spent the summer I was five in Lithuania, in the Baltics. Everything that was made there, so close to the West, was made better, and I was outfitted in turtlenecks, sailor shirts, jeans, overalls, ski hats, leather jackets, and tailored school uniforms that actually held together. It was all new, and itched me horribly; like my father, I hated having on more than I needed. When my mother's best friend came over with her daughter, the girl cast longing looks at my clothes, and I at all the food she left on her plate.

It was after the following summer, when I was six, in Crimea, on the Black Sea coast in Ukraine, that things changed, that it came time for knowledge. It's the first summer I recall with my own memory, instead of through stories told by my parents about some other boy with my name. Crimea was fabled: the Soviet Riviera. They had peaches down there, cherries, apples, and pears good enough to ship home. The seawater was like velvet. My grandfather had been stationed in Crimea in the 1940s, and my parents had honeymooned there in 1975, if you could call a month in a shed a honeymoon. But even this wasn't easy to come by: A friend of my grandfather's—also named Arkady, so they were Arkady the Black and Arkady the Red, for the color of their hair—knew someone who knew someone. And you paid these people directly, a forbidden private transaction that increased the sensation of being away from the norm.

In 1975, my parents had gotten more than the shed. The female half of the couple that owned it worked as a cashier at a café on the beach. My parents would try to pay, but she would wave them off: "It's a drop in the sea." And she would point to the sea outside the window: the black, silky sea that was as luxurious as everything around it was humble. Her husband delivered dairy products, and never failed to unload some of his burden at home. For the honeymooners, he saved the delicacies known, for lack of better translation, as glazed quarklets: small rectangular bundles of *tvorog*—a firmer version of quark cheese—infused with vanilla extract, then dipped in chocolate. The little things were quick to sweat in the heat; there being no refrigeration, my parents had no choice but to eat them at once.

In the decade since, Crimea had not changed its balance of plenty and want. The sea was so clement—not too cold, not too warm, with pockets of both—that I lived in it, once I no longer feared going in. But the summer quadrupling of the population strained the city's supply networks so badly that there was hardly any food in the stores. Only an official sanatorium for the employees of a military hardware factory (free massages, mud baths, mineral water treatments) was well stocked. We could hear the clamor of knife and fork from the outdoor café behind its raised walls. Word was they even had a dietitian on staff.

Mortal people—even my grandfather couldn't get us into that sanatorium—sent ahead nonperishables from home in slatted wooden boxes. This was called "savage leisure"—vacation the primitive way. The same boxes returned home filled with southern fruit.

The compound that enclosed our rental had a great olive-green gate, a massive red star at its middle. When we pulled up, we found a woman in a long, dark skirt and shawl, lengths of gray hair gathered above her sun-creased face—she could have been a hundred, or a hundred and twenty—sitting on a rickety foldout chair trying very hard not to move. "Hot," she declared. She rapped on the gate, and the red star snapped in half. Within, we were besieged by a herd of squealing pigs; it was our fate to spend summers in homes owned by men who kept swine. But Victor, the owner, did not slaughter his—he fed them peaches from the trees on his property.

Victor never wore shoes, and rarely pants, showered in the sea, and left the fraying, graying cloud of his hair to dry in the briny air without the aid of a comb. His wife was just as slim and attractive, and if they were slightly leathered by the year-round sun, they also shone with it, a bizarre, life-lived-outside vitality you would have had to assume was a foreigner's until they opened their mouths and Russian came out. Victor also grew cherries and grapes, from which he fermented wine, which, in the name of science and progress, he constantly sampled. In a month, we never encountered him sober—but never drunk, either. Just as we never saw his gray-haired, long-skirted mother anywhere but sitting sentinel by the gate, as if diamonds were concealed in the careless impasto of its paint job. "Hot," she said when we passed.

A sack of salami, black bread, hard-boiled eggs, thick-skinned tomatoes, peaches, and apples: lunch on the beach. One afternoon, I was so dazed from the sun that I drained the water in the cup the adults had left out before they headed down to the water. But Soviet people didn't drink water with their meals—"It'll just take up room in your stomach," Faina had explained once—and I, smashed from the vodka, collapsed under the little table and was snoring like a hopeless drunk, sand in my mouth, when the big people returned.

Otherwise, I wouldn't let my father alone, sitting on his head or crawling across the great fur of his chest; it was the color of night and billowed off him in tumbleweeds. (A Soviet vacation lasted nearly six weeks, so he'd come along; it was altogether too much rest for my grandparents.) Sometimes it was Soviet life that wouldn't let him be: "They've got potatoes at the store!" the call would go up and down the beach; my father would bolt to his feet and sprint off, shirtless, shocking the masses; haul two bags, the handles eating his skin, up to the Compound of the Red Star; then return for one more swim before dinner. Savage leisure.

The women—my father's older brother and his wife had come with us—left the beach first, to make food. At home, they usually discovered Victor's wife frying tomatoes in sunflower oil; these went onto a hunk of garlic-rubbed rye. There was nothing at the store, but at Victor's there was fresh pork, sun-fattened tomatoes, and sunflower oil that was like toasted seeds in your nose. In Russian, it was *podsolnechnoye* ("under the sun" oil) and, they said, "had the entire periodic table in it"—that is, every vitamin.

Returning later, my father, uncle, and I always took the way past a row of houses with blackberry brambles so high and thick they swung out over their fences. After hours of sun, so many berries had dropped to the ground that it was smeared violet. Sometimes they fell on your head as you walked. Admonished to keep my fingers clear of the brambles, I was allowed to pick those that leaned into the street. For every two I put in my mouth, I fed one to my father and one to my uncle. As their mother's children, they knew how to allow themselves a treat.

When we reached home, hiding our violet tongues, we found the table set with food enough for a dozen. If anyone could work the odd mix at her disposal into sigh-worthy meals, it was my aunt. She had grown up in a village, and cooked like it. She pan-fried flour-dusted pike perch in sunflower oil until it gleamed like the cheeks of a teenage girl after a snowfall, or so Victor said, summoned by the scent. The bones and the tail were so sweet we sucked them between our fingers. The cabbage that the store could be counted on to have even after the apocalypse she transformed into *salat provençal*—shredded cabbage, sweet onion, grated carrot, vinegar, sunflower oil, salt, pepper, and a teaspoon of sugar. (These ingredients would seem to have nothing to do with an actual Provençal salad, but Provence sounded exotic, so why not.)

PAN-FRIED PIKE PERCH WITH CREAMY
MASHED POTATOES AND CABBAGE SALAD

Time: 30–45 minutes   Serves: 4

Note: Pike perch, or zander, is as ubiquitous in Europe as it isn't in the States, so substitute another fish with meaty, flaky, sweet meat. Walleye comes closest (if you have a fishing rod and a lake, you're in luck), but a branzino or porgy would work fine as well. Or do as I do and throw yourself on the mercy of your local fishmonger.

SALAD

¼ cup diced red onion

2 tablespoons white vinegar, plus additional to taste

1 teaspoon sugar, plus additional to taste

½ pound green cabbage (¼ of a medium-size head), cut into small pieces (the size of a pinkie nail)

½ carrot, grated

Kosher salt and black pepper, to taste

Sunflower oil, for drizzling

POTATOES

1½ pounds Idaho potatoes, peeled

½ onion, chopped

1 bay leaf

Kosher salt, to taste

⅔ cup milk

1 tablespoon butter

2 garlic cloves, put through a garlic press

FISH

2 medium-size whole fish (about 1 pound each), rinsed and patted dry

Kosher salt and black pepper, to taste

½ cup flour

Sunflower oil, for frying

FOR THE SALAD:

1. In a small bowl, toss the onion with the vinegar and sugar.

2. Ball and squeeze the cabbage as you move it from your cutting board to a salad bowl, so it starts to release juices and flavor. (A good, well-mauled cabbage has a peppery, horseradish-like bite.) Add the carrot, the onion mixture, and salt and pepper to taste. Taste for tang and sweetness and add more vinegar and/or sugar until you have the flavor balance you want.

If you don't mind a little bite, you can add up to 3 more tablespoons of vinegar. If a hint of sweetness doesn't throw you off in salads, add up to 3 more teaspoons of sugar. Drizzle with a little sunflower oil, mix well, and let sit, so the flavors can exchange information.

FOR THE POTATOES:

1. In a medium pot or saucepan, place the potatoes, onion, and bay leaf and cover, by one inch, with well-salted water. Bring to a boil and cook until a knife goes through the potatoes smoothly, about 25 minutes.

2. Meanwhile, in a small saucepan, warm the milk and butter over medium-low heat.

3. Drain the potatoes and return them to the pot, leaving the onion and bay leaf in the strainer. Mash the potatoes while adding the warm milk mixture, a little at a time. Mix in the pressed garlic and season with salt. Cover to keep warm.

FOR THE FISH:

1. Snip any fins off the fish using scissors, but leave the tails and heads—they add flavor. Salt and pepper generously, both outside and inside the fish. Sprinkle the flour on a plate and dredge each fish, on both sides, until well coated; pat off any excess.

2. In a large nonstick pan, heat a generous amount of sunflower oil over medium-high heat. When the oil has had several minutes to get very hot, add the fish—taking care not to get splattered by hot oil. Cook on each side for 3–4 minutes.

3. Serve all together. For extra sinfulness, pour a spoonful of the oil in which the fish cooked over the mashed potatoes. The crisp, tart cabbage salad should complement and cut the creaminess of the potatoes and the richness of the fried fish. And the smell of fried fish, that staple of seaside places the world over, should give a hint of what it was like to walk into my aunt's kitchen after a long day pickling in the Black Sea. (For the record, unlike most of the recipes in this book, the Black Sea is blissfully undersalted.)

✦

Periodically, some of the adults vanished outside for a smoke—they were on vacation, after all. Then a round of tea with the jams

my aunt made from the blessing of peach, cherry, and grape outside. There would be jams again in the morning, with her *bliny*—
crepes. Thinking of that, who wanted to fall asleep? But I had
to—my uncle snored like thunder, so that if you weren't asleep by
the time the great bulk of him touched down on the other side of
the cardboard wall, you were doomed for the night. (Science must
study how my aunt managed to stay asleep with Krakatoa erupt-
ing by her a thousand times every night.) I was made to lie down
immediately after the meal, so the fat could "cohere." A skinny
child wouldn't do. At the beach, a new apple was jammed into my
mouth as soon as I finished the previous one. I wouldn't have the
same fruit back north. But I was being insulated against more than
a fruitless Minsk winter.

One evening back home that fall, dusky and cold, I was playing in
the sandbox with my classmate Sasha when two men approached
to ask if we knew the way to the school. Sasha was smarter, but I'd
never lied to anyone about anything, and agreed to show them.
When we reached it, I turned around but saw only one of the two
men behind me. The other was fifty meters away, by the back door
of an idling yellow car, waving *Come on*. That was when my father
rounded the corner, bursting in on us—he had come downstairs; it
was dinnertime. There was no altercation; in a blur, he swept me
up and we vanished. He carried me home in his arms, as if setting
me down would make me a flight risk, and I wept into his shoulder.
    Curiously, neither of my parents remembers this episode,
whereas I do, with painful clarity. Perhaps they don't because
they'd failed—the world they worked so hard to keep outside my
fantasy shell had trespassed inside. I had never even been allowed
to find out what my grandfather got up to—often, conversations
fell silent as soon as I joined the dinner table. But the older I became, the more the real world wanted to flicker through, like the

sun breaking the foliage of the chestnut trees in the massive yard of our apartment building.

One night, unable to sleep, I tiptoed into the hallway and overheard my grandfather telling a table of acquaintances about the expensive Armenian cognac with which he had once plied the surgeon who was going to remove my grandmother's gallbladder the next morning. They drank so much that the surgeon was still drunk when he picked up the scalpel. The table roared, though my grandmother did not.

In that place, no fantasy shelter could hold. Bigger boys from another yard might come and demand last names to see who among us needed a whipping because he was Jewish. (My Russian Orthodox alias was Novikov—the New Man, or the Rookie, depending on how you translate it.) When, in second grade, older boys encircled flame-haired, perennially snot-nosed Eugene, his miserably ill-tailored school uniform on him like a sack, I broke in and shouted until they dispersed. Perhaps I did this because I had been misled by my family into believing that we lived in a country of justice and valor. Perhaps because I had somehow osmosed from my grandfather that they always dispersed if only you fought.

Sometimes I was the one who attacked. One late-autumn day, standing in the big yard before my skinny friend Pavel—a too-thin nylon brown coat with a fur-lined hoodie; always-chapped lips; bright-white but uneven teeth; a stream of snot at his nose—I wound up and smashed my fist into his belly. No reason. No one else was around. Pavel doubled over but said nothing and did not defend himself, as if he understood such things as his fate.

The following summer, Pavel drowned in the Black Sea. For months, I was sure it was because I had punched him. However, I hadn't told anyone that I had, and neither had Pavel, and in this way I escaped justice.

CHAPTER 3

1988

What to cook to win over a former countrywoman made good in the West

How to eat when you've sold your stove because you're emigrating halfway around the world

What food to pack to get five mouths through one Iron Curtain

✤

You won't live like that at first," the woman at our dining table said, gesturing toward the closet, where her fur coat hung. My grandfather had insisted on helping her out of it, ostensibly out of chivalry but really so he could paw it and see what you could get in America. Chinchilla, she'd said, but he knew what he knew: That was rabbit. It was a good copy, though—the coat light, the hair dense. He had held the coat closet wide open so she could notice the blue German lamb's wool there, the minks, the French shearling knee-length. He was doing just fine without the wisdom of people like her.

It was 1988—Soviet Jews were leaving in droves for America. (During this period, the word "leaving" came to refer to a single thing requiring no clarification.) That it was easier to leave didn't mean it was easy—as always, only certain things worked at certain times for certain people. For instance, not only were letters from abroad getting through to us—opened and read, but with almost nothing crossed out—but the émigrés *themselves* were sometimes permitted to return and sit in former friends' living rooms without ideological coaching, all while the authorities continued to menace and demoralize those trying to leave. But we had slipped through.

On this go-around, my father and grandfather went into the visa office when called. We were leaving, and we wanted to know what to expect.

My grandmother didn't know how to set the table for our guest—would Soviet food seem paltry next to the glories to which this former countrywoman now surely had access in American supermarkets? My grandmother decided on the opposite of what she had served all those years ago to the safety instructor from my father's technical college: In times of uncertainty among kinspeople, lean on the Jewish regimen. Dill-flecked chicken bouillon with *kneidels* (matzoh balls, from matzoh baked and delivered by secret couriers at night); a chicken stuffed with macaroni and fried gizzards; the neck skin of several chickens tied together and stuffed with caramelized onion, flour, and dill to make a sausage-like item called *helzel*. For excess, there was deconstructed, or "lazy," stuffed cabbage—everything that would have stewed inside a cabbage leaf shredded and shaped into patties instead—and a chicken *rulet*: a deboned chicken layered with sautéed garlic, caramelized carrot, and hard-boiled egg, then rolled up and fastened for cooking with needle and thread. It had a noble pedigree: In 1941, with the Nazis beginning to starve Leningrad, the Soviets discovered two thousand tons of mutton guts in the seaport and made *rulet* out of them. As always, my grandmother made too much, but you had to show you didn't lack for things.

"You'll have to eat a little shit to start with," the woman went on, wiping her mouth; on sighting the food, she had forgotten her queenly hauteur. "But one of my friends owns a Hallmark franchise—greeting cards—and would you like to know what she hauls in in a day?" She allowed a pregnant pause to expire. *"Two thousand dollars."* My mother, eager to show gratitude, gasped in wonder. My grandfather selflessly refrained from raising his hands in mock worship—he had the equivalent of that in his pocket right now. My father uncrossed the arms he liked to keep at his chest in a kind of preemptive objection. "But what about crime?" he said. "It's all they show on television."

The woman swished around her bracelets. "I walk like this all the time," she said. "Just don't bring hats. Everyone has a car and drives everywhere, so you don't need a hat. If you're wearing one, that means you're an immigrant. In fact, don't bring anything. They have everything there. And it costs next to nothing." Perhaps it was because my grandfather couldn't tell this high-handed hag what he really thought that the first thing he stuffed into our luggage was the gray mink hat that sat on his head from September to April.

It was like one of my father's strange fairy tales: Little by little— for free, for favors, for pay—the apartment began disappearing. The vanishing of the television, taken by one of my mother's co-workers, caused me special grief. When my grandfather and I weren't "polishing" the cold concrete seats of the soccer stadium itself, it was where I watched Dinamo Minsk go up against Zenit Leningrad and Torpedo Moskva. The separation of twenty-two previously indistinguishable men into two adversarial uniforms, the pride of a city behind each, was a gnomic, primitive message from some other dimension in which, as the pig slaughterer whose summer cottage we rented had so essentially put it, "there will be you—and there will be them." The television alone knew my guilt for rooting—the Russian word is *bolet'*, to be ill for—for the Finns instead of the Soviets in hockey. The Finns had such mellifluous names, vowel after vowel, like Arctic Hawaiians. And they were so clean and crisp in their white-and-blue jerseys, so calm against the tense red of ours. They looked like our players—tall, fair-haired, light-skinned—but without the roughness and disfigurement of our faces. Disfigured by hockey, but also by how we ate and drank, by the expressions into which our faces were fixed.

My bookshelves were attached to the wall, so I believed they were safe, but one day they were gone, too. Then the Persian rug on which, on all fours, I read the sports pages. Then my bed. The kitchen went last. A friend of my mother's hauled away everything in it. They agreed on a price, but the woman gave us no money; she had a relative in America, and since each emigrant could take the equivalent of only $90 in currency (and $250 in possessions), the woman's relative would pay 50 percent of the agreed-upon price when we got to America—for us, a way of getting out more currency than was allowed. Our position was weak: Who knew if the phone number the woman scrawled on a piece of graph paper corresponded to an actual human. But if it did, that poor person had to shell out money on behalf of a Soviet relative for nothing in exchange. So 50 percent was the actuarial measure of the exposure and risk for all involved.

You can sleep on the floor, but you can't eat the air; how to survive without a stove or a fridge? For the first time in my life, I experienced the dread of not knowing from where the next meal would come. No one had explained that those relatives and friends who did not fear associating with us—"men would not come to our plague-stricken house, but sent their wives instead," as Nadezhda Mandelstam, the condemned Soviet poet Osip Mandelstam's wife, wrote in more severe circumstances—would come with everything from utensils to foldout tables. My aunt brought braised beef with cubed potatoes and marinated peppers; blintzes stuffed with ground beef and caramelized onion; and a chicken stuffed with crepes and more browned onion, then roasted. All this disappeared quickly. Departures like ours meant more helping hands, but also more mouths.

Though my grandparents' home never lacked guests, this was a different kind of assembly. The smartest people congregated in the kitchen, where the constant replenishment of the foldout table turned the day into a single, unbroken meal. But there were people standing—with glasses, or arms folded, or consoling hands atop grieving wrists—in every room, even mine. (Evidently, its emptiness had re-registered it as common property.) Periodically, these congregants would make a pilgrimage to the kitchen like steam bathers who'd spent too much time in the cold and down thimbles of cognac or vodka. Often, no one had to be anywhere in particular. There was nothing to do in the Soviet Union other than the obscene number of hours you spent queueing for food. You could go to the cinema, you could go for a walk in the park, you could watch a sporting event, and on a special occasion you could splurge in a café. Otherwise, you sat in people's kitchens, ate, drank, and talked.

The apartment hummed with festiveness, nerves, and anticipation. Even my father strode around with a strange gregarious bloom. Not long before, he had kicked in the television—the thick, greenish glass shattered—and vanished for days. Nothing was explained to me—a new TV appeared right away—but I knew it had to be another argument about my grandparents making all the decisions, and was filled with anguish. But now he and my grandparents smiled and laughed with each other. How? The only thing my father hated more than too many people was falsehood.

People came and went, but my grandmother's older sister, who never took vacation days and disliked socializing even more than my father, came for the entire day every day, which indicated just how extreme our situation must have been. As did the rolls with sugar and cinnamon she brought, still warm, the crowns shining with egg wash like little brioches—you never saw extravagance like that from her.

The war had orphaned the two sisters. When the Nazis invaded, their grandmother, not a slim woman, had squeezed behind the furnace and suffocated herself. Their parents and grandfather were killed in the pogrom that finished off those Jews in the Minsk ghetto who had survived the previous three. (My grandmother had managed to slip out the month before, but her grandfather was ailing and her parents would not leave him.) When the sisters returned home after the war, they found it occupied by an ethnic Belarusian who had collaborated with the Nazis. He gave them a corner. When they were out one day, he stole and pawned all the clothes the Red Cross had given them, leaving one dress apiece.

ROAST CHICKEN STUFFED WITH
CREPES AND CARAMELIZED ONION

Time: 2 hours   Serves: 6

My Aunt Lyuba is one of those fabled ex-Soviet women who can "cover" a multi-course table for a dozen guests in an hour without advance warning. This dish takes a little longer but is worth the trouble for an unusual, homey take on a roast chicken.

4 tablespoons vegetable oil, plus additional for the pan	4 large eggs
	²/₃ cup flour
1¹/₂ onions, chopped	1 teaspoon sugar
Kosher salt and black pepper, to taste	¹/₄ teaspoon salt
	1 whole chicken, 5–6 pounds (a
1¹/₄ cups milk	larger chicken means a larger
¹/₄ cup water	cavity for stuffing)

1. Heat 2 tablespoons of the oil in a pan over medium-low heat. Add the onions and cook, stirring once in a while, until golden brown. Season with salt and pepper.

2. While the onions are cooking, make the batter by mixing the milk, water, and 2 of the eggs. Then whisk the flour in, little by little. Then add the sugar and ¼ teaspoon salt. And finally, add the 2 remaining tablespoons of vegetable oil, whisking well. Your batter should be pretty liquid.

3. Warm up a small (8- to 9-inch) crepe pan or nonstick skillet over medium-low heat. Add a tiny amount of oil (or cooking spray), give it a little time to warm up, and roll it around so it covers the whole pan. Raise the heat to medium.

4. Lift the pan off direct heat—otherwise the batter sticks too quickly—and add enough batter that it expands to the edges of the pan (around 2 tablespoons), swirling the batter until it forms as perfect a circle as possible. You want a thin crepe, so try to add as little batter as necessary to reach the edges of the pan after swirling. Return to direct heat.

5. After 2 minutes or so at medium heat, the crepe should be sufficiently browned underneath and crisp around the edges for you to be able to use a spatula or a fine-tipped wooden skewer to lift it. Now you have to flip it to the other side. The difficult truth is that there's no better instrument than your fingers, if they can withstand the heat.

6. If the crepe tears, don't worry: The first crepe always comes out sideways, as we say. You can "darn" the hole by pouring in a little new batter to fill it. Either way, this is a forgiving dish for ugly practice crepes—they will end up out of view. After 2 minutes on the other side, the crepe should be ready; set aside and repeat with the remaining batter.

7. Stack the crepes on top of each other and cut into quarter-inch-wide vertical strips, and then cut those strips into thirds horizontally. Mix in a large bowl with the cooked onion, and then add the 2 remaining eggs. Mix thoroughly.

8. Preheat the oven to 450 degrees. (The high heat will give the skin a nice crispness.) Rinse the chicken and pat dry. Season generously, inside and out, with salt and pepper. Then fill the cavity with the crepe-and-onion mixture, closing the skin flaps around it as much as possible. Lay the chicken down gently in an oven-worthy pan, breasts down so they absorb the dripping juice and the fat of the thighs. Cook for 10–12 minutes per pound, until the juices from a thigh run clear when pricked with a fork.

✦

This affected the sisters very differently. My grandmother became flamboyant and unsparing, her hair half a foot high and her nails always painted; my grandmother's sister was humbly clothed and allergic to makeup. She took advantage of none of the private perks of the government job she got after going back for more school after the war. She barely touched food. Held on to every ruble. Didn't drink, didn't smoke, didn't laugh with everyone else. If her son was going to the theater, she had to go there after curtain to check that his coat was on one of the hangers and that he'd arrived safely. (Soviet cities not having anything like American traffic or sprawl, it didn't take her long to get there and back.) In the evenings, the young man hardly late, she'd begin calling police precincts and hospitals. To her husband, his family already lost to Communist purges by the time the Nazis arrived, nothing was holier than fresh lamb "forgotten about" at low heat for hours, or slices off a crescent of veal tongue with horseradish and chased with cold vodka—his last name was actually Golod, "*Hunger*"—but she always badgered him to cook less. She didn't hug my grandmother, didn't kiss her. But they had sat in each other's kitchens almost every day for forty-five years.

Her severity had its uses. Every fall, when the cabbage came in, the cellar disgorged a contraption resembling a cross between an ironing board and a giant mandolin, through which the women ran giant heads of cabbage, shreds leaping into the air like wisps of hair when my grandfather barbered. These went into jars the size of a boy's torso, with peppercorns, bay leaves, rings of onion, and cranberries. When they reemerged, a month or two later, they bit the tongue in a way that was rare during those dead winter months. It was a group job, but when my grandfather's brother appeared to "help," he sat down and filled the kitchen with bitter, cheap smoke, which meant the kitchen window had to come open, which meant the boy might catch cold. So he was eased out. Then his daughter came and drank instant coffee and dropped rumors. She was less harmful, but useless, so she was creatively disappeared as well. The job "moved" only when it was my grandmother and her sister.

UNCLE TIMA'S BRAISED VEAL TONGUE

Time: 2 hours   Serves: 4

The beauty of this recipe is that it requires no vigilance—cover the tongue with water, overload the liquid with spices, bring to a boil, and let simmer at a low setting for ninety minutes. (More if the tongue is bigger than the one used below.) Tongue might take a minute for American eaters, but give it a try and you'll see what Mexican taco makers and Slavs have known for a long time: There are few tenderer proteins. And it'll follow your lead: You can pile in whatever spices you want, after the essentials of bay leaf, garlic, and allspice. (You can also go with fresh versions—fresh dill, fresh parsley; you're creating flavor for the stock.) Veal tongue is more expensive than cow tongue, but not by much, and, for obvious reasons, it comes in smaller, more meal-friendly sizes.

1 veal tongue (about 1¼ pounds)	25 peppercorns
12 garlic cloves, peeled and cut in half lengthwise	1 tablespoon coriander seeds
2 tablespoons salt	1 tablespoon whole allspice
7 bay leaves	1 tablespoon caraway seeds
	1 tablespoon dill weed

1. Rinse the tongue under cold water. Put into a pot and cover, by 2 inches, with water. Add remaining ingredients and bring to a boil. Lower the heat and simmer, partly covered, for 90 minutes.

2. Stick a sharp knife into the tongue. If it goes through like butter, you're done.

3. Remove the tongue with tongs and run it under cold water. As soon as it's cool enough to touch, peel off and discard the pale casing.

Slice and serve with **Homemade Horseradish** *or your condiment of choice.*

✢

Aunt Polina was so undone by my grandmother's leaving that she even let her husband bring his tongue and braised lamb. Making the most of his rare dispensation, he snuck in a new pièce de résistance: potato latkes drizzled with goose fat and honey.

The various discouragement taxes remained in place: It cost seven months' salary per adult to renounce citizenship. The white identity papers we received in exchange were so flimsy that someone figured out how to doctor them: Move up the birthdate and retire sooner in the States. We were all becoming new people; no one needed to know. But the bejeweled and false-furred acquaintance who had visited from America had said no one lied there. If you did, your name went into a file. To a Soviet person, that made perfect sense. My father said no to the age adjustment.

Émigrés were allowed to ship things forward, but the boxes were rummaged at Soviet customs. People who owned diamonds threw them like beads into the boxes and container units they sent—they might never find the diamonds, but neither might customs. Those shipments that made it to New York encountered new, American dangers—two boxes of my father's construction equipment were stolen out of the trunk of the relative who received them.

After the construction equipment, we sent nothing ahead. Our visitor had said America had everything, and for pennies. So we crammed a century of Russian life into five suitcases. The things we carried included a single photo of my parents' wedding; my checkers set; cupping jars and mustard plasters; the cobalt West German tea set; Italian enamel cooking vessels; my grandfather's French shearling coat; and three books, the comedians Ilf and Petrov sandwiched by Bulgakov and Pushkin. (This was an American sandwich—Soviets ate only open-face sandwiches.) And we carried everything we had been told would sell in the secondhand markets outside Rome, the next transit point after Vienna: electric drills, Zenit cameras, peaked army caps, Lenin pins, good Soviet linen, Armenian cognac.

We did not carry my mother's wedding ring, alone worth more than the allowed limit per person; the Yugoslav entertainment center; my grandmother's Finnish leather boots; my mother's Austrian suede heels; my grandfather's collection of Italian leather shoes; Jules Verne, Alexandre Dumas, or the Soviet writer Ilya Ehrenburg; my mother's wedding dress; or the ice skates I never learned how to use. Outside of his tools, my father possessed almost nothing and so had nothing to part with. But we also did not carry the cast-iron cooking pot. It was too heavy. It would have made one last loss to that place that had already taken so much were my grandmother Faina not more than happy to have it back in her hands.

The train left at six in the evening—it would go to Warsaw, then Czechoslovakia, then Vienna: thirty-six hours. No one knew how long customs would take, so we appeared at the station in the late morning; no one could sleep anyway. First we had to fill out a declaration listing everything in the suitcases. I had been turned into a mule—a gold necklace had been hidden under the top button of my checked shirt, filling me with dread. I fidgeted with the top button, which was eating my neck, but stopped after a tight-jawed look from my mother.

When our turn came, the customs agent cast out everything my mother and grandmother had so carefully packed—clusters of émigrés were reassembling their crudely dispersed lives all around the hall—and checked it against their declaration. "And this?" he said, holding a kind of briefcase from which gleamed rows of gold-plated utensils, each corseted by a burgundy band. (These, too, were meant for pawn down the line.)

"Cutlery," my mother said. "It's under the limit."

"Where is it here?" He waved the declaration.

He wouldn't give my mother the form, so she had to try to read it while he fluttered it just out of her reach. It wasn't there. "I made a mistake," she said. "I have a terrible earache. I didn't mean to hide it—you see, it was on top in the suitcase." The part about the earache was true; she always had inflammations. She reached for the form: "I can add it."

The agent moved the paper out of her reach. "It's confiscated," he said.

"She made a mistake!" my grandfather said, his eyes lighting up.

The agent looked down at him—he had a head over him. "One more word, bitch," he hissed, "and these spoons won't be the only thing staying back." My grandfather's eyes burned terribly. He had heard such a thing a million times, but every time, he had been able to answer, usually by arranging an encounter between some very hard object and a vulnerable part of the offender's body. We watched his pride war against his responsibility—almost wearily, because so many times he had chosen the pride. Eventually he stalked off, though the words "fucking fascist" could be heard out of his mouth if you were young enough for sharp hearing. In the heat of the altercation, I had forgotten about the gold around my neck.

They did not take our salami, hard-boiled eggs, or tinned sprats. Perhaps even a Soviet customs agent would not have taken away a loaf of Borodinsky.

Not everyone who wished to see us off came to the farewell platform: Things were changing, but who knew where they would end up. My mother's best friend came, but not her husband, a lauded opera singer and stage actor: things to lose. "You can't eat two dinners," he had said when he learned we were leaving. "What do you need over there?" ("Over there" had boiled down to the same single meaning that "leaving" had.) *Easy for him to say*, the people with one foot on the ledge of the Vienna express may have wanted to think. But it would've been false to deny the progress our country had made in the thirty years since my father looked in vain for fruit at the fruit-and-vegetable store.

When the train moved, we opened one of the bottles of Armenian cognac—damn the lira we could collect for it from the Italians. The adults clinked, uttered brief toasts—"Forward," "Let's go," "To leaving"—and drained the filigreed crystal thimbles that had survived the pillage in the customs hall. These, too, would get sold to Italian cupboards. No one had an appetite, but it was gauche to take alcohol down empty, so a cucumber was dug out and passed around amid remarks that a semi-sour pickle would have done better. My grandfather waved off the cucumber and sniffed hard from his sleeve—what uneducated people did when there was no chaser—and my mother paused her sobbing to glare at him in reprimand. Who was there to be embarrassed in front of now? But the readiness to be—the extreme consciousness of what others would think, with which everyone in that place, but especially Jews, lived—did not let go just because she was finally crossing the border. My mother was thirty-three, my father thirty-five, my grandparents sixty-one. And a Soviet year, like a dog's life, was like ten years elsewhere.

My mother had been crying since she reached the platform. It was September; the air was autumnally crisp; she kept saying things like "We will never see this again" and "We will never smell that again." And then, just like that, we were forever out of the only city we'd known and into the birch-studded countryside where we'd spent so many campfire weekends and my father had picked plums for Grandma Daria (for Grandma Daria's *pigs*) all those years ago.

A mere day and a half later, we rolled into the Other World, Vienna, the *West*. Living up to her reputation for militant independence, Grandmother Faina had declined to join us—she'd follow six months later with my father's older brother. Hers were the last family hands to let go of the cast-iron pot, which stayed behind in its (adopted) homeland, and is quite possibly serving someone decently to this day. Belarus may have changed less in the past thirty years than in the thirty years prior.

A year after we left, the opera singer who had no use for two dinners would turn out to want them as well. He and his wife had a nine-year-old of their own to rescue—the girl who had longed for my clothes while I lusted after her food.

CHAPTER 4

September 1988

What to cook on your first night in the West

What to cook when you miss your sister so much you want to die,
or your husband needs to ingratiate himself
with a black-market middleman

✴

My father woke first—inside one of his fairy tales. Neatly marked roads, tended fields, country homes carefully painted white and yellow—the suburbs of Vienna were turning into the city. Nabokov, the forced exile, kept writing stories about fairy-tale portholes in Europe on whose other side the narrator's acquaintance—always the narrator's acquaintance—finds himself magically transported to the pre-revolutionary Russia of his youth. My father was having a similar experience in the other direction.

Soldiers in black uniforms with guard dogs clustered on the train platform, though only beside the car that held the émigrés. (In 1973, Palestinian militants had taken hostage a train of Vienna-bound Soviet Jews.) A half century earlier, men in similar dress had overseen, perhaps from the same platform, the shipment of Jews out. Now they were protecting us on the way in. It wasn't difficult to pick out the Jew in their midst, the local representative of the Hebrew Immigrant Aid Society (HIAS), the American organization sponsoring our passage. Following him out of the station, we passed a kiosk into which we peered like Kalahari tribesmen sighting our first spaceship. The kiosks in Minsk offered two newspapers—*Trud* (Labor) and *Pravda* (Truth)—and maybe some pens. This kiosk looked like the Ark. "*Guten Morgen*," the vendor said in the language of the people who had destroyed my grandparents' families—it fell on my grandmother's ears for the first time in forty-five years. "*Gut margn*," my grandfather answered him, stunned, in the language of the people destroyed. They were almost the same.

Not only was every vehicle parked in the station lot a Mercedes, but the *minivan* that would convey us to our hotel also bore the three-pointed star. Perhaps cleaning women also drove Mercedeses here! However, the Germans had not designed for political refugees—not one row in the minivan was large enough for even one of our jumbo suitcases. But then our minder yanked a latch and the row of seats . . . fell away to lie flat. A man acquainted with the darkest recesses of the Soviet black market, another who had immunized himself to sincerity outside the safety of his household—they gaped like children too young to be embarrassed about their enthusiasm, and like men who had to wonder about just how many years they'd squandered on *that* place.

The setup that awaited us at the Pension Rose, where we would lodge until our documents were in order and we could go on to Rome, was equally wondrous: separate rooms for the families (what had been one family would henceforth be two); a private backyard with benches, flowers, and trees; if a shared bathroom, then a spotless one; and from every scrubbed corner an aroma of some kind of soothing, herbaceous detergent—all this in an establishment of only two stars. Only the communal kitchen on every floor was familiar.

There my grandmother went, leaving, over the next weeks, only for showers and sleep. The first meal of our new lives used up the last of the old: hard-boiled eggs, salami, cutlets, and beef tongue. A young fellow-traveling couple contributed fried liver with buckwheat, and a young man named Ilya who'd been sent on alone—my grandmother found this inexplicable and placed herself in charge of his feeding—contributed a jar of jam made by his mother. But there was no more bread. My father was chosen to go out into the city. My grandfather questioned the wisdom of using Yiddish in a German-speaking city—in truth, he was afraid to go out there—whereas my father had memorized the odd English word on the way.

That morning, for the first time in memory, my family ate without bread: My father had vanished. When he finally appeared, two hours after he left, everyone began shouting with relief and reproach. "I'm sorry," he said. "I lost my mind." He had gone only a block. The supermarket door had *slid open by itself*, whereupon he nearly toppled the tiny old Austrian woman coming out, her scream loud enough for the other shoppers to stare with cold shock at the bearish man who had accosted Frau Fichter. But this my father, ready for error and penalty, only imagined: Frau Fichter did exclaim—but then smiled. Smiled! Like an idiot, my father smiled back. No one smiled socially in the USSR. They didn't have automatic sliding doors there, either.

Inside he found grapes from Chile (Chile?! How about the moon!), rose-rumped chickens, tortes too pretty to touch, and a machine that produced what he could only conclude was *fresh-squeezed* orange juice. At checkout, these goods were placed inside plastic bags, on which my father had never laid eyes, either. Soviet shoppers used "perhaps" bags: netted string bags named after a word that meant, vaguely, "and maybe I will," an incantation of hope for luck on the shelves. Because my grandfather had regular access to such luck, he couldn't use a see-through "perhaps" bag; he had a special "definitely" bag, with handles to withstand concrete. "His arms live below his knees," people said about him as he carried his load, admiringly and not.

That evening, we went on a walk and saw what my father had. Only my grandmother wouldn't go out—she couldn't handle the sound of German. She would make dinner from the bounty my father had hauled home, and wait at the Rose. But her waiting was disappointed again.

This was not a place you could walk through quickly, the tidy Austrians striding past, the lindens swaying in the light breeze of early September, the blaring lights from every imaginable shop. On one corner, we came upon a cart with bratwurst. Street food didn't exist in the USSR—it was considered primitive, unhygienic. But everything in Vienna looked as if licked clean. I looked up expectantly from below, like a cat. Hands reached for the dowry of shillings that sat heavily in our pockets; each of us received a subsidy of a hundred per day—only seven dollars but, between five people, enough to feast over and over.

The bratwurst man tonged one into a paper boat and incised it, whereupon a pungent melted cheese gushed out over the herb- and fat-studded meat. Into the gash he poured a stream of grainy, olive-colored mustard, moving his wrist back and forth the way my father did when he painted with a brush instead of a roller. He extended it to my mother, the woman, but she nodded gratefully and pointed at me, in whose wavering hands the boat finally landed. The man pointed at his mouth—hot—but I couldn't wait and incinerated my tongue. I was on my last bite when, sheepishly, I looked up to find three adults looking down with envy and love. It had not occurred to me they wouldn't get one, or three, for themselves.

The next block offered a cart that sold ice cream. In this country, the sausages melted like ice cream, and the ice cream came wrapped at the ends with striped twine, like cured sausage. Again, only I got one—the reason, I was assured, was that my grandmother was waiting with dinner. The ice cream was only vanilla, but the vanilla and cream were in perfect matrimony, and platonically suspended between solid and liquid, though I did my part by licking so hard that the ice cream hardly had time to think about melting.

My grandmother had made chicken-under-a-brick, one of those broilers with asses like the cheeks of a teenage girl after a snowfall (Crimean Victor's expression had worked its way into our lexicon), butterflied and pan-fried in oil infused with garlic (and cayenne

and coriander she had found in a cupboard) under a plate held down
by a drill my father had brought to sell in Italy. My parents and
grandfather covered for me. Whenever my grandmother turned
away, a fork appeared over my plate, stabbed a drumstick, and vanished. Every plate was cleaned to the last shred of garlic—the walk
had left the adults with a remarkable appetite. We finished with a
plum strudel that the young couple who had contributed the fried
liver earlier had ferried from home. Young Ilya sliced it, because he
had somehow managed to smuggle an enormous knife—a scimitar,
really—past customs. I felt what I had two nights before, when
out of the bedlam of our suitcases my grandmother had conjured
a meal that looked exactly as it had at home. I wished I could be
hungry again.

The next morning, we went for our medical screenings—the
gravely ill and mentally unfit would not qualify for America. Chernobyl had blown up two years earlier. The wind had blown north
that day, away from nearby Kiev and toward Minsk, two hundred
miles away. It had been raining, but my mother and I had gone for
a walk. The puddles on the ground were oily and yellow, but that
was pollen from the flowering lindens. The next day, my mother
received a call from a boy she'd passed over when she was younger,
now a cyberneticist at the Academy of Sciences. "Close your windows, and don't go outside," he said; as someone closer to government information, he knew. "Why?" she said. "I can't tell you," he
said, and hung up. Several days later, on May 1, we were made to
march for Labor Day as if all was normal. Since then, no one in the
immediate family had developed symptoms, but there was no telling what European X-ray technology would discover. (I did have a
second cousin who had been born without hair.) My mother wasn't
sure whether to mention the earache still tormenting her—who
knew what these people considered gravely ill.

She felt deranged. She had cried most of the way to Vienna and
had resumed shortly after settling at the Rose. She joked sourly

that she would be singled out, but for the mentally unfit category. She took a chance with the physician, pointed at her ear, and made an expression of pain. He examined her, then brought a jar of pills with a childproof safety feature that he had to show her how to overcome. Then he drew a picture of an ear, a mouth, and one of the pills. He circled the pill, drew an arrow from it to the mouth, then crossed out the ear: *Put the pill in the mouth, not the ear.* In the Soviet Union, earaches were treated with alcohol-soaked overnight compresses kept in place by a scarf wrapped like a war bandage. After enough émigrés had tried to put the pills in their ears, the doctor had decided he needed a diagram.

The following day, we went to the synagogue: A Jewish organization was sponsoring us, after all, and it was September's march of Jewish holidays that had extended our magic stay in Vienna. (You couldn't work on these, it was explained.) The HIAS van dropped our group off on a canyon-like street concealed from the sun by tall residential buildings. We looked around but saw nothing. Admittedly, no one knew what to look for, never having seen a synagogue.

"They call these streets the Bermuda Triangle," the guide declared—they were winding and narrow; one was guaranteed to get lost. He pointed to a building indistinguishable from its neighbors except for the Hebrew script above its entry. When it was built, he said, the facades of non-Catholic houses of worship could not look out into the street, so the Stadttempel was made to look like the homes it was next to. This saved it during Kristallnacht—you couldn't burn it without burning the neighbors. No other Viennese synagogue survived the war.

Services were in progress, so the guide called us away, but my grandfather hadn't been brought all this way to look at a door. He split off and went for the entrance, my hand in his. Carefully, he opened the door and we slid in our noses. It looked like an opera house. In the middle of the great hall, men shrouded with fringed, striped garments, their heads covered with skullcaps and their ears hung with sidelocks, pitched themselves forward and recoiled while chanting, the place humming like an apiary. My grandfather twisted his finger into his temple—the Soviet gesture for *crazy.* "Fanatics," he shrugged, and closed the door.

My grandfather was young enough to have had a grandmother who spoke only Yiddish and observed the Jewish holidays and dietary restrictions. But we, like most Soviet people, genuinely regarded religion as mindless cultism. The activists on both sides of the Iron Curtain who fought so hard for our release were impelled by the injustice of the discrimination people like us endured no matter how much we tried to blend in. But we weren't emigrating for the freedom to worship. Ours was a "salami immigration," as people called it—all we wanted was the freedom to make money.

At the Rose, my grandmother, who had declined to join the synagogue outing with an authority none of the rest of us thought we possessed, was pounding the last of dinner together: chicken stuffed with prunes, apples, and apricots, summer's last bounty at the market. During those first days in Vienna, she was periodically pleaded with to relent and to rest, but she missed her sister beyond language and could bury it only at the stove—in the unambiguous goodness of feeding people. If she needed a butcher cut, she called over Ilya with his scimitar, and sometimes they spoke, like two orphans.

All the adults were beside themselves with the dislocation of what they were going through, but my grandmother's was of a different order. She had been separated from a sister who was her sole living connection to a family lost in the Holocaust. None of us had ever strayed from one another—ordinary people in the Soviet Union almost never traveled outside of it, and hardly even within it. But our genes also carried generations of anxiety about safety as Jews—if we went to the wrong place, or left the relative safety that came with community, the panic that set in was as intense in the person leaving as in the people being left. (My father left behind his brother and mother, but they weren't as close as my grandmother had been with her sister.) There must be no one for whom this is less natural to comprehend than Americans, whose country enshrines mobility as a national virtue—unless you ask African Americans about their elders, perhaps. It isn't only that Americans don't fear going from one place to another; it's also that they don't fear letting each other go there and don't use guilt to discourage it, while those who go don't feel ashamed for wanting to.

ROAST CHICKEN STUFFED WITH DRIED FRUIT AND APPLES

Time: 1 hour, 15 minutes Serves: 6

12 dried apricots
1 whole chicken, 5–6 pounds (a larger chicken means a larger cavity for stuffing)
Kosher salt and black pepper, to taste
12 pitted prunes
3–4 Granny Smith apples, cut into eighths and seeded

1. In a heatproof bowl, cover the apricots with boiling water and let soak until softened, about 20 minutes.

2. Preheat the oven to 450 degrees. (The high heat will give the skin a nice crispness.) Rinse the chicken and pat dry. Season generously, inside and out, with salt and pepper. Drain the apricots and stuff inside the cavity, along with the prunes. Close the skin flaps around the dried fruit as much as possible so it doesn't fall out during cooking. Lay the chicken down gently in an oven-worthy pan (make sure there's room in it for the apples—see step 3), breasts down so they absorb the dripping juice and the fat of the thighs. Cook for 10–12 minutes per pound, until the juices from the thigh run clear when pricked with a fork.

3. About 25 minutes before the chicken is done, scatter the apple slices in the pan around the chicken. Return to the oven for the remaining cooking time.

That night, there was an unfamiliar body at the dinner table. From behind, he looked like Sharansky, the dissident: same height, same bald pate, though the leather jacket was expensive. No, it was Sasha from Moscow. Sasha had been part of an earlier immigrant wave, had looked around Vienna and thought: *Why not here?* The Austrians didn't mind, even put him on social assistance. He padded his income by reselling to the locals what the émigrés brought. That night, after wiping the chicken fat from his mouth and all but kneeling before my grandmother, he gave my grandfather $250 and left with a blue-on-white Chinese rug we had hauled with us. He returned the next night to buy more. He made sure to arrive right before dinner.

That night, the Rose was in disarray—Meyer, an old émigré, had gone for a pre-dinner walk and vanished. The table was set, but who could eat. Sasha tried to tell stories about Vienna, but no one listened. Then he proposed to call on some people—what did Meyer look like?

"What kind of people?" he was asked.

"People who find people," he said.

Meyer had looked old since boyhood—all wrinkles. Wore a cap. Other than that, even his son couldn't say. Sasha was about to make a call when the doorbell rang downstairs. The whole party rushed down, young Ilya reaching the door first. On the other side stood two policemen and old Meyer, short as a child between them. He'd gotten turned around and, on sighting the law, jammed a finger into his sternum and begun shouting, *"Ya Moskva! Ya Moskva!"*—"*I am Moscow! I am Moscow!*" Everyone knew where the Soviet people were staying.

Meyer's recovery was toasted with cognac. Were there more bottles, Sasha wanted to know? "Depends on the price," my grandfather said. That evening, Sasha left with two, and the next night with three more. It was *The Thousand and One Nights* immigrant style—with short, bald Sasha instead of Scheherazade and, in lieu of tales, cognac, cameras, wind-up toys, and locksmith equipment.

When Sasha found out my grandfather cut hair, he submitted himself to the maestro. Hair sprouted only from the sides of his head, but what he had, he wanted to have looking nice. Done and dashing, he gave my grandfather a handful of shillings.

"Dollars," Arkady said.

"What do you want with over there so badly?" Sasha said.

"You're asking me why I want to go to America?" my grandfather said.

"Look around yourself," Sasha said. "What else do you want? What is it with all of you, stampeding over there like a herd?"

My grandfather stared at Sasha—a little man working the black market and living off social assistance. He was comparing Austria to America?! And Sasha stared at my grandfather—what did this know-it-all know about America? Sasha shook his head and paid in dollars.

The next day, we finally made our appeal to the Americans. This was a formality—the official interview would take place at the American embassy in Rome, after the medical results and the rest of the information gathering had come in.

"What do you mean, 'information gathering'?" my grandfather asked the Russian-speaking staffer at the American consulate.

"Membership in the Communist Party, that type of thing," the man said. "Drink or smoke, any of you?"

"Holidays only," my father joked. Vienna had released in him something that had been constricted in Minsk. He neither smoked nor drank.

The man peered at him. "You're making a joke?"

My father's smile vanished. "Yes, just a joke."

"Don't joke that way in Rome. I'll put down 'no.'"

The travel authorizations to Rome came through soon after that.

Sasha invited us to celebrate our last evening—there was an organ concert at the cathedral in our neighborhood; we passed it every time we went to the metro.

"We're saving our money, Sasha," my grandmother said.

"So that's why you've got me," Sasha said.

Even my grandmother came. My grandfather pulled out his striped silk shirt and gray blazer. My father agreed to tie the arms of a sweater around his neck so he looked like a rich American. My grandmother wore a sleeveless dress of overlapping bright circles cinched by a tan belt, and wedge heels. My mother got into a below-the-knee skirt and a wool cardigan. I was resettled into the checked shirt that had fooled Soviet customs, the top button that had been used to conceal the gold unbuttoned this time.

For some reason, Sasha made us wait outside while the Austrians, their dress neither as festive nor as motley as ours, streamed in. When they opened the door, I caught glimpses of a thousand-foot ceiling, stained-glass windows sparkling in the hall's low light. The clock was at 8 p.m., but Sasha said to keep waiting. Then the light in the vestibule went off, the doors closed for good, and he summoned us. He slid the door open slightly and slipped through, motioning us to follow. We crept through the dark until we reached the last pews, which were empty. "Your Majesty," he bowed to my grandmother. She sneered at him, but sometimes she flirted that way.

When the music finally sounded, it was as stupendous as a nuclear cloud. Soon a chorus joined in, and my arms ran with goose bumps. I felt the music everywhere—in my ears, in my feet. I was so consumed that I didn't notice the hand on Sasha's shoulder, and his passionate whispering with its owner. In German, no less. We caught words we recognized—*Juden, die Immigranten, Geld*: "Jews," "immigrants," "money"—but the guard, despite a kind face and nods of understanding, didn't relent. Rules were rules. Sasha and the Jewish immigrants without money were gently ushered out as the people around us turned to look. Outside, you could still faintly hear; there was no law against standing on the sidewalk and listening. But now my grandfather sneered—*So good your life in Europe, Sasha, that you have to sneak into concerts?*—and began striding toward the Rose, leaving us no option but to follow. But Sasha had the last word—my grandfather was walking in the wrong direction.

CHAPTER 5

October–November 1988

What to cook when you've been let through to
a vita *so* dolce *you can't stop eating*

What to cook when the product is Mediterranean . . .
but the shopper is Soviet

What to cook while you wait for the most fateful verdict
of your life

✦

The pilgrims set out after breakfast, pausing now and then to check the street signs against their directions. They had arrived in Rome from Vienna the previous evening. They'd been told that the train would pause in Rome for only five minutes; if they did not extract their possessions in time, they would keep going. The trip was spent pondering this restriction. There was the opinion that their minders, the Hebrew Immigrant Aid Society, wished to burden their Italian hosts as little as possible, and there were enough families on the train for an orderly exit to take half an hour. This was countered by the view that the train had departed Vienna an hour and a half late—the Italians did not seem concerned about punctuality. Perhaps that was why they needed to make up time, someone else said. Eventually, this useless wondering—they were at the mercy of opaque, greater forces, and for this they had received a fine preparation in the Soviet Union—was replaced by the more practical issue of how to remove hundreds of suitcases, boxes, and duffels in five minutes.

A mechanically enlightened passenger had an idea. When the train stopped near Venice—it stopped for a full fifteen minutes, though the passengers could not disembark and had to content themselves with nose-to-glass squinting at the City of Bridges from across the lagoon (the insistence of one older man on packing binoculars was now vindicated)—he fiddled with the window and was pleased to discover that it detached from the frame. When the train stopped—Arezzo, Chiusi, Orvieto—the man performed demonstrations, and everyone practiced. Having acquainted himself with who was where, the man drew up a plan: Half the ablest men would be at the doors when the train stopped in Rome, whereupon they would fan out across the platform while in each compartment a designated opener opened the window. The other half of the able men would then start pushing the largest luggage down to the platform while the women, children, and pensioners scurried out with the things light enough to carry by hand. As the Rome suburbs loomed into view, some hearts in the group beat faster than they had at Soviet customs.

The train had hardly halted when everyone charged into action. (Though enough immigrants had congregated in Vienna to fill half the train, the only security greeting them was a single carabiniere, a pistol in his holster, who ran up and down the platform shouting in his beautiful, incomprehensible language.) The plan worked so well that the entire party—sixty or seventy people—was out on the platform in less than five minutes. The riders replicated the system for the loading of everyone's things into the canvas-covered beds of the trucks that awaited them. It wasn't until they were done that they noticed that the train was still in the station, a half hour later. One man dared to inquire of a passing agent in a boxy hat why—he pointed to his watch, pumped his arms, and said, "Choo-choo-choo." The agent spread his hands to indicate something large, said "Roma!" and then pointed to *his* watch and said, "*Un'ora.*" One hour.

The arrivals were dispersed between two hotels on the outskirts. The Marco Polo, from which the twenty-five pilgrims set out the next morning, had been a monastery; its cave-like rooms were a dismal welcome, especially in the darkness that had set by the time they reached it. In the banquet-size dining hall, the party was served a dinner of macaroni, some kind of cutlet, and salad. They didn't know what to think—macaroni was poor man's food in the Soviet Union. Even more oddly, the salad was served last, and consisted mostly of bizarre green leaves. The bread was the true sin, an eclair-shaped roll with nothing inside, not even dough: It was hollow. This seemed to symbolize everything that had transpired over the preceding several hours. In the morning, after breakfast disappointed again, they flung open their balconies and set up small tables with their remaining nonperishables: canned sardines, the salami they eternally carried. They tried to ignore the clouds of exhaust belching up from the ground, where the morning's traffic was crawling into the city. The Eternal City versus the Eternal Salami.

Then the Marco Polo–vites set off for the Nostrand, the other hotel, for a briefing. They were late. On the way, they encountered a man selling grapes, the bundles cradled in tissue paper and seated in tiered rows like guests at an opera. To some, the grapes looked like little green globes about to burst. To others, as if filaments of sun had lodged inside. To a third group, like the amber jewelry they'd left at home, not realizing what profit these Baltic deposits could bring in the West. "Moscato," the vendor announced to the group. He held up his left index finger, then his right. One kilo, one thousand lira—seventy cents. The group swarmed the seller until each family held a newspaper cone containing a kilo of grapes. Near them, a fire hydrant slowly pumped water into the street, of which they availed themselves, not understanding the seller's shouts of *"Pulite!"* ("Clean!"). Who knows what the Italians rushing to work all around made of this tribe. Well, you couldn't say they were rushing.

At the Nostrand, the other immigrant group felt despair. They'd received a funereal breakfast—instant coffee, the same accursed hollow bun, and a hard-boiled egg that the uniformed but slovenly waiter *hurled* out of a giant bowl using tongs. ("Like pig slop," someone said.) Some insisted on lodging a formal complaint; there were predictable arguments for and against. This was when the Marco Polo contingent appeared, their bellies full of burst globes, sun rays, and amber. What had *they* been fed, the Nostranders wanted to know? A travesty, the Polovites said: macaroni with a cutlet, then salad of nothing but leaves. This took the Nostranders' sense of persecution past endurance: They'd gotten the same—minus the cutlet.

A woman with rudimentary English was sent off to confront the front desk, where, after elaborate miming, the waiter was summoned. (Like the waiter, the receptionist also wore a suit made for another, whereas the entire Soviet contingent had turned out in finery.) The waiter listened, his brows pursed in confusion, then let forth a stream of Italian elaborated by reenactments of the egg's journey. The receptionist tried to translate to the lady from Mosca (who wasn't from Moscow, but that was the hotel's umbrella designation for the group): "Yessa, he flying the egga because then the shella break just enougha," and the egg wouldn't roll off the plate. It was a gesture of care, not the opposite—and a bit of an art, actually. If signora was so doubtful, the waiter said, she could try it herself. Then he stalked off.

The briefing was to tell the immigrants they were now on their own. The aid agency would still pay for lodging—in a coastal suburb called Ladispoli—but they had to arrange it themselves. "In what language, exactly?" someone called out. After generations of being told what to do by our homeland, the refugees had taken naturally to HIAS's babying. In fact, it would be even more difficult to deploy initiative here—we didn't speak the language. Somehow, this paralysis coexisted with the daring to leave our lives for the completely unknown. (Even my grandfather, who feared no one

but my grandmother, expected to find in America "a big man—
tall, in a hat, big stomach, in a striped suit. He's smoking a cigar.
And he's squinting at me because I'm nothing. And he says: 'I'm
gonna make a puddle out of you.'") The dictionary of words and
phrases with Proustian power over an ex-Soviet person—the use
of which can make every non-Soviet in the room, even a spouse
or child, suddenly seem irredeemably foreign—includes *"dayut,"* a
verb in the third-person plural that forms a complete sentence by
itself and means *giving,* or *handing out,* or *distributing.* The pro-
noun and verb—*They are*—are unnecessary. Who *they?* The *they*
who decide.

Ladispoli, a half hour west of Rome, didn't have much, and didn't
need it—it bordered miles of azure Tyrrhenian coastline. Soviet
refugees had been staying here for years, so it wasn't long before my
grandfather had a piece of paper with an address. At the Ladispoli
train station, my father offered it to the ticket vendor, who opened
fire in Italian and flung her hands in so many directions that, not
wishing to harm her feelings, he nodded vigorously and ran off.

I needed the bathroom, which, instead of being marked DONNE
and UOMINI (words I already knew), carried the international sym-
bols for "male" and "female"—those circles, crosses, and arrows that
correspond to nothing male or female at all. I waited for someone
to emerge to clarify which was whose, but nature made it hard and
I took my best guess. It didn't matter—the bathroom was empty.
It was only after I heard heels clopping on the tile outside my stall
that I understood that some kind of free-world hygienic sophistica-
tion was not the reason I'd seen no urinals upon entering. I heard
more heels. Then the unclasping of a purse, something skittering
down the tile, laughter. Then pulling and snapping that could only
confound a nine-year-old boy, followed by—here my chest filled
with terror—a stream very assertively greeting the water. I knew,
by then, that women peed just like men, but the patriarchal force

of my birthplace must have led me to expect a decorous trickle instead of the torrent next door.

The illicitness might have been arousing were I not crouched on my toilet seat, my heart in my throat because I was certain that my parents—who would have, rationally, confined their search to the men's bathroom—were frantic. It's one thing to find Via dei Tulipani without Italian, another to file a missing-person report: "Parted black hair, eats well for the most part, head in the clouds—once he forgot to throw out the garbage and took it to school." When the sounds finally ceased, I hurled open the stall and flung open the bathroom door with the full force of my fear, thrusting myself upon a young woman trying to enter.

On Tulipani, my knocking—I'd learned a dozen words of Italian, so I was out front—was answered by a well-fed man with mussed hair, wearing a robe. "*Apartamento!*" we sang out. "*Momento,*" he said, wagging his finger in apology, and shuffled away. This, too, we understood—we were getting the hang of things. He returned wearing a shirt, tie, slacks, blazer, and dress shoes, his dark hair wet and scraped over his head. He led us to his garden, took out an arrow-tipped pen, and wrote a number with so many zeros that even the exchange rate couldn't help.

"*Momento,*" he said again to the fallen faces around him, and vanished again. He returned with a woman. Her face was dark from the sun and her bun of hair had silver threads, but her grayish-green eyes were pellucidly young. She wore men's black leather oxfords over bare feet, a long, loose dotted black skirt, and a black cardigan over a blouse. She may have been the first woman for whom I felt desire—primed, perhaps, by my initiation in the women's bathroom of the Ladispoli train station. Signora Limona had a two-story villa with a large kitchen, fronted by an orchard of persimmons and pears that she had abandoned to nature—the ground was littered with fruit. Miraculously, the number attached to this extravagant place—a villa!—was right. *"Bene,"* she nodded, and receded toward a side dwelling, positioning herself on a bench in the sun with that day's copy of *Ladispoli Oggi* (*Ladispoli Today*).

At 5:00 p.m. on Tuesdays, Wednesdays, and Thursdays, we reported to a synagogue to learn who'd been granted "interviews" at the American embassy, and who had done well enough at theirs to get the green light to go. Then everyone went to "the fountain"—a cracked, weathered goblet at the entrance to town. All sorts of plant life, including a palm tree, had sprouted in its murky waters, clogging things up for the koi-like fish and turtles that made it their home. Periodically, the turtles emerged onto a green metal landing where, like synchronizing Olympians or castaways fleeing ecological ruin, they climbed one another's backs and retracted their heads until they resembled a stack of giant mushroom heads. All in all, the thing resembled something out of the deep. But there was a wide plaza with benches and a border of high bushes, so here the Soviets of Ladispoli whiled away their evenings as they awaited release.

In one corner huddled members of a "mafia," all from the same Belarus town, who rented apartments and subleased them for more to new arrivals who preferred not to venture into Ladispoli and become trapped in the wrong gender's bathroom as they tried it themselves. In another corner were the people selling, buying, and trading to improve their offerings at the secondhand market, or unloading final possessions because they'd been waved through to America. In a third corner were the children, squealing and jumping, save for a pair of exceptionally well-behaved young people, a girl and a boy, who sometimes brought construction paper, scissors, and markers. Out of the paper, Alina and I cut cucumbers, tomatoes, apples, pears, eggplant. With the markers, we raised a crop of goose bumps on the cucumbers; draped the tomatoes with green vines; dotted the pears (these would be on sale because spotted). Then we—she was the daughter of new acquaintances, a platonic interest, as my heart belonged to Signora Limona—pulled on our parents' pant legs until they parted with real lira for our supply. The adults were usually grouped around some sage who knew everything because he'd had his consular interview that afternoon. The grandparents were exiled to the rim of the plaza, ostensibly to keep an eye on the children but really to spare their blood pressure while the middle generation sifted through rumor. This chaos also supplied cover for certain men and women who wished to whisper with each other without their spouses seeing.

In the morning, everyone fled the villa—we went out of our way to use that word; when else would we get to say such a thing?—because my grandmother's longing for her sister had reached a hysterical level. My grandfather and I went to the beach, gorging on the persimmons and pears that, heavy with a day's heat, thudded to the ground as we fell asleep. My father went to the secondhand market.

There, former engineers, scientists, and physicians wrapped themselves like ancients in high-quality Soviet linen and shouted, "*Russo producto!*" The spark kindled by my father's time in Vienna was still fizzing—he relished the same ploys that had killed his spirit back home. Before leaving Minsk, my grandfather had "confiscated" his barbershop's supply of aftershave, whose label claimed production facilities in Moscow and Paris. "*Parizh!*" my father yelled as its cloying scent drenched the air. Sometimes he sprayed his compatriots and, by pointing at his own nostrils and then their necks, urged the passing women to consider a gift for *signore*.

The Soviet men had been sent off with thermoses of tea with lemon and honey and bundles of bread lined with cold cuts and vegetables, but sometimes they allowed themselves the roasted peanuts and chocolate sold by the Italians. They sat on overturned milk crates or construction equipment, shelled nuts, tested their dental work on the chocolate, and strategized. What if they took turns crowding one another's stalls so the Italians thought something good was on sale? What about a fake bidding game? The warm air hitting their faces, they crouched and debated like hustlers, like the Gypsies they had once pitied in the open-air markets of their Soviet hometowns, like the petty-merchant grandparents upon whose lot they had been meant to improve.

The cold cuts, bread, and vegetables in their satchels were nothing like what they'd been fed at their Roman hotels. No matter what the wives who did the food shopping brought from the local salumerias—soppressata, capicola—the dinner table cheered and banged their forks. Mortadella had flecks of fat, like tongue, which the children prodded with their forks, hanging the giant circular slices over their noses; bresaola looked like Armenian *basturma*. The vegetables crunched and crisped in ways even fresh Soviet vegetables didn't.

In one of the bakeries, my mother found a bread—white, disk-like, a swirl at the top—that looked exactly like the *polenitsa* my grandmother had loved in Minsk, and bought two loaves, hoping it would spell her mother's heartache for an evening. She also bought cookies filled with chocolate, raspberry, and cream that melted on the tongue like communal wafers. One day, the counterman steered her toward a jar filled with a paste of dubious color. She shrugged— why not. It survived in the cupboard for less than twenty-four hours, the adults sneaking spoonfuls when no one was looking. Each of them meant to apprise the child of the treasure behind the cabinet door but somehow never got around to it. The Nutella did more than the Soviet-style bread to briefly turn my grandmother. Only the strange coffee the Italians consumed remained outside our ken—gleaming machines large as generators huffed and rumbled until they released a pitiful trickle into a thimble the size of two thumbs. We chased our cookies with instant.

After finishing at the market, my father wandered the town, savoring the unfamiliar delight of not being expected at home. He especially enjoyed passing by an open-windowed bar-café whose patrons clustered at small round tables, seemingly doing nothing other than talking. No one met in a café in the Soviet Union just to . . . talk. Going out was so momentous that one could hardly bother with something so serene and prosaic.

One day, he watched a postman seat himself at the counter and remove a newspaper from the leather satchel over his shoulder. Without taking an order, the barman withdrew a glass that he inspected for dust, then set on a coaster. Then he reached into a lowboy and reemerged with a small, bulbous jar of pear juice. Gently, he turned it upside down and back, then popped the lid. The barman held the bottle over the lowball for what felt like an hour, not a word passing between the two men. The drink stood untouched for another eternity. Then the postman brought it to his lips, took an invisible sip, and returned it to the coaster.

My father had come from a country whose waiters and salespeople watered down sour cream and vodka, and left a pinkie on the scale when weighing out sausage, the saved amounts siphoned off for personal use or sale on the side. From a country where food was fallen upon as if it would vanish. Whereas this ordinary postman had been served like a king given his nectar, and sipped it as if he planned to be there till dinner. It didn't escape my father that his afternoon walks were his own humble version of the same. But he didn't dare spend the money he'd made in the market, and never ordered a juice. Perhaps it wasn't money and he was simply shy.

At the beach, I tried to memorize words from a Russian-to-English picture book, but it was early October, the sea was warm, and it wasn't as if my grandfather could test me. In lieu of English, I mastered the art of lying beached on the sand, my stomach swelled with the Moscatos my grandfather had bought, nagged only slightly by the perfect grades I'd left behind for this life of leisure and sloth. To prevent random spot testing at home, I made myself scarce in the yard, collecting fallen fruit, raking leaves, and trying to ingratiate myself with the woman I loved.

Every night, we ate turkey wings. We'd never seen turkey, but the wings were in every market here, larger than chicken wings, tender, and cheap. We called them Soviet Wings, after the soccer team once managed by Stalin's son Vasily. (By persuasion or worse, he induced players from other clubs to defect until he had a unit of all-stars.) They got braised with onion, carrot, and tomatoes. They flavored soups. They sat astride swirls of mashed potato like slingshots. The Italians ate indoors, but the Soviets always went outside. You knew dinnertime in Ladispoli because suddenly hundreds of windows flew open, Adriano Celentano or Toto Cutugno crooning from stereos set on the sills. The Russians sang along, though they hardly knew what they were saying.

> *Buongiorno Italia con i tuoi artisti*
> *Con troppa America sui manifesti*
> (Good morning, Italy, with your artists
> With too much America on the posters.)

"SOVIET WINGS" BRAISED IN
CARAMELIZED ONION, CARROT, AND TOMATOES

Time: 1 hour, 20 minutes   Serves: 2

2 turkey wings, about ³/₄ pound
each
Kosher salt and black pepper, to
taste
9 garlic cloves, divided (3 put
through a garlic press, 3
chopped, 3 halved)
2 tablespoons plus 2 teaspoons
olive oil

1 large onion, chopped
1 large carrot, grated
4–5 vine-ripened tomatoes, or 3
meaty, ripe, juicy beefsteaks,
chopped
1 tablespoon tomato paste
2 bay leaves

1. Rinse the turkey wings and pat dry. If you wish, using a sharp knife, cut off the wing tips so they fit better in the pan. Season generously with salt and pepper.

2. In a small bowl, combine the pressed garlic and 2 teaspoons of the olive oil. Rub onto the wings and set aside.

3. In a large, heavy pot, heat the remaining 2 tablespoons olive oil over medium-high heat. Add the onion and cook until golden brown, about 10 minutes. Salt to taste. Add the carrot and cook for 5 minutes, until softened. Add the chopped garlic and cook, stirring, for 30 seconds.

4. Add the chopped tomatoes to the pot and salt to taste. Cover, turn the heat to medium-low, and let cook for 5 minutes, so the tomatoes can start to throw off their liquid.

5. Add the remaining halved garlic to the pot along with the tomato paste, bay leaves, and 2 cups of water. Salt to taste. Add the wings, nestling them into the liquid.

6. Cook at a gentle simmer, uncovered, for about 30 minutes, turning the wings every 10 minutes. You may wish to poke some holes in the turkey skin and meat with a thin, sharp knife so the flavor soaks in.

Serve over your favorite grain to soak up the broth.

✢

One night, we arrived at the fountain to discover a larger commotion than usual. Someone had been turned away. Turned away? From where? *America, where,* came the answer. That evening's sages were proclaiming the latest—if you had higher academic degrees, that made you less rather than more desirable; the Americans wanted only those who could prove discrimination, and if you worked in some physics institute, what kind of sufferer were you? Those who'd joined the Communist Party, even for practical reasons, would also have problems, as would criminals, the seriously sick, and the mentally ill. "Who's sane, coming out of that place?" someone said, and the crowd huffed, but we were trying to cheer ourselves up: How many of the men present had feigned "fainting spells and periodic lost consciousness" on their physicals to avoid serving in the Red Army, where you were lucky to come out of hazing alive even if you weren't a Jew? The Americans had computers. They knew everything.

"Beware the female consul!" the speaker bellowed over the racket. "They've turned away seven families!" At these words, the crowd fell silent. A single rejection could be dismissed as anomaly—but seven? That couldn't be true. The man was bluffing to keep their attention. *Sometimes our people, really. Bragging because they're in and you're not. Seven families! If so, what do they have us here for? What, they'll leave us in Italy? Come on, don't be ridiculous.* In our family, there was only one advanced degree, and a membership in the Young Communist League, not the party itself. Surely we were in the clear.

Italy took longer than Austria, so the art historians among the émigrés organized tours. Sixty dollars to go north and forty dollars to go south—transportation, lodging, meals, and tours included. At the Uffizi, my parents stood next to a Soviet couple who had emigrated to America eight years before. They were wounded by the nothing price my parents had paid for their trip; they'd paid thousands of dollars. However, the man said, "I can buy this painting right now. Seventy thousand dollars? Easy." The Soviet ability to mourn having spent more than another—while brandishing wealth—had survived their years in America.

It was in the Piazza San Marco that, for the first time, my mother felt her dolor about leaving lift slightly. It had persisted for so long that she wondered whether it was a sentence for all time, at least for emotional people like her—clearly her husband felt the opposite. At first, she hoped her mother's louder sorrow would make her own subside, but the only thing that subsided was the right she felt to not conceal it. Until the sight of the piazza tipped the last month's accumulation of beauty, leisure, and free conduct over some edge and made her weep, the way you break out in laughter after a chronic pain finally leaves.

To celebrate, they tried pizza. They'd tried it before leaving Minsk, where a pizzeria had just opened, but for those pizzaioli, it was a cake of fried dough baked with cheese and tomatoes. This was different. They were given knife and fork. Then they were gouged at the till. But they were light-headed from the indulgence. Then they tried espresso. They took it, strong as narcotic, with their elbows on the copper counter just like the Italians, and became even more light-headed. Then a second—he with tiramisu, she with fruit conserves plumped with whipped cream. Then a third. They couldn't sleep that night, but they didn't mind. The next day, they shelled out another irresponsible cluster of lira for a gondola ride. Gondoliers charged per ride, not per passenger, so a Soviet immigrant joke, circa 1988: How do you know where the people in that gondola come from? If it's two, they're American or Japanese. If it's ten, they're ours.

My parents would come to regret the money they'd spent so freely up north—even in Italy, it turned out, you couldn't relax without paying a price. They returned to a Ladispoli changed. The news of the seven families had been true. More rejections had come through, families bewildered amid rumors that stipends would end. One older man, inadequately shielded by his stunned children, suffered a terminal heart attack; a funeral cortege took him to a cemetery with spare plots. The word refusenik took on a new meaning.

The Soviet Union was liberalizing—the Americans weren't as keen to take in economically rather than politically repressed immigrants; neither were American Jews to agitate on behalf of people who celebrated Passover with pork. Israel would take them, but to go to Israel "and fight Arabs in the desert" was as conceivable as a Jew in charge of the USSR. Our elders had saved us from the Red Army so we could join Israel's? Meanwhile, over phone lines full of static, we heard about Azerbaijanis and Armenians locked in slaughter, rumors of a pogrom in Kharkov. Who knew what was true—every mouth embellished in proportion to the anxiety of its owner. But this was the Soviet Union the Americans thought was free of oppression?

The fountain was never the same. It was as if people stayed away from each other to avoid being hexed. You no longer saw as many dinner tables outside, and suddenly the Italians' music was irritating and frivolous. What had seemed like a blessed bit of hooky for the children came to seem like an indefinite future without schooling. It remained illegal to seek employment as long as the stipends came in, but how much could you count on these stipends if you couldn't count on any of it? People quietly signed up for house-painting crews, or to attend at gas stations. They worked with the fear and fury of people who had allowed themselves to believe—of people violently returned to the feeling that they had only themselves and their loved ones to trust. Impressed, their Italian employers asked if they'd considered another option: Italy. They'd hire them formally, full-time, with benefits. But the immigrants couldn't imagine they would be made to remain. *Have you lived badly here?* they were asked. *You're in Europe, in the most beautiful country on earth. What do you think waits for you over there?*

Meanwhile, the older people kept dying. By the time we were summoned for our interview in mid-November, an entire corner of the cemetery had been given over to *i russi*.

In preparation, my mother wrote out scripts. My grandmother would talk about the Minsk ghetto, surviving on potato peels in the swamps, returning to orphanhood. My grandfather would talk about anti-Semitic slurs in the navy, at work, on the street. Dispensing with concerns about what I would overhear, my mother made him rehearse, so that the villa rang with the strange sound of a Jewish man calling out the vilest anti-Semitic calumny. My grandfather kept trying to elaborate by describing how he had avenged his honor—a knee to the kidneys; a dumbbell to the jaw—and my mother kept yelling at him to keep quiet so he could cut a more pitiful picture.

No one slept the night before. In the general anxiety, we forgot to plan what to wear. Something dignified enough to make us seem worthy of America, but not so dignified that we seemed to have been doing fine in the Soviet Union. The hour of the Rome train approaching, bodies blearily wandered from room to room, holding up various outfits. Neither my grandfather nor my father enjoyed dressing himself on a regular day, and my grandmother remained a shadow of her stentorian self, so my mother cut the air with her hand and said, "Enough! Wear what you wore to the concert in Vienna." And so we went to meet the consul dressed like evening revelers. I was tucked into slacks and a brown Lithuanian velour sweater bisected by a leather black stripe—the very picture of need or prosperity, depending on whom you asked.

Maybe it was the lack of sleep. Maybe the fact that when we walked in, we saw the very person we'd prayed we would not: the female consul. (No one had mentioned her attractiveness: It didn't agree with the picture in our minds.) My grandmother began talking about the war and then started weeping softly. Instead of focusing on his slights, my grandfather couldn't help pointing out, after all, about how he gave as good as he got. My father stumbled, too. Even I could see they were failing. The questions kept coming, businesslike—free of hostility, pity, and empathy all—but the consular officer was writing down less after the translator translated.

My mother tried to even the score. In a torrent, she let forth everything everyone had forgotten to say. "My parents are elderly— they're frightened and nervous," she said, and burst into tears. A long, crinkling silence followed, the consul watching inscrutably. Then she turned toward the window, where I sat slightly apart as if my fate were not interlinked with the others'. The translator conveyed her words: "And what about you? You're not such a young boy anymore. Did you know you were Jewish in the Soviet Union?" My mother quit crying and stared at me. She looked stricken with terror. A script for me she hadn't considered.

I leaned forward, placed my elbows on my knees and my palms on my temples. Then I slapped one of the temples. "They threw rocks at my head," I said.

"Who did?" the translator blurted out without waiting for the consul.

"The other children," I said. "They called me a kike and threw rocks at my head."

"Did you tell the teacher?"

"Of course."

"And?"

"What can I say?" I shrugged theatrically. "The teacher was silent."

The consul's brows opened and she leaned back in her chair. Her gaze remained unfathomable, but in a different way than before.

On the train home, we were silent. I burned with shame at having said what I'd said about my beloved teacher, the friends who wouldn't have dared throw an acorn at my head. *I* was the one who punched *them* in the stomach! Where did those words come from? I hadn't lied once in my life, certain my parents would see it blazing out of me like a poisonous light. I wanted the adults to explain what had happened, but for once, they seemed to have forgotten me. Perhaps a lie was all right if you did it on behalf of your family. If you learned it from them. Maybe that's what they were thinking about.

Returning to the villa, we ran into another émigré. "Who did you get?" he asked. "The woman consul," we said glumly. He whistled. "You're done for," he said, and went on his way.

Worse, the interview took place on a Thursday—we'd have to wait till Tuesday for the next synagogue readout of who'd made it. My grandmother went directly to bed. My mother followed. They lay next to each other in silence. My grandfather sat at the dining table, issuing monologues to no one about why he'd said what he'd said. Only my father remained standing. He left, returning a half hour later with a small bag. Soon there were five plates of pasta with olive oil, garlic, and lemon on the dining room table, a single piece of shrimp atop each. The women descended like zombies, protesting no appetite but saying they'd sit "for the company." But they ate. No one spoke except my grandmother, who reprimanded my father for spending money on shrimp.

"It was a gift," my father said. "He was closing."

"I didn't know you could cook," she said, not clear whether it was a compliment.

"You never let me near the stove." Ditto.

The next day, he took me along. The sun was cold, leaves rustling the pavement. "*Zuppa*," the grocery man called out—he understood my father was looking for bargains—filling our sack with day-old bread, cannellini beans, a sack of aged vegetables, and a meatless ham hock he went across the street to ask the butcher to give us for free. My father boiled the hock until the water turned cloudy, periodically skimming fat from the top. Then the vegetables went in, from hardest to softest. The beans toward the end. Once it was ready, he ladled it over the bread.

"But the bread's already in the soup," my grandfather objected. He'd never eaten bread other than out of his left hand while the right forked the food.

"Try it," my father said. The soup bowls were emptied. The next day, my father made sardines with garlic, white wine, and mint, the lattermost pushed on him by the grocer. No one touched the mint, but the sardines went down heads and all.

By Tuesday morning, my mother was beyond reason. The villa having no phone, she went to the phone booth down the street and dialed the HIAS office in Rome. The phone was answered by an Italian employee who'd managed to learn enough Russian. "If you don't tell me the decision," my mother said evenly, "first my mother will die of a heart attack and then my father will die of a heart attack. I know you're not supposed to—but they'll die." After taking surnames, the Italian put the phone down. When she returned, she said, "*Sì, signora.*" My mother stiffened for the verdict, but she'd misunderstood. That *was* the verdict: *Sì*. When she came home, she burst into tears, misleading everyone. Then: shouting, embraces.

Only I wasn't happy. Feeling like a traitor, I slipped out to the yard and began crying. Then I grabbed the rake and started scratching the lawn. The fruit had finished weeks before, but the leaves kept coming. Whimpering, I raised three piles as if I were going to build a leaf man, only how could it hold? I heard the tap of heels on cobblestone and saw Signora Limona, one finger keeping her place in *Ladispoli Oggi*. She said something in Italian, of which I understood only the last word, *bambino*, but I knew she was asking why I was crying. I poked a finger at the banner of her paper. "America—*oggi*," I said.

I did not realize it till then, but I did not want to leave. Why leave such a place? I couldn't understand why our friends wouldn't consider the offers of their secret Italian employers. Was it bad fortune or good that this was still unknown to me at the consular interview where my lie had saved us? It doesn't matter. I wouldn't have dared choose myself over the others in that way, even if ostensibly all this was for me. That was not how it worked in my family.

Signora Limona's eyes crinkled with what I wanted to imagine was understanding. She said something, smiled a little, and walked away. I went inside, where the adults swarmed me with embraces and kisses—I had saved them. My grandmother stormed the kitchen and began exhuming the fridge to conjure up lunch. My gaze went past her to the windowsill. There, three perfect persimmons sat like three little Buddhas, one for each pile of leaves. Like the three golden apples Hippomenes used to seduce Atalanta. If only that were my fate.

Not believing our fortune, we went to the synagogue to hear our names. We were told we'd be leaving on a 3 a.m. transport the next morning. Spotting the man who had discouraged us on the street, my grandfather couldn't help sharing the news. And the man couldn't help deflating us once again. "They're changing their minds at the airport now," he said. "You go to the airport and they turn you back." My grandfather had to be restrained from assault. But the words got through, our joy fell apart, and we spent the next thirty-six hours in repurposed anxiety.

When we reached the airport, we were ushered into a hall for a final roll call. As the HIAS employee went down the list, he held up a plastic bag containing the flotsam that constituted the sum of a family's diplomatic existence: X-rays, the old white Soviet-issued identity cards, the American visas. Our surnames were the first to be called. As we approached, the HIAS man held out our packet, then asked which among us was Sofia. My grandmother raised her hand. And who was Sofia's child? My mother raised her hand. The man took her aside.

"We made a special appeal for your mother's condition to be ignored," he said.

"What condition?" my mother said.

The agent stared uneasily. "Does your mother drink?"

My mother's face blanched. This all over again. "No," she said. "Never more than a glass of champagne on a holiday."

"It's her liver," he said. "The results were quite bad. It's the sort of thing that leads to cirrhosis. Has she ever had a transfusion?"

"She had her gallbladder replaced," my mother said. The gallbladder my grandfather was so intent on having removed with special care that he couldn't stop pouring cognac down the surgeon's throat the evening before. During the operation, my grandmother had required a transfusion, though who could say why.

"We made a special appeal," the man said again.

When my mother returned, her face had no color. She pretended it had been a formality. No one pressed her. We were leaving.

The rejections increased after that, some families remaining in their Italian limbo for as long as a year. We were part of the last wave of Soviet refugees to go through Vienna and Italy. Afterward, those who got through went by plane directly to New York. Or, just as often, Tel Aviv.

My grandmother left Italy with cirrhosis of the liver. My

grandfather with blood pressure of 280 over 140, nearly earning a spot of his own in what had come to be called, at the cemetery, the Russian Corner. I left with three persimmons that I'd have to give up at American customs, and three memorized words of English. My father left with three Italian recipes, my mother with a heart broken by news of her mother's illness. We still had the West German cobalt-blue tea set with gold trim from which we'd slurped tea on the way out of Minsk. We'd pawned everything else, and decided we'd left behind enough.

CHAPTER 6

Thanksgiving 1988

+

In one of those heavy-handed details you can't put in a made-up story, we touched down in America on Thanksgiving Day. We had never flown other than Aeroflot down to Crimea, where the dining service consisted of pre-landing mints on a round tray; had never had the exotic experience of being served by a male steward with a close, ash-colored beard who belonged in a fashion magazine rather than balancing drinks. (My father finally had his pear nectar.) Meyer, the pleated and furrowed father of the family that had been traveling with us since Minsk, demanded an Alitalia address for a letter of gratitude, presumably to be written in the same Russian in which Meyer was now perplexing the steward. The Russian for "letter"—*pis'mo*—comes close to the Italian for "to pee," so at first the steward tried to send the old man to the toilets, but when that turned out to be wrong, he disappeared and returned with two baby bottles of vodka. Then he patted the old man on the shoulder and vanished.

New York in November—it wasn't Ladispoli. A cold wind blew. The family friend meeting us—the one whose wife had sewn our names into his underwear—wrestled away the suitcase my father was holding and hurled it at the luggage cart with all the force of eight years of waiting turned to relief at finally seeing us. My mother and grandmother winced—that was the suitcase with the tea set. We exited the terminal in a single file that repeated our friend's footsteps. A uniformed black man in a cap stopped us and said something while pointing at the luggage—we stiffened; to us this could mean only another inspection, and a black person was as unfamiliar as the language he spoke—but then our friend not only answered him in fluent English but *made him laugh*. This kind of ease seemed unimaginable.

At our friends' apartment, my mother and grandmother stole off to the bedroom and, their eyes half-closed in anticipation of disaster—when they make statues of us, this will be our eternal repose—unwrapped the issue of *Ladispoli Oggi* they'd used to buffer the tea set. A miracle, of sorts: Only one cup and saucer had broken.

It was Thanksgiving, we were informed. Our hosts couldn't say thanks from whom to whom and for what, but that thing was a turkey. So that was what it looked like whole instead of just wings. Otherwise, every item on the table was identical to our cooking at home. Herring in oil, vinegar, and sweet onion; "uniformed"— unpeeled—potatoes, quartered and pan-fried; slices of smoked salmon spread like a lady's fan. And fruit, though it was almost December.

"When does your fruit start?" my grandfather asked in astonishment, even his out-of-season feats outdone.

"6AM," our friend said, meaning the local grocery. It turned into a standard exchange. Every new arrival asked that question, and every old hand answered the same way.

None of us could put turkey in our mouths—it was indivisible from the misery of the previous weeks—so we pleaded nostalgia for home dishes. These, however, did not taste like home. The stuffed carp—here called gefilte fish—was a dense, deboned, jellied mass tasting of nothing but wet fish rather than a braised, melting wonder swimming in sweet broth. The black bread was stale, or so we thought; it had been toasted—you kept it in the freezer, then toasted it. (My grandmother was scandalized by both parts.) We ate off plastic plates, at once revolutionary and insulting, which were then thrown out instead of washed (ditto). The 6AM strawberries tasted of nothing. You kept eating them only because it was surreal to put in your mouth something that looked like a strawberry, and was three times as large, but had one-third the taste. Only Saran Wrap earned our unqualified admiration.

Over time, we understood: Here, the same food item existed in two different castes. You could buy the cheap version, made with the assistance of chemicals or lower-quality ingredients, or you could buy the expensive version, which tasted the way things had tasted at home, though there they cost ten times less. In this way, we were introduced to an American innovation that to Americans symbolized freedom, but to us seemed tyrannical: choice. If you felt financially secure, you bought the right-tasting version; if you didn't, you bought the shit. Because there was shit on offer, new terms such as "cholesterol" entered our vocabulary, and my mother's chemistry took on new utility. Most émigrés bought the cheap versions, then endlessly debated fat content, blood pressure, and salt intake as they never had in the USSR.

The Americans ate strangely, too. One time, while painting an apartment—it was Christmas Eve, extra pay—my father observed the woman of the house, who had mimed that family was coming, setting out tubs of what he would later learn were tuna, macaroni, and potato salads. Then a bowl of white dressing next to dwarf carrots and celery sticks, their leaves cut away. He assumed this was the appetizer table, but it was the main event. A Soviet person would have fallen through the ground in shame before serving this and nothing else.

Some things did work similarly: You had to bribe a building super to let an apartment to you instead of another; you had to bribe the housepainting union for a spot on the rolls. You had to bribe Americans as much as the Soviets, though here, refreshingly, it was done virtually in the open and you didn't have to invent ruses to get your taker to feel less guilty the way one had to in the USSR;

here, it was my father who was embarrassed. All the same—even as we belatedly learned that the day our friend-of-a-friend's Hallmark franchise hauled in two thousand dollars happened to fall during *Christmas week*—my father earned in a day what took a month back in Minsk. So, at the supermarket, Faina's son didn't buy the tub of fat-free—fat-free!—Breyers ice cream that we were told we must buy because it was both health-conscious and economical, but individual bars that reminded him of silver-wrapped Soviet Eskimos (vanilla ice cream in dark chocolate) or Chocolate Loaves (hazelnut-studded chocolate ice cream, ditto).

Instead of the Russian grocery, my father went to a local salumeria for sweet rather than painful reminders of Italy. He spent as much time in the kitchen as my grandmother, who was washing floors and babysitting for three dollars an hour. As he walked around, he encountered a mystery: A different perfume wafted out of every home on the block. Was this what private ownership meant? The houses in America smelled like perfume! Eventually he understood that each—each!—home had its own washing and drying machine; he was smelling laundry vapor. With time, he became a connoisseur: This was a Tide home. This one was All.

Almost nothing else smelled like perfume in those first months in Brooklyn. It was ugly—squat and low-slung blocks, where we once had prospects and boulevards. There was shit everywhere—literal shit, left by dogs (or, more correctly, by their owners). The metro, instead of chandeliers and marble, had painted graffiti. After a life of Polish and Bulgarian products, we'd finally made it to a place where we could buy things that said MADE IN AMERICA. Only nothing seemed to be made in America: It was made in China. The three-dollar slippers tore the day after you bought them; the watch died before you got home. They had street carts with frankfurters here, too, only they swam in gray water and tasted like rubber. There were forms—for credit cards, health insurance, used-car purchases—to shame Soviet bureaucracy, but these came with riders in small print that (it took us a while to gather this, because it didn't seem possible) listed all the ways in which you couldn't count on the thing the big print said was yours. It was the same with the ads that surrounded us like an army whose weapon was noise—there was no commercial advertising in the Soviet Union—and lied about what was really on offer. Here, these lies were called business.

My mother and grandmother were crying again, though for different reasons: Where had they brought me? Once, just back from English lessons, my mother called out a quick greeting and ran into the bedroom. I knocked on the door and opened it softly. She was wearing a knee-length black skirt, a blouse with a little bow, and one of her nicest brooches—she always dressed up for the lessons, an hour and a half each way by subway. She was weeping. I pulled her hands away from her face. "What is it?" I demanded. "I don't understand . . . anything," she said, and went back to crying.

Our Soviet minds hadn't believed that the construction equipment we had sent forward to Brooklyn had been stolen—the addressee must have kept it. But then the hubcaps were taken off our pitiful Oldsmobile Cutlass Ciera. Our Brooklyn apartment was robbed. And then—sunny weekend day, busy street—I was. It was because of the boy I was with, who was draped with so much jewelry you could see it from a block away. I wore only a silver bracelet and necklace, even these concessions to my grandfather's insistence on showing the world what we already had. My friend was three years older and had been studying karate, his kicks always flying very close to my face because—*watch this*, and *watch this*, and *I could really fuck you up*, and so on. His talent melted away before our assailant, however, a Russian man in his twenties who took the trouble to explain that he was facing prison and needed money for a lawyer.

That night, my grandfather prowled our neighborhood with a knife in his pocket—the same knife with which my grandmother had hacked off bread for me on the train out of Minsk. We still have the knife, the bevel scuffed from decades of Soviet sharpening. We did not have grindstones there: You waited till the sharpener showed up with his pedal-operated sandstone wheel, and then there were a hundred people in the yard, brandishing knives. My aunt, who cooked three times a day and couldn't wait for the sharpener, sharpened her knives on the edge of the stairs outside her apartment.

The dread was so thick over our Brooklyn lives that it lodged in your throat. I wanted to help. When I learned that American supermarkets gave back five cents for every returned empty—some states, like the mysterious Michigan, its very name like a granite monument, gave you ten cents—I decided I would return the twenty-four Pepsi cans we'd received in some charity food bundle and give the haul to my parents. The problem was that the adults didn't dare touch this indulgence—it was for me—but I could hardly drink it all, and it felt terribly profligate to waste it. One weekend afternoon, however, my parents and my grandfather out and my grandmother resting, I couldn't wait any longer. Gingerly, I closed the bathroom door, opened each one, muffling the noise with a towel, and, my heart squirming, poured the contents down the drain.

I washed each can as if it were a newborn—water, soap, swish, repeat. I didn't know how stringent the inspectors would be—I would give them no excuse. I dried the cans with my mother's hair dryer and restacked them carefully in the case. However, I couldn't help catching a whiff of the Ivory soap that—fool!—I had used; we bought the cheapest, and it smelled that way. The apartment ticking with a weekend afternoon's silence, I crept into my parents' bedroom, where, on a lacquered tray, my mother kept her single indulgence: a bottle of Climat perfume from Paris. I tiptoed to the bathroom and sprayed the Climat twenty-four times, into twenty-four Pepsis.

My heart beat so hard when I stole out of the apartment, my grandmother snoring lightly, that I don't remember the walk to the supermarket. I do remember the lines—the Italian mothers of Bensonhurst, Brooklyn, were doing the week's shopping. When my turn came, I gazed at the cashier with helplessness and preemptive resentment. Please, I thought. *Please*. She ran the cans through the scanner with all the ceremony of, well, a bottle return, and handed me a dollar and four nickels. I don't think she looked at me once. I stood there, vibrating slightly.

The English that didn't matter in Ladispoli seeped in so quickly I didn't notice it happen. The forms with riders went to me. So did the bills with inexplicable taxes and surcharges, the calls to dispute this or that, the letters of complaint and appeal to all the imponderable American institutions gouging us, we knew, because we were immigrant rubes. Now I was the first to speak when we appeared before some plenipotentiary, our fate in her hands; into many rooms—interviews, mixers—I was sent by myself, my mission to seduce those present with charisma and wit so they'd give me—us—what they had the power to give. I passed my days feeling a mix of the terror and ecstasy you feel at match point. But this match point went on for days, weeks, months, and years.

Eventually, I came to know how to feel little else. Everything felt like the end of the world, every resolution a miracle. Terror and ecstasy, with nothing between. When I think of my first years in America, I see a quartet of tight, anxious faces awaiting my verdict as I emerge from the bedroom, from the privacy of which I have been making an assault on some inexplicable letter or scandalous charge. "I did it," I tell them, and they swarm me the way the American football players on television—baffling sport, but sometimes I steal my mother's shoulder pads and run around the living room with a tiny plastic football in my hands—swarm the guy who caught it forty yards out. I am the king. The mighty and petrified king.

Outside our home, I am not even a plebe. I am the boy with the barbaric name, the freak who got an 85 on his spelling test without knowing any English, the boy in the very strange clothes, the one with the deadly part in his hair. They call me Commie and tell me to go back to Russia. They throw a football at my head when I am not looking. After Diana Gencarelli (not her name), she of the cascading black hair and Neapolitan fuzz on her lip—in another life, we could have been hirsutely non-Anglo-Saxon together!—finally relents and agrees to sign my autograph book at the end of fifth grade, her message advises me to go and learn the facts of life. So in school it is petrification as well, only for the opposite reason, for how much tighter can I be holding on to the facts, Diana? I am clutching them in my fist, so the others can clutch onto me. Given a tube of strange Pez-like mints at school lunch one day, I . . . shit my pants. I defecate in my pants, like an infant. I sprint home, three blocks away, but I don't cry. It doesn't occur to me to cry. I fix it, and start over.

Of course, I didn't understand what all this meant, the oddity of losing oneself even as one "took control," a mask settling before anything had cohered underneath. That it was so odd—I was out front, after all; the adults did what I instructed—only helped to conceal that loss, as did the urgency of my desire to help, perform, meet the goal, ease the set of their jaws. But other parts of me noticed. For a while, before going to sleep, I took to barricading my bed with our high-backed kitchen chairs; couldn't say why, just wanted to. Then I began to feel a siege of invisible lines of yarn, which I had to keep to the right side of or I would be struck by terrible luck. I was always twirling my hands and feet, hoping no one would notice.

My parents developed tics of their own. They'd never bothered me about schoolwork, but now, in a false tragedy familiar to any immigrant child, a 94 led to a crestfallen family council. What went wrong? Why not a 100? It wasn't in them to yell, so they counted on my sense of duty, and my ear for what was meant rather than said, to make sure it never happened again. (The ability to hear that way is invaluable for a writer; they gave me my first practice.) They didn't know how to live without expecting the worst; they'd only switched reasons.

They became obsessed with my weight. "You've rounded a little, haven't you?" they began saying, trying to sound casual. But they kept putting full plates in front of me, and I kept finishing them off as they watched. So much had turned upside down; food was one of the few things that worked as it used to. The more I became the person they brought me to America to become, the less we seemed to share, and the harder all of us tried to pretend it wasn't happening. Wasting no time, my grandfather had gotten involved in some scheme that left him with tubs of pharmacy goods. Relentless offers of these replaced dinner conversation: shampoo, deodorant, toothpaste, loofahs, cologne, pumices, any medication I wanted. The only medication I wanted was understanding, but this one they didn't have. Not that I could have put it that way. But once in a while, I saw something different transpire between my American friends and their parents. Different *how*, I wouldn't have been able to say—but better. For my part, I was fed.

I let my hair grow long, and once a neighboring boy played me some heavy metal, I listened only to that—Testament, Sepultura, Overkill, Suicidal Tendencies. But I kept making calls, writing letters, seducing the room, clutching my racket as the ref called match point again and again, no matter how many times I had won it— surely the only long-haired teenager in a Megadeth T-shirt in suburban New Jersey whose mother's hand hid in his when they were crossing the street.

PART II

CHAPTER 7

2005

What to cook if where you're going, they're not going to feed you

How to cook like dancing without legs

What to cook when you're allowed to go all the way

✤

In a simpler world, they'd always remain apart, safe
in their sense of enmity.
—PICO IYER, *The Man Within My Head*

Not many people visit Midwood, in south Brooklyn—even for the Dutch, it was the Midwout, the "Middle Woods" that separated the proper towns of Boswijck (Bushwick) and Breuckelen—but if you were passing through early on a blustery day in November 2004, you might have seen a woman on Avenue P, her fingers clutching the upper flaps of her nylon overcoat. There wasn't proper nail polish on the fingers, though she came from Ukraine, where only dead women went without painted nails. And she wore no rings or bracelets, though only poor Ukrainian women went without jewelry—poor, or poor in love. At forty-four, Oksana was neither—in Ukraine, she'd left a man, a salary, and a life with nice things, though she had them only because she knew how to hustle outside the official channels.

In America, Oksana was a home aide—the person a home-care agency, contracted by the city and paid by Medicaid, sent to look after an old person with the right social benefits. At the training—it was conducted in Russian; in this part of Brooklyn, all the home aides came from former Soviet republics—the instructors had said:

No jewelry. The "clients" were invalids—you wouldn't want, as you pulled and pushed and lifted and lowered, to scrape a cheek or snag a bouffant with the clasp of a bracelet. And the aides should forget their home cooking, too—the Uzbeks with their *plov* and *kharcho*, the Georgians with their *khachapuri*, the Ukrainians with their fried this and that. Medicaid wouldn't keep sending money for a dead client.

Oksana was walking down Avenue P that morning because she had a day off. But she didn't want a day off. She called the agency to see if anyone needed a sub, and lucked out: There was an old man on Avenue P whose usual home aide was not above a vacation day. She was going to my grandfather's house. Their encounter would lead to something neither of them could have imagined, and they would recall it often in the years to come.

Oksana carried a Tupperware filled with *grechanniki* (greh-CHA-nee-kee)—patties made from caramelized carrots, ground chicken and pork, and buckwheat (*grechka*), finished with parsley or dill. The mosaic they made in the stewing pan always transported her to her small kitchen in Ivano-Frankovsk, a midsize city in the foothills of the Carpathian Mountains, in western Ukraine. She was bringing her own food because her usual client wouldn't share.

Nothing Oksana did was right for that woman. There was a perfectly nice bedroom, but the old woman locked it and slept in the living room with Oksana. In the morning, she sent Oksana into the forbidden room to fix the bed even though it hadn't been touched. *Make it again, that side is not even. Make it again, I see a bubble.* The woman was so frugal she wouldn't give Oksana a dollar to wash the window curtains in the laundry room downstairs. The curtains hadn't been washed since man touched the moon, but Oksana was too frugal to spend her own dollar and ran her hands raw in the bleach-filled sink. What was the point of painting her nails?

The "clients" were all Jews—political refugees from the USSR—and the home aides all Christian, here because the economy was dead in Ukraine. The old people didn't speak English, and neither did the aides; they were made for each other. But it was quite a reversal for these ex-Soviet people: Christians waiting on Jews. Oksana thought maybe this was why her old woman, who was Jewish, was so rough with her—revenge, of a kind.

Oksana didn't have to take the woman's abuse—she wasn't illegal. But she didn't want to make noise. She didn't speak English, and the Russian women who ran the home-care agency seemed decent but perfunctory in the American way. Besides, Oksana wasn't here to make a life, only a living. She would work eight days a week if it meant more to send home. She didn't even have an apartment. She lived with the old woman because the assignment was for round-the-clock care, and for the odd night off, she rented a cot (and a mailing address) from a friend.

One-thirty Avenue P was nearly a block long. The recessed, colonnaded entryway reminded her a little of the pastel-hued Hapsburg beauty of the central district at home. This was what passed for decorative fretting here. Surely it was different in Manhattan; she hadn't been. On the tenant list, almost every surname was Slavic. She crossed herself and pressed 5J.

On the fifth floor, the door opened to reveal a man of medium height in a blue tracksuit, slight except for his belly, which looked like he'd eaten a basketball. Unlike Oksana, he wore lots of jewelry: a square signet ring on his pinkie, and gold on his wrist. The left hand bore a tattoo of a ring buoy, the right of a knight in panther's skin.

"I'm your sub," she said. "I'm sorry—I should have come earlier so as not to delay you. Is the client sleeping?"

The man laughed. There was more gold in his mouth. Gold was manipulable, did not corrode, and made a hard biting surface;

half the Soviet Union had gold teeth. "*'Is the client sleeping?'*" he mimicked her genially. A smile moved over his eyes. "The client is standing in front of you!" He bowed his head—a coquet.

"You're Arkady?" She couldn't help her own smile. "Excuse me. You're so . . ."

"Young?" he said. "Seventy-eight."

"I would say sixty-five," she said without false compliment.

"Then say it; why not?" He reached for Oksana's coat. She accepted the gesture.

She stepped into a bright, spacious living room, with its black lacquered wall-length entertainment center, though its television was a sideshow to all the crystal and china in the display cabinets: a Soviet home in absentia. The furniture set—beige leather bordered by curvaceous armrests made from expensive wood—said the same: Money had been spent on these things. The room was suffused with an agreeable warmth—the radiator clanked as if to confirm the impression. Outside, the cold sun shone on a field of low rooftops, the occasional window fronted by a rope of late-season laundry. *Those are Russian-speaking windows*, she thought. She and her old woman saved another dollar by tying a clothesline to the fire escape.

Above the small dining table was a portrait of a woman with a high hairdo and over-rouged cheeks, drawn up in an uneven, scowling smile. A photo of the same woman on the entertainment center made the painting's features seem distorted.

"I'm here just a year," Arkady said, losing his gleam. "We had a good apartment on Eighty-fourth Street. But I couldn't live there after Sofia . . ." He wavered.

"It's a beautiful portrait," Oksana lied.

"A friend," he said. "Paints icons. All the churches want him." Oksana nodded eagerly.

Back home, good apartments being hard to come by, every visit began with a tour; she wanted to give him the chance to show off.

In the bedroom, a bookshelf held clowns rather than books: a jester in a two-pointed hat, a clown in a ruff astride a check-patterned clock, two others riding a bell pepper like a bobsled. "I bought one to cheer me up," Arkady said. "Now the guy won't let me alone—calls every time they get a new clown." The wood of the bed was curvy and lustrous—same set as the living room. The kitchen was small, a galley with a good countertop, but the usable floor had less than two feet of width. Well, she would only be here for the day.

"Not bad for an old man," he said. "But life alone—I wouldn't wish it on an enemy."

Oksana sighed. "God holds the key."

"And you, my bird?" he said. "Ukraine, they told me."

She nodded. "Let me put a bowl of something warm in front of you and we'll talk. I'll just change quickly." She was in black dress pants and her square-heeled black shoes—the nicest clothes she had. When she arrived in Brooklyn, she thought everyone was poor, because they wore such shoddy clothes. It had been a cold, gray, humid October, the wetness so thick it seemed to hang on the trees. The train rumbled endlessly above Eighty-sixth Street, garbage piled all over, and the doorways to the Chinese fishmongers ran with fetid, off-color meltwater. The whole place was gray—even the people in their sweatpants. But then she understood that they wore sweatpants because here people felt free—the number one thing was to be comfortable.

"Is there anything you have to take care of today?" she said.

"Just food shopping," he said.

Oksana opened the fridge. "You want to go food shopping? There's not even room here for my Tupperware." The vegetable crispers were full, and the shelves held a dozen plastic containers with labels from a Russian grocery—stuffed cabbage; schnitzels; beet salad. Only one item seemed homemade, though, a tall jar of chicken soup. But it looked sickly and thin.

"I'm waiting out the Chinese at the fish place," he said. "They raised the carp to $1.99 a pound for Passover—they know the Jews are making gefilte fish. But guess what—Passover ended six months ago, and carp's still $1.99."

Oksana was opening and closing the kitchen cabinets. Every imaginable grain, a hundred teas for taste and for health, canned goods to survive a world war. She turned to Arkady—"You can open up your own store."

He smiled mournfully, but not without satisfaction. "My fighting days are over."

"How about some millet with pumpkin and dried fruit?" she said. "A recipe from home."

He shrugged good-naturedly. "Will you help me?" she said. He seemed to perk up when he had the chance to impress her. "If you could measure out two cups of millet while I change."

"Yes, commander," he said. "I was in the navy—I obey orders."

She laughed. "Today, at least, my life will be easy."

"Why? You have a difficult client?"

"I'm grateful for what I've got," she said, and thought about it. "You know how it is. Things can always get harder."

She wasn't sure he heard her—he was staring past her shoulder. "Junior Seaman Arkady," she called. He shivered out of his daze. "Two cups of millet, okay? I'll be right back."

"Senior Seaman," he corrected her, and saluted.

While she boiled water for the pumpkin—he had never had pumpkin, but it was on sale after Halloween, so he and his usual aide had bought two, what the hell—he tried to measure the millet. She'd changed into work clothes: netted slippers; tights printed with wild patterns; a short-sleeved shirt with swirls, rhinestones, and curlicues; and a small silver cross on her neck. There was a gold Star of David around his.

Oksana had skinned the pumpkin and chopped it into small

cubes and was stirring it hard—she wanted a puree. She set water to boil for the millet.

"Can you have salt?" she called out.

"Why not," he said.

"Just a little," she said.

She could cook from scratch quickly; if there were unannounced guests, there was something bubbling on the stove by the time they had hung up their coats. She had to set up the children with new apartments, to buy her son Misha a new car, to renovate the small country home they shared in the summer. But if something was left, and she could manage the bribes, sometimes she thought about returning home to open a little café.

The pumpkin puree went into the millet. For sugar, she substituted a cap of vanilla. She liked crystallized better than liquid—it tasted less bitter. She decided on a mix of dried cranberries and plums. She glanced over at him. "At home, if the parents like the groom when he comes asking for a bride," she said, "they bring out the runners that we drape over icons. But if they don't, they bring him a pumpkin."

"So I am rejected?" he said.

"Some rejection!" she laughed. In the bowl, the millet was bright yellow, the flecks of cranberry and dried plum like dark little stars.

"And where's your bowl?" he said.

"Oh, I'll just have some coffee here in the kitchen."

"Don't be crazy—sit with me. You want something stronger than coffee?"

She laughed. "In the middle of the morning?"

"Don't tell me you've never!" he said. "Look at this." He opened a covered section of the entertainment center in the living room: rows of bottles, shelf after shelf.

"I can't stand a cold meal," she said. "Eat, please. You'll show me everything later."

Between spoonfuls, he asked questions. Had she come to be a

hamatenda? (They all said "home attendant" that way.) No, she had started out in a grocery in Detroit; she'd worked in a supermarket for twenty-seven years in Ukraine. Why that? She wanted to be a teacher, but money was short. How did she make money? Same way he did. Everything was loose rather than packaged in a Soviet supermarket, easy to siphon off and sell on the side. After 1991, the money went to shit—inflation, deflation, who could make sense of it. But the border had opened. To the Bulgarians she sold electrical equipment, stainless steel, and coffee. To the Poles, down blankets and children's clothes. When she went to Turkey, she had to buy two tickets—one for herself, one for the rug she'd buy to resell down the line.

"So you've seen the world," he said.

"From the sole of a shoe, maybe," she said. "You're finished?" His bowl was half-full. "Was it sweet enough? Cooked enough?"

"Good, good," he answered vaguely, nodding his head.

Maybe he wasn't much of an eater? But look at that belly! But she didn't press. "You get dressed, I'll wash the dishes."

Ten minutes later, she was done, but he was still standing in front of his closet. It contained cashmere sweaters, corduroys, wool socks—he kept to the old ideas about dressing up for the street—but he couldn't choose what. "The red sweater, you think?"

"He can score a twenty-four-hour *hamatenda* even though he's hale as a bull," she said, "but he needs a lady to choose his wardrobe?"

"I'm accompanying the lady—it's no casual matter," he said, arching his eyebrows.

She laughed. "The red one, sure."

"And what pants?"

So she dressed him. The red one, dark-brown corduroys, and white leather slip-on loafers. When she was helping him out of the tracksuit, she saw the long keloidal scar on his chest: quadruple bypass. It made her think of her mother; she sent a prayer five thousand miles away. Arkady flashed a gold smile, looked in the mirror, flipped up his collar, and said, "Forward!"

When they got to the produce store, she understood why he had made her take a little carriage on wheels. In the fruit section, he went through the cherries one by one, boxing out an old woman shopper with his belly. "It's okay to turn them over like that?" she said carefully.

"I buy so much here I could look through his wallet if I wanted to," Arkady said, meaning the owner, then moved on to oranges, apples, kiwis, and strawberries.

"You already have two containers of strawberries!"

"But look at them!" he said. "Big as a finger." But before he could finish with the strawberries, he moved, as if in a trance, toward a tray of red peppers, so red and plump they looked ready to burst. "A sin not to buy peppers like these," he said.

He was right about the owner, who mewled "Hi, hava yoo?" when he saw the old Russian man who came all the time. It came to twenty-eight dollars and change; Arkady gave the cashier thirty, winked, and patted her hand. She tried to force change on him, and he made an insulted face. So she went to the produce aisle and returned with two heads of cauliflower. "Fresh!" she said.

"She couldn't gift us something lighter?" he said under his breath, and Oksana laughed.

Arkady was a boulevardier, his currency goods rather than gossip. He liked having this woman half his age on his arm. Not to be mistaken for a wife—to show the local people that he was a man taken care of. So the little carriage kept wheeling toward Eighty-sixth Street, the commercial thoroughfare that runs through Bensonhurst, the subway clattering on the raised track.

They walked past the pizza parlor where he used to buy his wife a slice. She had cirrhosis of the liver, so she wasn't supposed to— all that salt and fat. They always got the pizza bianca—ricotta was healthier, right? It looked healthier. In his pizza pidgin, Arkady would ask the Italian to heat it up less—too crispy was too rough on the roof of her mouth. She pulled at the soft dough with her lips, a moment in heaven, as he pleaded with her to eat slowly, it's hot. It was the only thing she craved from an American kitchen. Back in Minsk, Sofia's chicken schnitzels were such that the next-door neighbor would stumble out onto their shared balcony and bang on their door. And even though he was a bit of a drinker, how could you refuse him one of those chicken steaks fried to a golden crisp in their airy egg batter?

At the fishmonger's, the carp was still $1.99. The Chinese man in the bloodstained apron behind the counter had no English, only a sharp cleaver in his nicotine-stained fingers. He smiled tooth-lessly at the Russian man with the round belly—he was like a Bud-dha. Arkady stuck out his index finger to mean one; then nine of the ten fingers twice to say "ninety-nine"; then he jabbed the finger at the fish and waved it back and forth: "No!"

The fishmonger laughed and pointed up—to indicate his boss? God's will? The Russian's index finger turned admonitory—he wanted to impress his new home attendant with his bargaining skills or, failing that, his outrage. But eventually he gave in— "Okay, fish, yes." The fishmonger smiled—he could have been twenty or eighty—and yanked the carp, with its stunned mouth, from the display.

Now the old Russian swiped his index finger across his throat. Was he threatening the man's life? For God's sake, Oksana would pay the difference. But Arkady meant he wanted the carp weighed without the head. He got his wish, and then—because rewards come to the far-seeing—he insisted the head go into his bag anyway, be-cause what was the guy going to do with a carp head? Meanwhile, Arkady's home aide could use it to make stock. He got the head and, because he got it for free, a lower average price on the buy after all.

"You belong on the stage," Oksana said, marveling. "Can I buy some things for lunch? I want to make something fresh." She was still smarting from the mixed reaction to the millet. "And then we'll buy a second fridge on the way home."

"You can buy whatever you want," he said.

While Oksana picked beets for borshch, cabbage for salad, and kidney beans for her kidney-bean patties, Arkady went to the flower stand and came back with a single rose for Oksana. When they checked out, the pair of young cashiers broke into applause at the gallant gesture and insisted the rose would be free. They knew him here, too.

"Where next?" she said when they were outside.

"I wanted to go to the cake store for my birthday," he said. "But I'm ready for home."

"Are you feeling all right?"

"A little nap, that's all. Tell me a good story and we'll be home quickly."

"I don't have any stories like you do. My stories are sad. I'd rather you told me a story."

He stopped. "A woman like you? No."

"A woman like me, yes," she laughed mirthlessly. They walked for a block. Finally Arkady said, "So you're alone?"

"You know what it is, Arkady Kharitonovich?" She used his patronymic—the respectful form of address. "When you grew up—on the one hand, it was the Soviet time, it was bad, right? But things feel uglier now. Even though there's no war. Even though everyone's free."

He liked being addressed as an authority. He shrugged modestly.

"I was seventeen years old," she said. "This young man walks into the store—he's in the oil-and-gas department at the college, they're done with exams, he wants champagne and chocolates for their celebration. I was in the back; he got impatient and plopped his champagne bottle on the scale. Nearly broke it. I came out and gave him a piece of my mind. I guess he liked it—he came back in the evening. 'I'm glad they make you work a long shift,' he says. 'The hours are on the door,' I said. 'I know,' he says, 'I checked on my way out before.' A regular Romeo! He walked me home; we started seeing each other. Soon after, we had to go to a wedding on my mother's side. Somehow, they forgot the onions—can you imagine a Ukrainian table without onions? So he got in his car, drove to his village, and came back with twenty kilos of onions. My mother's heart was his for eternity."

"Smart man," Arkady said.

"Only that was the last decision he ever made. He got me, and he didn't want to try hard ever again. I was the go-getter. Also, he cheated on me. I guess he needed to feel like a man."

Arkady walked silently, and Oksana worried that she'd spoken vulgarly. But then he said, "I can't make sense of it. And now, no one?"

"Six years ago, I met someone else. I was thirty-eight, I thought it would look strange if I was without a husband. But again, I was the husband. The earnings were mine, I brought in the food, the apartment I paid for. It's fine, I didn't need material things—all I wanted was someone stronger than me. 'Strong woman' is a foolish notion—I wanted a real man. He and I were walking by the river once, and he was complaining again, and I remember looking at the water and praying, 'God, please grant me a green card to America.' And God heard me."

They were in front of Arkady's building. "Sad talking makes quick walking," she said. "Let's go up—you take a nap, I'll make lunch."

"What's for lunch?" he said.

"It's a surprise—you can dream about it."

"I want a *gogol-mogol*," he said. It was the Russian version of eggnog, only that among Russians it counted as a cold remedy and all-purpose aid.

"Can you have all that sugar?" she said. "I'll adjust it."

The adjustment, once the refrigerator came to look like the last train out of Paris before the Germans rolled in, was hot milk with buckwheat honey: no sugar, no egg yolks.

"It's a hardship regime," the client complained. He'd changed into pinstriped pajamas.

She laughed. "Very. I'll take some of those peppers and marinate them in this honey." She puckered her hands in front of her lips the way she had seen Italians do. "Gorgeous!"

"Okay, gorgeous," he said. He declined his head obediently and downed the hot milk. "Don't be lonely. I won't sleep long."

While he napped, Oksana cooked. She worked handicapped: no caramelized onions and carrots in the borshch, because of the amounts of oil required; no sugar in the salad dressing. Only the kidney-bean burgers could keep to the original recipe: semolina flour, a little sour cream, nothing terrible. If she had to spare oil and fat, she'd get her flavor from spice: the borshch would get parsnip, potatoes, and—you wouldn't find the housewives at home using it—jalapeño. She'd made other discoveries in the New World: basil, cumin, curry. At home, it was all root vegetables.

When the client emerged from the bedroom, the ash-colored hair that had been neatly parted now up in a coxcomb, the borshch was "breathing" on the stove and Oksana was at the dining table writing. It would be a late lunch.

"Writing up a report?" Arkady said, and he produced a long, satisfied yawn.

She swiveled in the chair and threw the paper in her purse. "It's nothing. Let's go, it'll be three soon! What a day."

"There's a sweater in the bedroom," he said. "Little dots all over. Can you get it?"

When she walked out, he went to her purse and pulled out the piece of paper. It had a line down the middle—one side said "good," the other "bad." Under "good," it said: "1) children, 2) Mama,

3) health." Under "bad" was written a female name—it must have been the old woman she looked after—and then "love" and then "no English."

He heard her approaching and tossed it back into the purse. "I couldn't find the one with dots," she said. "I got you another."

"I must have got rid of it," he shrugged.

At the table, she held her breath as he slurped the borshch. He kept rotating his shoulder—maybe he didn't sleep well? Maybe, God, he *liked* watery chicken soup!

He lifted his head. "Won't you eat?"

"No one less hungry than a cook," she said. "Tasting and trying as you go." She added suggestively, "You want to know how it came out, you know." She waited. "Oh, Arkady Kharitonovich, I can't keep on like this. I see you eating like it's homework. Don't you like it?"

His eyes became big. "Don't I like it? I love it!"

"You're a flatterer—tell the truth. What's wrong with it?"

"It's good! Oksanushka, it's fine!"

She was touched by the diminutive. "It's not fine," she said.

"It's a little lean, that's all," he said. "Good for me," he said unconvincingly.

"But what could I do?" she said. "It's like dancing without legs, this cooking. A Ukrainian dish without salt, without caramelized onions?" She shook her head.

Arkady put his spoon down. Her eyes followed him to the liquor cabinet, from which he withdrew a bronze-colored bottle and two shot glasses. These had narrow necks, but for pouring his hand was steady. She watched him, uncertain.

"Oksanushka," he said, "let me introduce myself again. I'm Arkady—you can call me Arkady, don't bother with the patronymic." He waited for her to raise her glass, clinked it, and drank in one gulp. "And Arkady," he said, giving her that coquettish look again, "can have whatever he wants." She couldn't believe she was about to drink on the job, but it was a strange day; she drained her glass. The warmth went right to her head. It was good cognac.

"They said diet food," she said.

"And do I look like the rest of them?"

"And what about that?" She pointed at the ropy scar on his chest.

"So what the hell did they clean them out for?" he said, pointing at his arteries.

"Then I disown this table," she said. "Let me do it again."

"Fine," he said. "I'll read the newspaper."

"Read out loud," she said. "I feel like a worm who's been down in the soil. It's always bad news at home. Here, I feel like it varies."

An hour later, the kitchen deep in a new round of cooking that would have to become dinner, he was reading out proverbs and humor from the newspaper when the doorbell rang. They looked up. The doorbell was tricky for Soviet people. It rarely meant something good.

"I don't know," he shrugged. "I'm not expecting anyone."

Oksana cast a parental look at the ribs in her pan—she had to keep the braising liquid from getting too low. At the door, they discovered an old man in blue workout pants and Fila slippers over brown socks. It was Yasha, the neighbor.

"Excuse me, people," he said. "I'm out for my exercise, but who can exercise with these smells floating around? I've been sniffing doorways for ten minutes."

"Yasha does stairwells before dinner," Arkady said. "Fitness fanatic." Yasha was of medium height like Arkady, but he didn't have Arkady's belly. But Arkady's hair had stayed gray, whereas Yasha's had gone white. These men compared these things—out loud when the comparison favored them, to themselves when it didn't.

"So if it smells good, come in," Arkady said. He turned to Oksana. "What do we have?"

"Crispy potatoes, stewed chicken—and dry ribs if I don't run back to the kitchen."

Yasha slapped his hands together. "I knew I knocked on the right door."

"Here, I know your favorite appetizer," Arkady said, and filled a new shot glass.

They drank, they screwed up their faces, they chased with lemon slices. "You got any quarters?" Arkady said. Yasha was the super's assistant and got paid in laundry quarters, so his pockets were always drooping with coins.

"Of course I have quarters," Yasha said. "You need for the laundry?"

"Wait, wait." Arkady left the living room. He returned with a pink plastic pig.

"You're obsessed with that pig," Yasha said.

"I'm a collector, what do you want?"

"Yes, I've seen your clowns."

"Just change me a twenty."

"You're going to change a twenty into eighty quarters to dump into that piggy," Yasha said, "so you can take it to the bank and enjoy getting a twenty back. Your dementia's starting."

"Who cares—change it. I'll give it to my grandson. He's too proud to take money, but trifles like coins, he might give in. I'll tell him the pig's too heavy, can't he help?"

Yasha started dropping quarters onto the oilcloth; Arkady arranged them in piles of four.

"Better to count quarters than pills," Yasha said.

"Fifty-six," Arkady announced.

"I'll bring the rest down after dinner. Or you want some fish next time I go to the pier?"

"What's the best fish?" Arkady said. "A piece of meat. And what's the best meat?"

"A sockful of cash," Yasha finished for him.

"So here's the twenty dollars, and you bring up the rest after dinner. I don't eat fish from the river."

"And where do you think the Chinese get it? Deep in the ocean?"

Arkady shrugged and poured another thimble. "It's all bullshit," he said.

"It's all bullshit," Yasha confirmed.

Eventually they gave up on forks and gnawed on the ribs until it was too much for dentures. The chicken stew was so good that Yasha asked forgiveness and just drank the broth straight from the bowl, dodging bones. When he returned it to the table after a satisfied belch, two carrot shavings remained on his nose, almost a cross.

"Her food is so good, she converted you," Arkady said.

After Yasha left, the living room gained a slight mournfulness—the daylight gone, the meal gone, Oksana's shift almost gone, too. Oksana had never been mournful about the end of a shift; so life still had surprises for her. When she was cooking—the potatoes blistering, the ribs braising—it was all ahead. A meal went too quickly.

"Excuse me for a minute," Oksana said.

Arkady remained at the table, pushing around crumbs with his pinkie. He was thinking about Oksana, and about his wife, and about nothing at all. Finally he rose and went toward the pillbox—less box than chest—in the bedroom. His evening friends awaited him: Toprol and Ranexa and Plavix and Flomax. Passing the bathroom, he stopped. She was crying in there. Had he done something? He tried the door—open—and pushed.

"Oh, goodness," she said. "Forgive me."

"But what is it?" he said.

"Nothing! Just silliness."

"I won't let you be—please tell me."

"Oh, Arkady Kharitonovich. Arkady—" She was drying her eyes with the shelf of her hand. "A pig without manners, to cry like this." Finally she turned to him. "In eight months in this country, not one person has asked me half of the things you asked me today. That's all."

He smiled, proud of himself but embarrassed that she'd been treated without courtesy and frustrated that she was around just for the day, not enough time for him to fix it. He reached out and gently touched a clump of her hair. "What's on your head?" he said. "I've wanted to ask all day. You look like a tree and someone's lopped off the branches."

"Somebody in Detroit practicing," she said. "They did it for free. It doesn't matter."

"Let's go," he said. "My equipment's in the living room."

"You still cut hair?"

"On special occasions."

"Cognac doesn't loosen your touch?"

"Steadies it."

"I don't want to trouble you."

"Stop it, please. You want to be looked after, let people look after you."

It was true—he hadn't cut hair in a long time. After the trading post into which he'd turned his Minsk barbershop, working in So-and-so's salon on Avenue J for pocket change held no appeal. So he barbered the occasional head in his building, but since Sofia's death almost no one.

When he finished, Oksana looked in the mirror and gasped. "You've taken ten years." He knew men's hair better, so the cut he'd given her was a touch boyish, but she liked it.

They embraced and wished each other good health. The Tupperware in Oksana's plastic bag was as full of *grechanniki* as it had been that morning. Otherwise, the bag bulged with half the fruit and vegetables Arkady had bought. The rose he'd given her sat among them; she arranged it so that it peeked out past the bag handles. She wanted them to see in the street.

GRECHANNIKI (BUCKWHEAT BURGERS)

Time: 1 hour, 30 minutes   Serves: 6–8

1⅓ cups buckwheat groats
2 tablespoons vegetable oil, plus
    additional for cooking the
    patties
1 large onion, chopped
1 large carrot, grated
Kosher salt, to taste
1 tablespoon tomato paste, plus
    additional to taste
1 bay leaf
Crushed red pepper, to taste

¾ pound ground chicken
¾ pound ground pork
1 egg
½ bunch fresh dill, roughly
    chopped
2 cloves garlic, put through a
    garlic press
1 tablespoon ground coriander
1 tablespoon curry powder
1 teaspoon black pepper
¼ cup flour

1. Inspect the buckwheat for black groats and remove. They're bitter.

2. Dump the groats into a fine-mesh strainer and rinse with cold water, riffling through them with your fingers.

3. In a pot, cover the groats with 2⅔ cups of water, add salt, and bring to a boil. Turn the heat down and let simmer, a lid on most of the way, till the water has evaporated, 15 to 20 minutes. Set aside to cool. Alternatively, you can cover the buckwheat with the 2⅔ cups of water and let it soak overnight—it will be "cooked" by morning.

4. Meanwhile, in a large, deep sauté pan, heat the 2 tablespoons of oil over medium heat. Add half the chopped onion and cook, stirring frequently, until golden brown, about 10 minutes. Add the carrot and cook until softened, about 5 minutes. Salt to taste. Add 2 cups of water (or use vegetable or chicken stock if you prefer), the tomato paste, bay leaf, and crushed red pepper. Bring to a gentle simmer. Taste and add more tomato paste if you like and season lightly with salt. Turn the heat down to its lowest setting and cover the pan (to keep it warm while you prepare the patties).

5. Combine the chicken and pork in a large bowl. Add the cooled buckwheat, the egg, half the chopped dill, the remaining chopped onion, the garlic, coriander, curry, and black pepper. Season with a teaspoon of salt, or to taste. Mix gently until well combined.

6. Using your hands or a spoon, shape the mixture into small patties the size of mini-burgers. (You should end up with 30 or so.) Put the flour onto a plate and dredge the patties lightly on both sides, patting off any excess.

7. In a large pan, add enough oil to coat the bottom well, and warm over medium heat. Brown the patties, in batches if necessary, 5 minutes on one side and 3 on the other.

8. Place the patties into the pan with the braising liquid (the patties should be half-covered by the liquid) and cook, covered, over medium-low heat for 30 minutes, stirring gently every 10 minutes. If you would prefer a slightly thicker broth, dust in a little flour after the first 10 minutes, or cook uncovered so the liquid can boil down.

9. Crown with the remaining dill.

Serve over your favorite grain: quinoa, couscous, bulgur wheat. The grains will soak up the braising broth.

✧

ROASTED PEPPERS MARINATED IN BUCKWHEAT HONEY AND GARLIC (V)

Time: 1 hour, 15 minutes   Serves: 4

The pepper needs to be meaty—like a person.
—Oksana

PEPPERS

3 large red bell peppers	Kosher salt, to taste
6 cloves garlic, put through a garlic press	

MARINADE

¼ cup white vinegar	1 tablespoon sunflower oil
2 teaspoons sugar	(sunflower oil doesn't become
¼ teaspoon kosher salt	solid in the fridge)
1 teaspoon buckwheat honey	Chopped fresh dill, to taste
(substitute another honey if	
you can't find buckwheat)	

1. Preheat the oven to 400 degrees. Place the peppers, whole, into a pan and roast in the oven, turning them every 10 to 15 minutes. After 45 to 60 minutes, the skin should have a golden-brown crust and seem like it'll peel off easily.

2. Meanwhile, combine all the ingredients for the marinade in a bowl.

3. When the peppers are cool enough to handle, remove the skin and seeds. Do this over a bowl to catch the peppers' juices, and add them to the marinade.

4. Slice the peppers lengthwise—6–8 "leaves" per pepper—taking care to remove stray seeds.

5. In a container, layer the pepper slices, covering each layer with some of the pressed garlic and a generous pinch of salt. You should end up with 3 or 4 layers.

6. Pour the marinade gently over the pepper layers, making sure it penetrates all the way to the bottom. Gently spear the peppers in several places with a fork to get the marinade to penetrate better.

7. Generously sprinkle the uppermost layer with dill, and refrigerate for a day.

✤

A STOVETOP ALTERNATIVE, WHICH USES A SLIGHTLY DIFFERENT MARINADE

Time: 45 minutes   Serves: 4

PEPPERS

2 tablespoons vegetable oil
3 large red bell peppers, sliced
   lengthwise into quarters and
   cleaned of seeds

The cloves of ½ a head of garlic,
   peeled and minced
Kosher salt, to taste

MARINADE

¾ cup water
⅓ cup white vinegar, plus
   additional to taste

Juice of 1 medium lemon
1½ tablespoons sugar, plus
   additional to taste

1. In a deep sauté pan, heat the oil over medium heat. Add the peppers and cook, stirring occasionally, until softened, about 15 minutes.

2. Meanwhile, combine all the ingredients for the marinade in a bowl, adjusting to taste. As Oksana says, "This dish is all about the contrast between sweet and tart, sugar and vinegar."

3. Add the marinade to the pan with the peppers, throw in the garlic, season lightly with salt, and cover the pan. The lemon may turn the garlic blue, but it won't affect the taste. Bring to a gentle simmer, tasting the marinade every 5 to 10 minutes; if it's too vinegary, add a little sugar. If you're running low on liquid, make more of the marinade according to the specifications above, or see the note at the end of the recipe.

4. When the liquid in the pan—the *yushka*—has turned cloudy, the marinade will be flavorful, but the peppers will probably need more salt: They can absorb a lot without becoming oversalted, thanks to all their moisture. Add more salt now and, as Oksana says, "don't be stingy with it."

5. After 30 minutes, the peppers should be fully soft without losing shape.

6. Let cool, transfer the peppers to a jar, and cover with the marinade.

7. Refrigerate overnight—they are a cool, refreshing side to starches or meat dishes.

Note: If you end up with extra marinade in the first variant, it serves most suitably if the second ends up needing more liquid.

⁜

CHAPTER 8

2006

What to cook for Passover if you're an atheist

What to cook for a bunch of Jews on Passover if you're an Orthodox Christian

✤

Passover—one of the non-negotiable gatherings. I had been a perfunctory presence at the mandatory family assemblies for years now, but I hadn't managed to work up the ruthlessness to break my mother's heart and fail to appear altogether. I was weary of south Brooklyn the way you give up on someone you cared for once because they're still addicts.

To sit at a table like my family's was to reinfect oneself with the addiction. They passed around conspiracy theories—George W. Bush had not said that; someone pretending to be him had given that interview. They shared medieval wisdom: Women in the Netherlands had a lower birth rate because it was cold there. They did not bother with innuendo, and enjoyed a powerful tolerance for cognitive dissonance—just because south Brooklyn was filled with ex-Soviets defrauding Social Security and Medicaid didn't mean the welfare rolls were anything but 100 percent black. Blacks carried generations of trauma passed down by slavery? But Jews had been abused—slaughtered, ghettoized, disadvantaged—in Russia for centuries, and that didn't stop them from high earnings in a country they barely knew. As for their own activity on the wrong side of the law, did they not deserve the perks after so much abuse? And, what, America had clean hands? Enough—pass the pork.

I had kept arguing, but then I gave up. When my father moved us out to New Jersey, I had tried to pass myself off as a Bobby. The shape-shift was short-lived, and I retreated back to bits of Russianness now and then. But for years now, it had taken more and more to make myself go down to my grandfather's neighborhood.

Passover seemed like an easy time for a no-show—we were atheists. In our first years, the American Jews had tried their best with us. They hired us; plied us with food bundles and free synagogue memberships; got their knife on my privates for a very belated circumcision, the pain of which surely would never leave my subconscious. It all came to nothing. My parents were fanatic defenders of Israel, and my mother liked Hanukkah so much, she kept the menorah lit well past the ritual eight days—why not, it looked nice. But that was it. The people who fought so hard for our release never imagined that getting us out would be the easy part.

But Passover was near enough my mother's birthday to make it an expensive collateral hit. In Minsk, it was Lenin's birthday, several days from my mother's, that always ruined her birthday weekend, because everyone had to spend the weekend after His birthday doing volunteer labor. And now Passover would do the same in America? Fate always gave us the short end.

So I went, though I made no effort to hide how I felt. And this time, at least, there was a palliating reason to join them. In the preceding months, we'd started hearing about a new home attendant with "golden hands at the stove." Oksana had been a day sub, but then the regular home aide had over-reported her hours and suddenly there was an opening for the weekdays. Previously, Oksana had been assigned to some lunatic ogress, but this was why my grandfather kept the ladies at the assignment agency in chocolates and perfume. A quiet reassignment. My grandparents had scrolled through a half dozen home nurses since my grandmother had been formally diagnosed. None had been singled out for her or his cooking. Singled out for anything. Passover would be our first time at Oksana's table.

I was coming from Washington, D.C., where I was bivouacked on a writing project, with a stop at my girlfriend Alana's apartment on the Upper West Side, where I was bivouacked while my apartment got some repairs. She wasn't coming to our phony version of Passover—her family did all of it: the prayers, the rituals, the restrictions. Except that she kept kosher only at home. This choice was supposed to indicate a conscious, personal engagement with religion, but to me it seemed like convenience, another version of our phoniness. What was the merit of doing something unless you did it all the way?

Before Passover, she scrubbed and boiled until the kitchen was pure, so I returned from Washington to half of it wrapped in tinfoil to prevent use during the holiday, which lent it the slightly touched look of a DIY alien-contact station. She was following obsolete rules, I wanted to say. Also, I could buy very tasty chicken for a third of the kosher price—in south Brooklyn, in fact, where produce and other groceries were often twice as good at half the cost. (Often, this was what tipped the scale toward going there, after all.) But I said nothing. It would offend.

On the subway down to my grandfather's, I carried an item as alien as a kilo of heroin—I hid it from view every time I opened my bag. I was a practiced concealer—abroad, I wrapped my guidebooks to avoid being exposed as a tourist; at home, I wrapped the books I was embarrassed to be seen reading. It was a Russian-language Haggadah, the ritual Passover text. For decades, Jewish dissidents in the Soviet Union had passed around the same text with the same secrecy. I was free not to bother, but I didn't have their devotion. I lowered my voice every time I said the word "Jewish," just as we had in the Soviet Union.

I'd procured it from a skullcapped Jewish Uzbek barber in my neighborhood. It was ugly and unceremonious—modern graphic design may never come to books in Russian. The cover showed nineteen guests—all men, all hirsutely Central Asian, all wearing versions of Joseph's dreamcoat—seated around a Passover table framed by a floating panorama of beet- and gold-colored crowns, Stars of David, and generic arabesques. It was 86 pages—128 if you counted the local-restaurant ads in the back. Or, rather, in the front—they wanted you to read it like Hebrew, back to front.

Eighty-six pages—I'd make them go all the way. If it was a Jewish holiday and I had to be there, my way would have to be taken into account. They did not restrain themselves with me, and so, them, I would not worry about offending. But the home aide was outside that circle. I wondered if it'd be awkward with her. She was Christian.

In the elevator of my grandfather's building, I held the door for one of "ours": sleeveless housedress, netted slippers, mail in her hand. She didn't know what to do with me. My darkness could have been Georgian, but Georgians didn't wear boat shoes and politely tight looks. "*Shlyut i shlyut*," she tried, shrugging at the stack of catalogs in her hands. "They send and they send"—there hadn't been a fraction of all this mail, so wasteful and oppressive, in the Soviet Union. I shared her bafflement. But I only smiled noncommittally. "*Gudbai*," she said when her floor came. "Goodbye," I said in clean English.

Oksana wore the other uniform of our women: tights and a close-fitting T-shirt instead of the housedress. She had close-set eyes and puffy white arms. She was first into the foyer after I opened the door, but stopped shyly.

"Your grandfather's told me so much about you," she said. She used the formal "you."

"And me about you," I lied. I had avoided my grandfather for months. Didn't visit, barely called. "Your buzzer's broken," I said when he appeared in the foyer. "I rang and rang."

He shrugged. "Everyone I need is right here," he said. "And your parents, of course."

"Well, they won't be able to get in," I said. "I'll wash my hands." I always washed my hands when I got in. Arriving home, I changed my clothes. Soviet notions of hygiene. This caused much amusement for my American girlfriends. I'd never had a Russian girlfriend.

"My father washed his hands for ten minutes after coming home," I heard him say to Oksana as I receded. "Scalding hot water. Then tea. Three glasses, four glasses. Then he was ready to talk. Though he wasn't much of a talker. My mother was the talker."

I'd never heard my grandfather talk about his mother or father. I pictured a man in a wooden dwelling, his suspenders around his waist, his shirt cuffed to the elbow. "Why did he do that?" I said when I returned.

"Who?"

"Your father, who."

"He delivered safes," he said. "Quarter-ton each. He'd haul them up the flights on his back. They didn't have a file for him at the medical clinic until he was seventy-two."

"So you're making up for lost time," I said. He glowered. Then he turned to Oksana and softened. "My father had the best horses in the city." He counted on his fingers: "Beetle, Pegasus, Boy. With the first set, though, he got taken in. At the horse market, it was all Gypsies. The horse can be young, good strong teeth, but only they know he's lazy. I had a talk with them—we were friendly, people didn't mess around with me. And they gave my father his money back."

Was he making it up? He'd never talked to me about these things. I'd filled out my grandmother's Holocaust restitution application a decade before and, as she told her story, he dropped a detail of his own now and then, but she silenced him—she didn't want me to know what he got up to. Occasionally I probed him for more, but he answered so vaguely I didn't know how to start clarifying. I'd quit asking. I wasn't going to chase him.

"Mama and Papa tell you how long?" I said.

"Traffic." He shrugged. "If they lived in Brooklyn, they'd be here already."

It was Paris that had made me avoid him. Some people fall in love there—and some people out. Early one morning the previous November, shortly after he and Oksana had met, the escalator rose out of the Paris metro, my heart thudding with each stair that vanished into its mechanical mouth. We had landed at Charles de Gaulle two hours before. I'd made him take the underground—the number the (brown-bagged) guidebook quoted for a taxi would have upset him as badly as me. There was another reason: The guidebook said the station exit let out onto a view of the Eiffel Tower, near which our hotel stood. It was a surprise. I planned to emerge out of the metro and—wham. The Eiffel Tower. *How do you like that?* I'd researched the exits and hoped to God this was the one.

It had been my idea. What would have been my grandmother's birthday was approaching, then his own (she had been eleven days older). A distraction: a trip to Paris and Israel, with me as his mule. For a person like him, the name Paris concentrated every romance and luxury absent from Soviet life. And half his old Minsk friends had emigrated to Israel. He hadn't seen them in nearly two decades. He wouldn't go to New Jersey, but he could brag about Paris.

The Eiffel was for him—I prided myself on avoiding this kind of kitsch. I did well—suddenly there it was, in its early-morning, unpeopled glory, only banks of flowers swaying in the wind. Triumphantly, I turned around to note his impression. But there was no one to impress. This option I hadn't considered. I swiveled frantically—there was no down escalator, and I hadn't researched how to get back underground and search for a lost grandfather. Then I saw him. He was at the window of a footwear boutique. "Look at these loafers!" he roared, banging the glass. A mustached street sweeper, a cigarette hanging from his mouth, looked up— the tongue of our nation was barbaric in all that quiet civility.

"Look at this goddamn tower!" I stuck a finger out at the international marvel before us.

"Oh!" he said, turning. "*Ukh ty.*" It was perfunctory wonder, embarrassingly obvious in its falsehood. Perhaps he felt he didn't have to try hard to fool me. He shuffled over for a photo, his gold signet ring sparkling in the sun and his big round belly pushing out his two-toned sweater—fabric in the back, leather in the front. He'd groomed his mustache extra neat for the trip—it had the shape of the Atari logo. Better than the Hitler-like square to which he sometimes inexplicably shaved it down.

On entering our bantam hotel room, the view from which caught a sliver of the tower (as I'd confirmed, in very bad French, via many calls to the hotel), he fluttered his lips in the way that meant *And how about this shit.* The bed nearly touched the wall, alongside which he squeezed himself like a victim. The shower was a coffin stood upright. I wanted to make him guess how much even this pleasure cost. But I had to choose what he was going to wear.

"The blue sweater," I proposed.

He shrugged and folded his lips. "I don't know . . ."

I put him back in the two-tone. Lunch presented a problem— the holes-in-the-wall I wanted to try were beneath him, but the menu of every bourgeois restaurant the guidebook recommended listed prices that would make him turn white.

"I didn't realize I would be touring Paris on foot," he said as I inspected our fifth menu.

"Let's just go in here," I said.

"What have they got?" he said.

"I don't know," I said. "I don't speak French. They have every-thing."

"It would've been good if you learned it," he said.

"Yeah? Did you learn English?"

"I'm an old man."

"Grandma Faina learned it."

"Yes, when you bother only about yourself, you've got time to learn English."

By now we were being fit around a bijou table by a waiter dressed better than we were. I knew we'd stepped in it—heavy white table-cloths, an expensive kind of quiet.

"Americans wouldn't fit at this table," he sniffed.

"Worry about yourself," I said. He had a belly like a beach ball, though the rest of him was tidy and slim. He was pinned like an insect.

I tried to translate the menu in my head, then render it for him in Russian. "They take a pork chop and stuff an onion in there, and then *lardons* . . . like salami. And they've got these greens they serve only in season. With garlic."

"The cigarette smoke!" he exclaimed, looking evilly at the other diners, who, for some reason, had failed to learn Russian to prepare for his visit and did not react. "Disgusting."

"You smoked for thirty years," I said.

"But I stopped."

"What are you going to eat?"

"I don't know." He shrugged. "What do they have?"

"I just told you what they have."

I repeated the descriptions, then again, and again, the dishes gradually dwindling to the main proteins: pork, chicken, fish, just as on the plane. Finally I gave up and just chose for him.

"An American wouldn't survive on these portions," he declared when the entrées arrived. Why was it necessary to go out to eat a stingy sliver of salmon for seventeen euros when he could get salmon for five dollars a pound back home? The sliver was actually twenty-five euros; I'd lied.

"They eat differently here," I said. "The portions are smaller, and they eat slowly. It's the culture. Look—there's not one fat person here."

"It's true, Americans are fat," he said. He didn't seem to mind the salmon itself—he was shoveling it into his mouth. I closed my eyes. I had no appetite.

"What's with work?" he said, sticking a finger into his mouth to clear a wet chunk of fish.

"Nothing," I said. "All the same. Trying."

"A novel?" he said. He read only the first and last pages of books.

"It's about you," I said, so he would value it more.

"*What* about me?" he said. He looked both flattered and wary.

"Why, you have secrets?" I said.

"Me?" he said. "I'm an open book."

"When Mama was filling out your Section 8 paperwork, I heard her say you were older than Grandma. But she's eleven days earlier in December, same year. So how can you be older?"

"You misheard."

"Why don't you just tell me?"

"Don't worry about it."

"So you're an open book?"

"With your degree, you could have done anything," he said, scraping roasted potato loudly enough to be heard in the street. "At least you're in Washington for this project. It's important, right? You work for the Senate."

"It's not what I care about," I said.

"They're paying you, though," he said.

"Yes, as I go."

His fork stopped. "Why would you allow them to do that? What prevents them from taking your work once you're done and just stiffing you?" He looked at me like I was an imbecile.

"My God—it's the United States government."

"Exactly—they can do whatever they want."

When the check came, I grabbed it so he couldn't see, but his gallantry wouldn't allow me to pay, so I gave him a reduced number and then, pleading the bathroom, added my own euros once

out of view. We stepped out into cold sunlight. The burn of having walked in without checking the prices—this is what happened
when you let down your guard—was compounded by that other
truism of spontaneous dining: If you'd tried just one storefront
more, next door, you would've found one of those solid bistros with
duck confit for half the tab.

He did like being photographed. At the Seine, the Arc de Tri-
omphe, the Mona Lisa, Notre Dame. A thumb in the air, a somber
look behind his tinted glasses.

"You choking?" I said. "Smile."

"I didn't know you were supposed to smile," he said, and lit up
like a lunatic.

Later, passing a store, he stopped me: They had a clown in the
window. No, I said—it was huge. Porcelain. We had so much far-
ther to go. But he was beyond reason, and we bought it.

By our last night, I couldn't endure one more meal out. I took
him to Le Bon Marché, and while he wandered the aisles in a
daze, I bought things that seemed most like what he ate in Brooklyn, meaning what he ate in the Soviet Union. Country pâté, hard
cheese, tomatoes, *saucisson sec*, *cornichons*, a baguette, éclairs, a
small bottle of cognac. At reception, I mimed a request for an extra
bedsheet, which I unfurled over the bed, the largest surface in the
room. Then I set it all out, using the mini ironing board as a table.
The bathroom drinking glasses sufficed for the cognac. The tomatoes and salami we ate without utensils, and the Cantal I contrived
to peel with a fresh razor blade. I sat on the floor, he on the bed with
his legs extended into the bathroom, a hand towel I'd tucked into
his collar serving as a bib. Periodically, we toasted. I had never been
drunk one-on-one with my grandfather. Blissfully, it was silent.
When we finished, he stared off and said, "They do live differently
here. We"—Soviet people—"were imprisoned." Sometimes he surprised you like that. I was about to press him for more but stopped
myself. No reason to ruin the moment.

French airport security wouldn't believe the clown wasn't for ferrying drugs and nearly broke it apart. "What drugs!" he shouted. "I'm an old man!" The guards contented themselves with a vibrator-size tube of toothpaste in his carry-on. I'd told him about the three-ounce rule many times before leaving home, but I should have known the home aide would have packed him, and she knew even less about American ubiquities than he did. It must have been in the checked luggage on the way over.

In Israel, he informed his old friends that he'd been to *Paris*, where he'd stayed in an *enormous* room, which was right by the *Eiffel Tower*, and had dined in the *best* places, and his *grandson* had arranged *all of it*. By the time we reached Eilat, on the Red Sea, the last stop, he was posing for photos in front of anything stationary. At the hotel, he corralled three young women dressed in fishnets, corsets, and feathered headpieces for some variety show, hoisted his thumbs, popped out a half-crazy smile, and waited while I searched for the camera. One morning, I awoke to the sight of him in wife-beater and briefs doing calisthenics, the sea shimmering outside. His hair was up like a wild plant, and he looked as focused as an Olympian. *Phoo*, he breathed out deeply with each jumping jack. So he took care of himself less vigilantly than Grandma Faina? But I decided to stay quiet, the slap of his feet on the floor the metronome to which I fell back asleep.

At my grandfather's, my mother embraced me as if we hadn't seen each other in years, not weeks.

"You stopped by Alana's?" she said. "How is it with you two?"

"Everything's great," I said. I knew she would ask; I had practiced.

"She didn't want to come?" she said.

"What? No, I told you. She's with her family. I told you several times."

"She's probably embarrassed about the way we do it."

"How many times have I said she doesn't care how you do it? She wants people to choose for themselves. She doesn't judge. How many times have I told you that? Why don't you hear what I'm saying?"

I could have remembered all this was coming, too. But I was able to control myself for only so long. There was a wounded look in my mother's eyes. Sometimes, I thought, she preferred to be hurt than deflected.

"Tell me about Washington," she said tightly.

"Marauding gangs," I snapped. "And hunger. I haven't eaten in weeks."

Her look turned to anger. "How long are we going to hang for that?"

Eight years earlier, late in my first year of college, I'd been chosen to move to Washington for a summer internship—a U.S. senator was working on a book of historic political speeches. I'd never gone that far from home for that long—gone from home, period. It was exactly the type of gratuitous voyage of which my people kept clear. But I had been writing some guileless poems and stories. And I was transfixed by the guile of American politics. And though dread was always with me, sometimes it felt even more dreadful not to try to beat it back. I was expected to strive, achieve, conquer. How to do that without taking advantage of opportunities like this one?

When I got the news, my parents congratulated me with colorless faces and said all the things that, for some reason, I'd hoped they wouldn't. Washington—that was far away. Where would I live? Where would I eat? I gave them a good lecture about their pathetic, embarrassing fears. Then I charged back upstairs, past two lacquered birch branches my parents had found in the local woods and brought back to remind them of all the birches in Belarus.

I was on hold with the senator's office when the door to my little workroom swung open. It had been a closet until my father cleared

it out and mounted waist-high shelving on the wall to make a kind
of desk. He could build a desk, a chandelier, or a flying closet to
hang off bicycle hooks in the ceiling because his son had been assigned to an eighty-square-foot double at school. But he didn't want
to turn this skill into a business. And he'd traded house painting
for a spot as a doorman at a tony building on the Upper East Side.
There he had the security and level of challenge he wanted. In the
closet office's little window, I could see the tree I'd planted with my
grandmother after we moved to New Jersey. The sapling had been
small enough to fit in the trunk of our battered blue Buick. Now it
stood higher than a person, aflame with white and pink flowers.

The office door revealed my mother, her eyes on the floor. She
slid a small slip of paper under my nose and fled. It said, for some
reason in English, "Please don't go." I stared at the wall, halfway
between numbness and tears. When the staffer finally got on the
line, I apologized and said I wouldn't be able to make it.

I was grateful, in a way: I'd yelled for my cause and given it up
for my loved ones—an honorable discharge. It was now, eight years
later, that I found myself filled with anger that wouldn't go away—
after the semester in Spain that unraveled, the Fulbright to Turkey
I turned down, the relocation to Mexico that I swore would be the
time I . . . but wasn't. By then, they no longer had to mainline the
apprehension into me, though they did anyway. And I kept trying
to persuade them. I couldn't manage to go without their blessing.

Eight years later, the Washington I'd finally gotten to see was
taking me in in a way New York never had. New York felt like it had
no need for people like me. There were thousands of freelance jour-
nalists there—disposable, and treated as such. Washington surely
had its own version of that, but writers swam in a smaller sea. The
committee staffers whose prose I'd been hired to edit for a government report on Hurricane Katrina seemed to like coming by to ask
which paragraph should go where. And for all the secret savagery
they must have dealt each other, these lawyers (lawyers!) went

about the Katrina investigation with an earnestness that moved me as the apparent mores of New York journalism never had. I had arrived with a New Yorker's condescension toward these supposedly square people, but I had come to feel admiration instead.

Earlier that spring, storm survivors had bused up from the South, dressed in the best Katrina had left them. The women in broad-brimmed hats and bright dresses reminded me of my grandmother Faina, now in Chicago with my uncle's family. Everyone was black. My suit marked me out as a staffer, so people pulled on my sleeve and tried to tell me their stories. That was all they wanted—someone to hear what had happened.

Several junior colleagues and I started writing these stories down and asking for more names to call. The report would focus on systems—interagency coordination and so on—but the introduction had no official mandate and, perhaps because it was assumed it would consist mostly of fluff, was relatively safe from political interference. Back upstairs, our little bullpen came to resemble a backwater broadsheet come upon some kind of local malfeasance— all hands on deck. We called, interviewed, and transcribed— morgue operators, surgeons, coast guard rescuers, parish officials, survivors—until we had enough to weave a real-time account of what these people had gone through during and after the storm. In New York, I'd been writing brief actress profiles for *Vogue*. For the first time in nearly twenty years in the States, I felt a sense of community, purpose, and belonging. I was electric with excitement. I know this because I ate Subway four times a day and didn't notice.

To this, at my grandfather's, only my mother was willing to listen. Oksana was laying out silverware, my father was sautéing shrimp on the stove, and my grandfather was staring at the blaring television as Oksana periodically checked that he was well propped on pillows (they would ward off the prostate cancer caused by hard surfaces). My mother would listen until day became day once again. I felt guilty about answering her sharply before and tried to give her the real answer, the one about finding belonging. But I couldn't explain my point very well.

Though she experienced her own lack of belonging with slashing bitterness all the time—her colleagues made fun of her accent, and she couldn't work up the courage to ask them to stop—my complaints must have seemed strange. To her, belonging was like finally figuring out the fucking difference between "a" and "the"—a luxury for somebody else. And what did I expect, anyway, considering the kind of work I had chosen?

After I'd announced I was moving to Mexico, having discovered on a reporting trip there some things I lacked sorely at home, she was forced to admit that she couldn't make sense of her son and made the first therapy appointment of her life. She couldn't understand, she said to the woman, why I would want to do something so reckless. "But how do you know it's reckless?" the therapist had said. "What if it goes well?" My mother sat there, stunned. Something as obvious as things turning out okay even if someone split from the pack had never occurred to her. Such a thing is obvious only to an American person—it had hardly occurred even to me. In arguing for Spain and Turkey and Mexico, I was trying to say how much I could use their support—not that I knew to put it that way—precisely because I was equally frightened of going. Her therapy session left her astounded and terrified both. She never went back.

The Passover table was set up under the portrait from which my grandmother squinted like a crazy person. All of us wanted it down, but, though the auteur who had produced it stopped by only once or twice a year, my grandfather didn't dare offend him.

"Before we begin—" I said loudly. Everyone looked up. Hands were already on forks. My father's shrimp was on the table, and Oksana was laying down appetizers—marinated peppers, smoked salmon, a salad of kidney beans and caramelized onions. Her repertoire was observing the holiday's dietary restrictions more than his.

"It's an actual holiday, right," I said. I withdrew the Haggadah and waved it at them. "So we should do it the right way."

My grandfather puckered his face as if to say *Not necessarily.* Oksana was the help—she'd go along with whatever. My father was squinting in a way that said *Not for me, please.* My mother was manufacturing an appearance of curiosity. "How interesting," she said.

"Where did you get that?" my grandfather asked, as if I was holding a crack pipe.

"From a barber, actually," I said. "Uzbek, down my block."

He perked up. "What does he charge for a men's?"

"I don't know," I said. "I only get my watch batteries there." Though it was on the Lower East Side, it was a true ex-Soviet shop: haircuts, batteries, orthopedic loafers, Haggadahs.

"This is our story—don't you care?" I said.

They exchanged glances I wasn't supposed to see. I pointed to the matzoh on the table: "Our ancestors ate unleavened bread"—I looked around; nothing—"because they were fleeing and didn't have time to bake bread that would rise." I looked at the slices of Borodinsky fanned around a wide dinner plate. Half was on its own, half slathered with butter and salmon roe.

"By the way, we recline," I said, "because God led them out of Egypt. They weren't slaves anymore. So they could relax." I looked around. "So relax."

My grandfather bent his head: "You want me to go to the couch?"

"No, just lean back and put your arm on the arm of your chair."

"The chairs don't have arms," my mother pointed out apologetically.

"Okay, forget it," I said. I began reading: "'If the Holy One, blessed be He, had not taken our fathers from Egypt, then we, our children and our children's children, would have remained enslaved to Pharaoh in Egypt.' Make you think of anything?"

"It was a very long time ago." My grandfather shrugged.

"That synagogue in Vienna?" my mother offered helpfully.

My jaw clenched. "Of us, of us! We were enslaved! We got out!"

"Oh," my mother said.

"The Torah speaks of four children," I barreled on. "'One is wise, one wicked, one simple, one that doesn't know how to ask questions.'" I stopped. You could see their jaws clenched, too. My mother inhaled and exhaled. "Maybe one of you has a question," I said.

"I do," my father said. "When will the service be over?" He had his arms crossed at his chest, his eyes almost closed—he had the graveyard shift in his doorman job. He nodded at the shrimp. "You can't eat cold food. There's your commandment." To enlarge my sense of guilt beyond family members—you could disrespect family members, but not outsiders—he added, "Oksana's been cooking all day."

"You can't eat shrimp, period," I said.

"Why don't we grow sidelocks and beat our heads against the wall?" he said. "This is how we celebrate. All of us together. It's the way we know. It's good enough."

"Don't worry about the food," Oksana said, rising. "Just give me a minute." She disappeared into the kitchen. The oven switched back to life.

"Grab the cognac on your way back," my grandfather called out.

"God visited plagues on the Egyptians for having kept the Jews slaves," I went on feebly. "He punished the—don't you see the connection? We weren't slaves, but . . . And we got out."

"Maybe if someone was actually punished for what we went through, I'd believe some of that crap," my grandfather said.

I slapped closed the book. "Forget it. You win." The table fell into an ill-humored silence. Oksana's return brought relief, as did the alcohol in her hands. She set down the cognac, then a cheap bottle of red wine. "My present to all of you on the holiday. I think you drink red wine on Passover. Because wine is joy."

"If wine is joy, cognac is ecstasy," my father said.

"Wait, wait," Oksana said. She went to the kitchen and came back with five little plates. Each had a dollop of horseradish and a date. She also held a bowl with water and five spoons. "You spoon the horseradish, and then you sprinkle some of this water on top— it's a little salty. And watch the horseradish! I just made it, it's hot." But everyone was already gasping and joking about Ukraine having gotten back its nuclear weapons. "Now chase with the date," she said. "Arkady, careful, there's pits." She held out her palm, and he obediently tongued out a thready pit after he'd sucked off the meat. "We have dates?" he said, still chewing.

Like children, they did what she said. You could not disrespect someone outside the family.

"The horseradish in salt water is because it was bitter for Jews in Egypt," she said. "And the date because then they got free and things became sweet. Let it be sweet for all of you always! Who wants cognac?" They all raised their hands.

"See, if you're eating at least, you can tolerate all this high philosophy," my father said.

"So let's eat," Oksana said. "Can I serve?" Everyone nodded, but she stood in place. I realized she was looking at me. She wouldn't do it unless I gave my permission as well.

"Of course," I said, defeated.

"God—he is good!" my father said in a needling voice, and everyone broke out in laughter, though Oksana only smiled politely.

As she served, I stared at my father. I'd never known my father the romantic, the individualist, the strummer of guitars. It was as if the States—where there was too much of the responsibility and risk of which there'd been too little at home—had finished off what was left when the USSR was through with him. "He's like a candle that's been snuffed out, but it's still smoking," one of my friends said once. It was as if the hardest parts of both places—the Soviet disinclination to believe; the tyranny of American choice, and the high cost of miscalculation—had fused within him to make a man whose first word was *no*. His former country had said *no* to him, and now he would.

"Oksana, but how in the world . . ." my mother said. The table had filled with . . . Jewish dishes. Jewish dishes we hadn't seen in a decade, since my grandmother became too ill to cook. No one else really knew how to make them, not the same way. *Tsimmes*, matzoh *babka*, potato latkes, kasha *varnishkes* . . . Quietly, Oksana had been keeping it all warm while I went on with my sermon.

"The Internet, how!" she said, and everyone laughed. "With adjustments." For a reminder of home, she'd also made sorrel borshch, the Easter soup in Ukraine. In Russian, the word for Passover and Easter is the same.

I couldn't compare Oksana's *tsimmes* to my grandmother's—it had been so long since I'd had my grandmother's *tsimmes*. And I couldn't trust my mother's exclamations over it—for her, politeness was more important than the truth. But Oksana's *tsimmes* was so good I heaved it into my mouth by the spoonful, too quickly. The pleasure daze sent me to the cognac along with everyone else. A Russian food writer—technically, Jewish-Russian-Latvian-Ukrainian; things got complicated over there—once offered a guideline for moderation in alcohol: "Drink only while hungry." But I couldn't stop being hungry. If I could pause for ten minutes, perhaps my brain would catch up to my stomach, but I couldn't manage to pause for that long.

Oksana herself touched very little—she reloaded serving plates, switched out dirty napkins, ignored our protests and pleas to sit down. She managed to not ask how it all tasted, but she hardly needed to, and we couldn't answer anyway—our mouths were distended with food.

On the subway home, even my postprandial stupor didn't conceal it: My grandfather had been speaking so openly about his past with Oksana because he trusted her. In a way he didn't trust even me, even if he "loved" me more. Oksana was a citizen of the same country. Same heart country, stomach country, prostate country. It was hard to say she didn't seem to deserve it. For the holiday, she had managed what I could not: only as much ritual as they could handle. I didn't care about Egypt any more than they did; I just wanted to hurt them. The heretical table I'd just left was more like my girlfriend's religion than me with my Haggadah: They were all picking and choosing. I was the fundamentalist. Uncommon achievement had always been expected of me, and you had to admit I had turned into something uncommon: a fundamentalist and nonbeliever at once.

OKSANA'S KASHA *VARNISHKES* (V)

Time: 20 minutes   Serves: 6

²/₃ cup buckwheat groats
¼ cup vegetable oil (preferably
  sunflower)
1 large onion, diced

¼ pound bowtie pasta
4 cloves garlic, put through a
  garlic press
Kosher salt, to taste

1. Inspect the buckwheat for black groats and remove. They're bitter.

2. Dump the groats into a fine-mesh strainer and rinse with cold water, riffling through them with your fingers.

3. In a pot, cover the groats with 1⅓ cups of water, add salt, and bring to a boil. Lower the heat and simmer until the buckwheat cooks fully, about 15 minutes. The buckwheat should be dry rather than soupy when finished.

4. Meanwhile, heat the oil in a sauté pan over medium heat. Add the onion and sauté, stirring occasionally, until golden brown, 10 minutes or so.

5. Cook the pasta in a pot of salted water. Drain and transfer to a large bowl. Add the buckwheat, the sautéed onion, and the garlic and stir. Salt to taste. If the mixture feels a little dry, add more oil.

6. Give the ingredients time to get to know one another. This is definitely a second-day dish.

+

POTATO LATKES WITH DILL,
GARLIC, AND FARMER CHEESE (V)

Time: 1 hour, 45 minutes   Serves: 4–6

Every housewife must decide when to flip.
—Oksana

³/₄ pound farmer cheese
1 bunch fresh dill, chopped
6 garlic cloves, put through a
   garlic press and divided
Kosher salt, to taste
3 large Idaho potatoes, peeled
   and grated
½ large onion, grated

2 eggs
1 tablespoon flour
1 tablespoon ground coriander, or
   to taste
1 tablespoon ground caraway, or
   to taste
Vegetable oil, for cooking the
   latkes

1. Mix the farmer cheese with the dill, half the garlic, and salt to taste. Set aside to let it warm up a bit while you prep the latkes. (This will make it easier to spoon out later in the recipe.)

2. Squeeze out most of the liquid from the potatoes and combine them with the onion, eggs, flour, spices, and remaining garlic. Season with salt. The mixture will keep letting off liquid, but that's fine: this will keep the latkes from being too dense.

3. Heat ⅛ inch of oil in a large nonstick pan over medium heat. Drop a tablespoon's worth of the potato-and-onion mixture onto the pan. Fill the pan with these proto-latkes, making sure to leave enough room between them to slide in a spatula and flip later.

4. After a minute or so—the bottom of the latke should seem like it's browning—carefully place a teaspoon of the farmer cheese mixture into the center of each latke and pat it down gently so it spreads, but not all the way to the edge of the latke. Running the spoon underwater or dipping it in a bit of oil beforehand will help the mixture move more easily. You can also use your hands to pat down the mixture while it's on the spoon before transferring it to the pan. Now cover the farmer cheese layer with another tablespoon of potato-and-onion batter.

5. The above two steps will take 2–3 minutes. When the bottom of each latke feels like it's getting ruddy—about 3 minutes more—flip to the other side.

6. Once the other side is equally brown (about 5 minutes), flip again, turn the heat down to its lowest setting, cover the pan, and cook for 2–3 minutes.

7. Remove the latkes, pour new oil, and repeat. You should end up with 20–25 latkes.

Serve with sour cream or mushroom gravy (see **Cabbage Vareniki [Dumplings] with Wild Mushroom Gravy***).*

✤

HOMEMADE HORSERADISH (V)

Time: 1 hour, 20 minutes   Serves: a very large and horseradish-happy party

If I was grating this horseradish at home,
you'd hear me weeping from across the house.
—Oksana

2 medium to large beets	Sugar, to taste
1 stalk horseradish, peeled	Kosher salt, to taste
9 percent white vinegar, to taste	

1. Cover the beets with water and bring to a boil in a pot with the lid mostly on. Boil until a small knife goes through easily. (About an hour— you may have to top up the water now and then.) After they have cooled, run them under cold water—the skin will come off in your hands.

2. Grate the horseradish and beets as finely as possible. A fresh horseradish will "smoke" hard enough to make onion-crying seem pleasant by comparison, so proceed incrementally. The measurements above are just a guideline: They're good for a horseradish with a kick. If you want your eyes to well up every time you taste it, cut down on the beet.

3. Combine the horseradish and beets with vinegar, sugar, and salt. A typical Oksana ratio: 5 tablespoons of 9 percent vinegar, 3 teaspoons of sugar, and a pinch of salt. ("Salt will take away the flavor, so no more than a pinch.")

This should produce about 3 cups. Grated horseradish evaporates, so keep the lid on, and every time you have some, add a bit more freshly grated horseradish to keep up the concentration and flavor.

✤

CHAPTER 9

2006

What to cook for a sister you haven't seen in a year

What to put on the table when introducing a Ukrainian home attendant and an Albanian super

What to make to get people to leave

✦

Intellectual things, learned things, ruin the appetite.
—CHEKHOV, "The Siren"

I t looked like the Last Supper: a dozen bodies around two foldout tables stacked end-to-end in my grandfather's living room. Everyone owned two foldout tables—if you had only one, must be people didn't like coming over.

I was surprised my grandfather didn't have *three* tables, for show if nothing else, but I couldn't recall the last time I'd seen even the second in use. Our Minsk had gotten scattered all over the world. But even those who chose New York couldn't re-create the frequency and revelry of their Soviet evenings. Work was different here—you had to get up early, because it took forever to get there; and you had to be there on time; and really work; and twice as long, so that by the time you hobbled home, you just wanted your bed. On the weekends, you tended to all the things that had been tended to for you in the USSR. This—private ownership, individual choice—was freedom. At least you made real money.

But there were two tables in my grandfather's living room now, and, around them, I recognized only three people: Oksana, my grandfather, and his neighbor Yasha, the one with the laundry quarters. Oksana brought me into the living room and waved down the noise. "This is Arkady's grandson!" she said. "We know!" someone with a Georgian accent shouted from the far end of the table. "You're all he talks about!"

"I'd give my right arm for him," my grandfather said solemnly from the king's spot at the head of the table.

"Better give him that silk on your head," a man with a belly the shape of a microwave called out, raising his shot glass. I was taking after my father's line—the hair was thick on my chest and thin on my head. Meanwhile, my grandfather's cap of ash-colored hair was as soft and dense as a teenager's, and his chest bare as a teenager's, too.

A week earlier, I had been sent home from the Passover table with *babka* and *tsimmes* that lasted a week. In Manhattan, I had to cook all the time—I couldn't eat out on freelance journalism— and Oksana's bundle had saved me many hours. But my fridge was empty again. My grandfather, my mother told me, was having Oksana "cover" a table and inviting people he knew because her sister was visiting from Albany. I could make him feel looked in on, and in doing so score another week's worth of leftovers.

"Sit!" someone yelled, and the table returned to its talk. Oksana went down the row: That was the man who had painted the demented portrait of my grandmother; that was his wife. That was Oksana's best friend—also named Oksana—and that man in the wheelchair was her home-care ward, an "intellectual" from Moscow. Yasha the neighbor had a home aide of his own, sitting next to him.

The man with the microwave belly lived upstairs with his wife and small boy. (From the back, ex-Soviet men like him seemed as slim as healthy people. Head-on, you encountered a rectangular escarpment that began at the sternum and ended at the waist, and refused gravity: It stayed aloft, tight as rock, not one inch of overhang.) Two weeks before, his wife was about to take the boy to school when her cell phone rang: Her elderly mother had to go to the ER. So Oksana and my grandfather walked him to school and—Brooklyn emergency-room wait times being what they are—picked him up, too. And if they picked him up, they had to feed him. He wanted cornflakes— that was what he got every day. No, Oksana would not give him cornflakes for lunch. She'd just finished boiling chicken soup and was simmering couscous. He got a cup of the soup—we always drank chicken soup out of cups—and a bowl of the couscous. He dug around it to show his resentment, but then he tried a small forkful, and then another, and eventually he ate it. That night, the escarpment man called and asked if Oksana and my grandfather would do that every day.

"That's quite a favor," I said.

"Who says it's a favor?" Oksana said.

"I see," I said.

"Where are they?" I said. Escarpment Man was flanked by no woman or child.

"He's making his own arrangement," she said.

"What does that mean?" I said.

She looked at my grandfather, who was going on to someone about how gifted the man who painted my grandmother's portrait was. The painter wasn't protesting.

"My grandfather told you not to tell me," I said.

"No, no . . ." she said unconvincingly. Now she had to tell me. "He's borrowing money. His wife doesn't know."

"From whom?" I said stupidly.

"From us, from whom. Your grandfather and I each put a little together."

"What percentage?" I said, trying to think of ways to sound less innocent.

"We said ten, but he himself insisted on twenty." She shrugged. "We'll see."

She finished her tour: That was the guy who gave my grandfather free rides in his Medicaid ambulette. That was the guy from the pharmacy. That was one of Oksana's friends—illegal. She was obsessed with immigration reform; during the day, she nannied two little girls; at night, she listened to Russian radio and wrote down what Dzhan Makeyn and Dzhordzh Boosh had said about the bills moving up and down Congress. This lawbreaker knew more about how American government worked than the rest of the room put together.

That man was a friend of my grandfather's—he was hale enough not to need a home aide, in fact hale enough for a mistress back in Ukraine. His wife knew, and let him go back to her every couple of months. And that was Oksana's sister Nadia, down from Albany, where she was an au pair for another Soviet Jewish family. She cooked Jewish dishes all day, so Oksana had dug deep in the Ukrainian repertoire: salted fatback on garlic-rubbed rye, ground-liver pie, polenta with feta and wild mushrooms, cabbage dumplings in wild mushroom gravy, barley-and-pickle soup with pork shoulder, and wafer torte with condensed milk and rum extract for dessert.

"It's all men," I said, gesturing at the pensioners.

Oksana shrugged. "The husband gets ill, and the wife dies."

As always, Oksana sat closest to the kitchen; she was gone half the time, reheating, replating, re-serving. Her plate was nearly unused, just a smudge of "little blues"—roast eggplant, peppers, and carrots, named after the color of the eggplant, perhaps by someone who was color-blind. Escarpment Man had to go upstairs to get me a spare chair. If it was the Last Supper, I was Judas.

I went to greet my grandfather. He rubbed his hands on the thick stubble on my cheeks.

"There aren't complaints?" he said.

"From whom?" I said. "About what?"

He lowered his voice. "The people at work."

I stared, baffled. Then I understood. In the USSR, unkempt people could be reported to work for disorderly living—in Minsk, every school day began with the vice principal checking the length of my nails and how neat the hairline was at the back of my neck. As an adult, you could be clean-shaven, and you could be bearded, as our fathers were—thickly but neatly—but not the five days I now had on my face. He knew I worked for myself—who could complain to whom? Perhaps every time I appeared before him, he hoped it would be as someone who'd wised up and become an employee of somebody else. Except that, in Minsk, he himself could stand to have superiors in name only. Maybe my grandfather thought working from home was unmanly. The poet Brodsky had been prosecuted for it in the USSR. My elders managed to venerate people like Brodsky while spurning the way of life that made them that way. I was so distracted by these thoughts I was looking right through him. Maybe these people drank so much because it softened the sound of each other's bullshit.

"How's Alana?" he said.

"To your health," I said, nodding at the shot glass in front of him. An effective distraction. They all drank Metaxa, the Greek brandy, perhaps because it looked like their Soviet cognac but went down more smoothly because it was really a botanical.

Alana and I had met in 2003. I was moderating a talk uptown, and she was a newspaper editor looking for new writers. In the post-event scrum, I barely noticed her. But when we had lunch in Bryant Park a while later, I realized that she possessed that rarest of qualities: She was not only beautiful and smart but *interesting*. For a season, we lived out that life that New York promises but so rarely delivers: hours of talk in elegant, low-lit places that seemed to have been built just for us.

We were opposites in so many ways. Three years older than my then twenty-four, she was in the exit lane of a failing young marriage; I hadn't had a serious girlfriend since high school. She was from a comfortable family, and I was a frugal immigrant. She loved New York, and I was overwhelmed by it. She loved journalism, and I resented it with all the bitterness of a twenty-four-year-old trying to publish. She was relatively at home in her skin, and I wanted to crawl out of mine. But the only thing that we remembered when we stumbled out of those bars at midnight and later was how interesting it was to talk to each other.

She wanted to settle down, but that was the last thing I knew how to do, especially with someone so different. "I wish I could meet you in five years," I had told her after it became clear we were interested in each other. "It's too good not to give it a try," she'd answered. She seemed so much more settled and knowledgeable— she had left her conservative religious community and gone to Barnard; was working, in therapy, through her parents' disapproval and her own questions—and so I agreed. Not every love involves the kind of attraction that would make Gabriel García Márquez sit up, and we'd been blessed with just that.

By that point in my twenties, I could tell I needed to answer some questions of my own. In my teens, something had begun to feel wrong about the responsibility that had been given to me as a boy; I realized I didn't know what it was like to feel carefree, adventurous, unresolved, unafraid. I felt angry all the time, but I didn't know the cause.

It was Alana who helped me find my way to it. It was because of her that I experienced the euphoria of inchoate self-understanding, of imagining life without so much confusion and discomfort. But it wasn't a clean line. There were a lot of detours. A lot of me yelling at her for something that had nothing to do with her, even if I couldn't be more certain it did. Alana led me to the powder keg, and got a lot of the shrapnel.

We still loved each other—even if it was harder and harder to be in the same room. I was constantly escaping to the Washingtons of the world, she into her career. It never stopped being interesting to talk—as long as the subject wasn't us. When it was, the more we tried to explain, the less clear things became. Our helplessness became frightened, furious, resentful: Individually, our lives were making more sense, but together they kept coming apart. In helping each other become the people we wanted to be, we were becoming people whose differences made being together impossible. Our practical differences didn't help. There was a map of rancor and heartbreak to be drawn, as there was for so many New York couples, of all the corners in Manhattan where we'd argued and said things we regretted.

"Another drink," I said to the cluster of men around my grandfather.

"But this is what I can't understand!" the Intellectual exclaimed from his wheelchair. "This. Is. What. I. Cannot. Un-der-stand! How can your husbands allow you to go off to another country by yourselves in this way?!" He slapped the table and drained his shot glass for emphasis.

"Let them stay where they are," one of the women said. I looked at my grandfather. Surreptitiously, he placed the nail of his middle finger against the pad of his thumb and flicked it against his neck. That was the Soviet gesture for "drunk"—the husbands were alcoholics.

"The alternative," the woman said, "is they come with you!" Everyone laughed.

"Is it true?" I asked Oksana when she came back from the kitchen. She was the person I felt safest talking to. Then I flicked my own finger against my neck.

"We're an unlucky generation," she sighed. She indicated one of the women. "Her husband came here with her. Every day, she watches him at 6:00 p.m. from their window, guzzling his last beer before coming upstairs. As if she can't smell it. Has he even gone to work? Supposedly—he has money. But where does he get it?" She closed her top lip over the bottom. "My sister was lucky—her husband was a good man. But then he died. If it's not one thing, it's another."

"The one who drinks," I said. "He was like that before he came? Or it started here?"

"Or take that woman," she said, speaking over me. "Her first husband died of cancer—he was younger than everyone at this table except you. So she remarried—"

"And the second one died, too?" I said.

She smiled; I was too naive to guess well in these situations. "Maybe it would be good if the two husbands reversed fates," she said. "No, he just drinks. But at least he's back in Ukraine. But she's got children there, too. To leave him, she had to leave them. And helping them means helping him. I understand this contradiction very well."

"She can't divorce him?" I said.

"She can divorce him," she said. "But how many of them can you divorce?" She smiled a crooked smile. "I'm lucky." She didn't mean herself. "My daughter, back home, she can be a woman—because she's married to a man who knows his responsibilities. They share duties, but she remains a woman. A woman must be *slabaya*." All the ex-Soviet women above a certain age said that. Their daughters didn't say it, because they were reared in America, but often they felt it, too—it's why I couldn't date them. Literally, *slabaya* means "weak," but in this case it meant that women had to be allowed to feel like women: supported and shielded, spared and saved, spoiled and surprised.

I wondered if I would've felt the same if we'd stayed in Belarus— or even if I hadn't left south Brooklyn. Alana had broken away from the conservative religious community in which she'd grown up, and Barnard did the rest. We referred to each other as "partner." She was the one with the office job and the more restrictive schedule, so usually I stayed at her apartment instead of vice versa, and—though she respected my work; she had been the first person to believe in it—I had to be the one to get milk if we wanted some in our coffee. I wanted to ask Oksana what we should do about our trouble—maybe she would have something different to say from my parents and grandfather—but I was afraid to ruin the good feeling between us.

My grandfather appeared next to us. "You haven't eaten," he said. "Have some of Yasha's whiting. Oksana Greeked it up—you'll bite off your fingers." For some reason, fish braised in a carrot broth was called "fish Greek style." The recipe was from Poland.

"Arkady, let him be," Oksana said gently. "He's an adult, he knows what he wants."

"I vanish, I vanish," he said like a clerk obeying his councillor, his hands raised in mock apology. He was flirting with her—not really, not in search of some kind of consummation, but as a man next to a woman. And she didn't mind, despite the more than thirty years separating them.

"What did you mean when you said you understand the contradiction?" I said after he left. "Helping the kids is helping the husband."

"I meant my son," she said. "He's very kind. He doesn't have any dirt inside. But he's like his father—the words go with the music, as they say. We had 'labor passports' during Soviet times; it said where you worked. Mine said the same place for twenty-seven years. It was like that for everyone. Whereas his father drifted between so many jobs, his labor passport ran out of room. That's my son, too. He worked at a beer distributorship. Then he sold eyeglasses. Then finance. It didn't take, so I got him into service industry management. He lost interest in that, too. Then he sold fridges, poured foundations, worked at a recycling center. He's not lazy. But he's had so many jobs, I've lost count. Searching, searching, and for God knows what."

"It sounds American," I said, wanting to be encouraging. "It sounds entrepreneurial. He won't stop until he finds the right thing."

"I don't know," she shrugged. She was being polite. She meant: *no.* "He needs the Soviet way—punch in, punch out. Your generation is a hustling generation, but he's not a hustler. And I've made it worse by sending money from here—he doesn't have to worry about work in the same way. He's always been surrounded by women— me, my mother, his sister."

She wished her son had more drive, but all the drive belonged to the women.

I'd walked in during that part of the evening when new courses had stopped appearing, and soon bodies had begun beaching themselves on the sofas. Now, like wounded coming to life, they were stumbling back toward the table. I took a triangle of pie—it looked like dessert. Oksana watched me excavate it carefully with a fork.

"Try it!" she laughed.

"But where's the liver?" I said.

"It's *in* the crepes." I stared at her quizzically. "It's *in* the batter," she said. "You grind chicken liver together with onion, and add eggs, flour, and so on. It comes out like a batter. And then between the leaves you can add whatever you want. I do garlic, dill, mayonnaise. Try it!"

Not wanting to offend, I took a bite. It was confoundingly delicious. I took another.

The talk at the table was slower, more slurred. I tried to remember if I'd had three or four shots. Manhattan felt so far away. My girlfriend felt far away. The one time I'd brought Alana to my grandfather's, she ended up working her phone surreptitiously under the table. Everyone had been trying to accommodate her by speaking English, and she seemed relieved when they gave up. But I didn't mind being at my grandfather's just then. Not in the way I'd minded for a while, my flesh burning with rage. There was something sweet about all those galactic bodies rubbing their bellies in near-catatonic contentment. Maybe just the booze in me made it seem so.

Oksana was huddled with the woman who must have been the illegal, because they were talking about green cards and lotteries and a certain kind of visa. Next to them, the one who had the mistress was telling them all that in Ukraine, he had worked near a meat plant that was particularly well policed by the managers, preventing the employees from ferrying out sides of beef for personal resale. So they had to resort to flinging them over the fence. *Chelyshki* and *okovalki* (brisket and sirloin), flying over the fence like God himself was tossing them down.

I poured myself a new thimble. "Sin to drink alone," Mistress Man said. The circle of men opened up to include me. I was gratified by it. "Tell us how the young live," he said.

My mind was warm from the drink. I tried to think of a story that would make them laugh. "Sorry to mention medical matters at the table," I said, and waited to gauge the reaction, but no one at this table was a stranger to medical matters. I barreled on. "I had this—I don't know what you call it. Inflammation. On my groin."

"Ho-ho-ho!" someone said.

"It was very sensitive. It got so bad I couldn't bear for clothing to touch it, couldn't sit down, nothing. So this woman we know, she says, 'You have to char a half-moon of onion and clamp it over the spot. It'll suck up all the bad stuff.' So I do it. Char half an onion on the burner and put it over my thigh with an ACE bandage, you know, those light-brown ones. But I have a date the next night. Date number three. It's time to—you know. Except I have a charred onion strapped to my groin. But it's not like I can, you know, without the onion, either."

They stared at me. Some curious, some confused. I thought my grandfather would like it. His great fear, impervious to all counter-evidence, was that I was gay. One weekend when he and my grand-mother had come to New Jersey—I was seventeen—I'd had a friend visit; eventually, she and I went upstairs to my room. When I came downstairs the next day, it was nearly noon and he was slurping soup. "So what happened?" he said. "Nothing," I said. "She's just a friend." He dropped his spoon into his soup. "When a girl goes to your room and stays there half the night, you fuck her, goddammit!" He used the word for "fuck" that sounds like artillery slamming its target. "I hope you're happy," he said. "Now she's going to tell all her friends that you"—he stuck out his finger—"are a homo." When I men-tioned a new girlfriend, the first thing he asked—his fear mixing with the need to speak decorously around his grandson, the result nearly biblical—was: "You lie down together, don't you?"

At the table, the curious ones joined the confused. "Yeah, couldn't get far with that one, could you?" someone said with unpersuasive camaraderie.

"It was people hiding beef under their clothes that made me think of it," I explained lamely. I thought I could buy their amuse-ment with self-deprecation, but in this group the only disclosure that went over was the self-flattering kind. If you represented your-self in an unflattering light, the fault was only your own, schmuck.

"When they arrested the great poet Mandelstam," the Intel-lectual took over, "they put him in a cell with an informer. Some-times they would take the informer out for 'interrogations,' so he could report on what Mandelstam said. Then one morning this fel-low comes back from questioning—and his breath reeks of onion! They'd fed him while he ratted. That's how Mandelstam knew he was a snitch."

He was rewarded with vague nods. No one knew who the hell Mandelstam was.

"Mark Twain was a Jew," my grandfather announced. "I read it in the newspaper."

"Men!" Oksana called out. She was emerging from the kitchen with a platter. "Dessert!" It was the wafer torte. That could travel well, I thought.

As she walked past me, she said, "When you need people to leave, serve them dessert."

They really did begin to stumble out after that, after embraces and wet kisses. Suddenly it was just four—Oksana and her sister Nadia, my grandfather and me—in a room too quiet.

My grandfather had a solution for silence. "How are things on the professional front?" he said, turning to me. He wanted me to impress Nadia. Alas, I told the truth.

"I'm trying to write a book about masculinity," I said.

"So it's a short one," Nadia said, and she and Oksana burst out laughing.

My grandfather stared at me in confusion. "Masculinity?" he said. "Is that like when they bomb a city and then you build it back up from the ruins?"

"What?" I said.

"So what is it?"

"What do you think it is?"

He thought about it. "When a man saves a woman from being beaten by another man. Or you save a child from a flood."

"Is it masculine to tell the truth or to lie?" I said.

"To tell the truth and it's against your own benefit, that's manly," he said. If I wasn't going to make up things to impress Nadia, then he would. "Girls, girls . . ." he said, sighing at Nadia and Oksana. "Both of you work so hard, and you're all alone. How I wish for you to find a man deserving of one finger on your hands."

Nadia shrugged, and Oksana folded her lips. "What will be will be," she said.

"Come on," he said. "One more for it." Everybody extended their shot glasses. I had had more than enough, but there were too few of us, and the toast's wish too important. We clinked and drank to good husbands. Oksana left and returned with her laptop.

"Arkady's weekend aide—we tried to find her a new man," she said.

"Her husband died in a hot tub," my grandfather said.

"How can you die in a hot tub?" I said.

"He overheated, I don't know. His heart gave out. In fact"—he pointed at me—"she's been wanting to sue those people. But she doesn't have the language. And if you took it on, she'd give you a piece of it."

"But I'm not a lawyer."

He opened his hands, meaning "Exactly."

"What are you looking for on that Internet?" Nadia said.

"Recipes," Oksana said.

"She needed an air conditioner," my grandfather said. "The building super says his friend has an extra. Albanian, too. And then he says the guy is a widower. So I say bring him, bring the air conditioner, I'll put a bottle on the table, and we'll introduce them."

"Does he speak Russian?" I said.

"He's Albanian—why should he speak Russian?"

"Well, the weekend aide doesn't speak Albanian."

My grandfather rolled his eyes. "People who want to understand each other find a way to understand each other. Anyway—I got out a fifteen-year-old bottle of cognac. Fifteen! They show up with the air conditioner. They plug it in, it works, everything's perfect. Finally it's time to go, and this specimen gets up and says, 'Thank you, delicious food,' and then he says to her—"

"'Twenty dollars, please, for the air conditioner,'" Oksana finished for him.

"This Romeo wanted to charge her for the air conditioner!"

"Did she give it to him?" I said.

"What?" he said.

"The twenty dollars." I was interested in the wrong details.

Oksana's computer pinged and she smashed her hand over her mouth.

"What? What?" they said in unison.

"Nadia, my blood, don't be mad at me," Oksana said. "I'm not looking for recipes." She looked up.

"*Kolis*," Nadia said. "Puncture," like a balloon. As in: give up the truth.

"There's a man Nadia knew," Oksana said to me and my grandfather. "A million years ago. They worked together. They got married to other people."

"So?" Nadia said.

"So his wife passed two years ago. I don't remember who told me—maybe when I was on home leave last year. And I didn't even think of it. But now I thought of it."

"Thought of what?" Nadia said.

"I got into your Facebook account. I blame Arkady—it's because he keeps pouring and saying these things that make your heart seize up. I found his daughter . . . I wrote her to ask if she would give me—I mean you—permission to call her father."

Nadia's eyes enlarged significantly.

"She answered one minute after I sent it," Oksana said. "She sent her phone number. And his phone number. His birthday is in a week. She said please call him."

Now Nadia's hand went over her mouth. "You criminal," she said.

"We drink again," my grandfather said.

It was after midnight by the time the subway dragged me home. It was unseasonably humid, and the train felt as sluggish as the whole city. It crawled half-heartedly for several minutes, then gave out a long sigh and fell silent, the kind of definitive silence you don't want to hear from machinery you're relying on to get home. Somewhere in the station, voices droned from the intercom. There was a lazy, distant blare from a maintenance train.

Before me sat a giant bag stenciled with Ukrainian lettering and loaded with Tupperwares full of pork-shoulder soup, *bliny* stuffed with chicken and onion, the liver pie, and wafer torte. I was so slow with drink I didn't remember to feel self-conscious about the foreign alphabet on my bag. I wondered vaguely whether the man across from me could smell what was in it.

When I got home, I pulled out a small book of poems by Mandelstam, the poet the Intellectual had been talking about. It wasn't until twelfth grade that I'd become curious about what we'd left behind instead of how to make it work where we'd gotten. A book did it. From the category that specializes in forcing a hard look at things: nineteenth-century Russian novels. Well, not all—the frenzied cold light of *Crime and Punishment*, earlier in the school year, had felt like reading a foreigner. No, it was Turgenev's *Fathers and Sons*, with its love, hand-wringing, and sentiment. At university, I majored in Russian literature. I felt for Russian books even if I didn't feel for Russian *people*; that happened sometimes, didn't it? But since then it had all somehow mixed together. It had been many years since I'd read a Russian novel, even in translation.

In the Mandelstam volume, I tried to find a poem about the informer who smelled of onion after his "interrogation," but nothing seemed close. I flipped to the famous execration of Stalin that eventually sent Mandelstam to his death and tried to translate what I could. My Russian had almost vanished during my years of trying to pass as an American, then revived to near fluency at university, then nearly vanished again. I managed to speak more or less comprehensibly with my family, but, I was now sadly discovering, I was no longer up to poetry. I went ahead anyway. Eight shots of Metaxa had loosened things up. You didn't have to be exactly right.

> *We live not feeling the ground beneath us,*
> *We speak so that, ten steps out, our speech is unheard,*
> something, something, and something,
> *They'll remember the mountain man in the Kremlin.*
> *The fat, greasy fingers like worms,*
> *The words, like ton weights,* something-something . . .

It was like trying to sprint for the first time after a decade of gluttony. Though it was late now, I turned to the previous poem—"The apartment is as silent as paper"—but beyond the first line, I foundered. I flipped to the one before, about Crimea, but even less success there. I couldn't grasp even the general meaning. And the Stalin poem I could understand only because it had entered general knowledge, enough of which had dripped down, over the years, into my drunk, not quite Russian and not quite American brain. My excitement turned doleful. I tried one more poem, then fell asleep in my armchair, the light still on above me.

OKSANA'S LIVER PIE

Time: 1 hour, 30 minutes   Serves: 8

It's good, but you won't kiss anyone after.
—Oksana

1 pound chicken livers
1 medium onion, chopped
4 eggs
3 heaping tablespoons flour (or less, if you like very thin crepes)
6 tablespoons corn or sunflower oil, plus additional for cooking the crepes

Kosher salt and pepper, to taste
4 heaping tablespoons mayonnaise
3 cloves garlic, put through a garlic press
1 bunch dill, finely chopped

1. Clean the livers—rinse, and cut off any film stuck to them—and pass the liver and onion through a meat grinder set to a fine grind, or pulse in a food processor until the mixture turns liquid.

2. Combine the liver mixture with the eggs, flour, oil, and salt and pepper. You're making batter for *bliny*, or crepes. "The first *blin* always comes out sideways," as Ukrainians say about far more than *bliny*.

A little batter hides all our sins.
—Oksana

3. Warm a small (8- to 9-inch) crepe pan or nonstick skillet over medium-low heat. Add a tiny amount of oil (or cooking spray), give it a little time to warm up, and roll it around so it covers the whole pan.

4. Lift the pan off direct heat—otherwise the batter sticks too quickly—and add enough batter that it expands to the edges of the pan, swirling the batter until it forms as perfect a circle as possible. You want a thin crepe, so try to add as little batter as necessary to reach the edges of the pan after swirling. Return to direct heat.

5. After 3 minutes or so (2 if the crepe is thinner), the crepe should be sufficiently browned underneath and crisp around the edges for you to be able to use a spatula or a fine-tipped wooden skewer to lift it up. Now you have to flip to the other side; the difficult truth is that there's no better instrument than your fingers, if they can withstand the heat. If the crepe is a bit thicker, a spatula will do the job. (As in the recipe for whole chicken stuffed with crepes, don't worry if you tear the crepe:

You can "darn" the hole—"reanimating," Oksana calls it, as if the crepe is a flatlined patient—by pouring a little new batter to fill it). After 2 minutes or so on the other side, flip again for a final 30 seconds, and set aside.

6. While the crepes are cooking, mix the mayonnaise, garlic, and most of the dill. (Save a little for garnish.) The creaminess of the mayonnaise works well with the tang of the garlic, the earthiness of the dill, and the taste of liver in the batter, but of course, the filling can include, or exclude, whatever you like.

7. Spread each liver pancake with the mayonnaise mix, layering the pancakes on top of one another until you have a stack you can cut into like a pie. (You may wish to make sure you have enough filling by laying out all the crepes and dolloping even amounts of filling onto each before proceeding with the stacking.) Decorate the uppermost layer generously with dill. Consistency and flavor are best after two hours in the fridge. Good both cold and warmed up.

✦

WAFER TORTE WITH CONDENSED MILK AND RUM OR VANILLA EXTRACT (V)

Time: 40 minutes   Serves: 8–12

It's the torte that never makes it to the fridge.
—Oksana

⅔ cup golden raisins
2 14-ounce cans 8.5-percent-fat sweetened condensed milk or dulce de leche (or a mixture)
2 sticks (1 cup) unsalted butter, softened to room temperature

Pure rum extract, to taste (if you can't find one free of artificial flavors, substitute vanilla extract)
Juice of 1 lemon
8 tort wafers

Sources: You can find 8.5 percent condensed milk at RussianFoodDirect.com. (American condensed milk tends to have a lower fat content, but you need thickness here so the frosting doesn't run.) If wafer sheets prove hard to find, Amazon can help.

1. Cover the raisins with boiling water and soak for about 20 minutes to soften them.

2. Meanwhile, using a whisk or an immersion blender, mix the condensed milk with the softened butter and rum extract. Proceed gingerly with the rum extract—too much will make the torte bitter. This means you have to taste the filling after every addition. You're welcome.

3. Drain and add the raisins and the lemon juice.

> Note: Acid like lemon juice can cause dairy to separate, but it's more of an issue with milk than butter, and it's less likely to occur here if you're using the immersion blender, as opposed to hand-whisking. But if you see modest clumping, don't worry—it won't affect the taste, and it will not be very visible in the result. That indelible kislinka (hint of sourness) in a sweet dish is a Ukrainian cook's first priority in such matters.

4. Brush the bottom of a wafer round with water so that it stays in place. (Don't run the bottom of the wafer round under water, as that'll get it too wet and begin to ruin its shape. Just brush it.) Place it on a plate wide enough to clear the wafer round by about two inches. Spread the remaining rounds out on a counter.

5. Reserve a scoop of the filling for covering the sides of the assembled torte. Divide the remaining filling among the 8 wafers. Spread the filling close to but not all the way to the edges of the wafer rounds. Make sure to get some raisins, which will have sunk to the bottom of the mixture, into every dollop.

6. Stack the rounds on top of one another and work your last scoop around the sides.

Refrigerate overnight to help the torte set. Decorate the top layer with your fruit of choice—strawberry halves add nicely to both the taste and the color.

✦

CHAPTER 10

2008

What to cook when the fusion is Argentina-Ukraine

What to cook if you're stuck in the Soviet Navy

What to cook when the cook can no longer cook

What to cook to unlock a man's secrets

✤

Families that make soup every day fall apart last.
—GENIS AND VAIL, *Russian Cooking in Exile*

He was twirling her in the street. Only a moment before, I had been holding his arm as he toed his way down Fifth Avenue, every sidewalk square a precipice—he'd seen Manhattan all of three times in twenty years. Then suddenly he let go of me and twirled Oksana.

They were going to see tango at City Center. Someone had been smart enough to advertise in the Russian papers—nothing more romantic to a Russian than tango. I imagined old Russian men, fumigated from their corners of Brooklyn and converging on Midtown, their home attendants on their arms. Oksana was wearing her Fancy Outfit—the black pants and square-heeled pumps—and I was their chaperone from the subway stop to City Center. I would wait while they watched, then escort them back to the subway. It was December and looking ready to rain, but this pair was not going to be splurging on a taxi, and the generosity of the ambulette driver who gave them free rides ended at the borders of Brooklyn.

The ad for the tango had sent him to the middle of the living room: He showed me the *bulba* (Belarusian), the *khapak*

(Ukrainian), and the *tsyganochka* (Gypsy), the dull-blue navy tattoos on his arms flying this way and that. He had to stop—he didn't have the wind for it anymore. "I could have been a dancer," he heaved out.

You had to give it to him. "You could have," I said. "Maybe without the tattoos. They gave tattoos out in the navy?"

"They grabbed me," he said. "I had no choice."

"What do you mean they grabbed you?"

"Don't worry about it."

The streets were slick by the time I found them in the crowd streaming out of the concert. I had made him confirm twice that he would turn his cell phone on after the show, but it remained off, and I found them . . . well, former Soviet people are easy to spot. They were giggly, rehearsing what had gone on inside. He kept making percussive sounds and playing air accordion. Oksana just sighed at the romance of it all—it was her first time in Manhattan. Feeling like a very sober designated driver, I pushed them toward the train.

The next day, Oksana went on the Internet and found Argentinean recipes that were sort of like Ukrainian recipes. Beef empanadas with raisins were sort of like dumplings with cabbage or pork, so she'd try dumplings with beef and raisins, why not. The Argentineans had lentil stew with chorizo—she'd use kidney beans and rib tips. But they were out of rib tips. The temperature had plummeted overnight, and the previous night's rain was now a thin coat of ice. Oksana wasn't supposed to leave Arkady at home alone, but she couldn't take him out into that kind of weather. So she ran out by herself. By the time she was rolling the dough for the dumplings, she could feel the fever. She had gone down ill, and now my grandfather—he relayed in a trembling, forlorn voice on the telephone—*was all alone.* She was in the next room, of course, but he could have been preparing to fend for himself on a cold, faraway planet.

"If she's sick, she has to take off," I said. "Imagine if a home aide gets an old person ill."

"Where's she going to go?" he said. The cot Oksana rented from a friend was not so much a cot as the space for one—in all her time in Brooklyn, she'd not had to use it.

"A hypochondriac like you is willing to have a sick person in the apartment?" I said.

"Don't worry about it," he said.

"Fine, fine, I'll come."

When I arrived, I couldn't find him. He wasn't in the living room, the only place I ever saw him. He couldn't be in the bedroom—Oksana was convalescing there, on the hospital bed he had somehow procured, the type with all the levers. One was courting bad luck by lying down in a hospital bed, but the alternative was to have her sneezing and coughing near him. (One was also courting bad luck by procuring a hospital bed, but a get is a get.) Even the television was silent. I'd never seen it shut off. That television would keep going after the End.

He was . . . at the stove. The kitchen was the smallest room in the apartment. I had measured once: two feet of floor space and fourteen feet long, so that from the doorway it looked like the galley kitchen of a submarine, especially because the small, frosted window at the far end, by the stove, always turned the outside light into a submerged grayish blue. So I had to squint. But it was him. With a spatula in his hand. I'd never seen my grandfather in front of a stove. Oksana must have cooked enough in advance and now he was reheating. But no—he was *cooking*. It was like seeing the pope at the batting cages.

He was making *ukha* (oo-HA)—salmon soup; he had the salmon steak cubed and ready to go. Everyone thinks Russians eat borshch, but borshch is the Ukrainian mother soup. Russians eat it, too, but a Russian's home soup is *ukha*. Root vegetables are all good, but without freshwater fish—pike, carp, sturgeon—Russia isn't Russia. (Literally: Siberia survives on pike. There's so much pike there, it's dog food.) I had tried to explain to the lox lovers of the Upper West

Side and the cedar-plank salmon eaters of the Northwest just what a thing *ukha* was, but they heard "boiled salmon" and tuned out. It was my mother soup. On a cold night, a bowl of *ukha* made things right for five minutes. We ate quickly.

Ukha always got many pages in Russian food books, because *there was that much to say about how exactly to make it.* "The age-old rules of preparing this traditional dish must be strictly observed to produce the right effect," as William Pokhlebkin, the epically named dean of Russian food writing, wrote. (Pokhlebkin translates to "Slurpkin"; he wrote a book about vodka, too.) The word "may" appears only once in his instructions; mostly they say "should." Or "must."

The man at the stove was ignoring the age-old rules, which said the broth had to be transparent. Oksana's *ukha* was "clear as a tear," but he would thicken his by mashing cooked potatoes that Pokhlebkin explicitly warned should not disintegrate into the liquid.

I kept staring silently down the long tunnel of the kitchen. "You can cook?" I said.

"Why not," he said.

"I've never seen you anything but served," I said. "Do you . . . need help?"

"You know how to peel and quarter potatoes?"

"Who doesn't know how to peel potatoes?"

"Drop them in water so they don't discolor." He wanted everything to be perfect for her.

"Yes, I *know.* How do you know?"

"The navy, how," he said. "I watched my mother, too."

"What did she make?" I said. I was handling the potatoes like newborn kittens. I wanted everything to be perfect for him.

"Same as all the mothers: *tsimmes*, latkes, potato *babka*, chicken soup. Everyone had pigs and cows, everyone had a garden. I spent a lot of time in other people's gardens. This one old man had everything: cherries, gooseberries, red currants. We'd pick him clean. He knew it, too, but he liked having kids in his garden. When he was coming home, he banged his cane extra loud on the sidewalk so we'd scatter before he had a chance to catch us."

"And the navy?" I said. "How many potatoes you want?"

"Two. No, three. The navy what?"

"Cooking. Or—in general."

"In the navy, you take a tin of American beef and spread it around a whole pot of macaroni—that way it looks like the meat's everywhere, but you've used up only one tin. But you can use half a tin, and the rest . . ." He looked up: "You want to see the navy?" He plopped down the spatula and went into the living room. Then suddenly he was dancing the *yablochko*, the Little Apple, a sailor dance.

> *Oh, little apple,*
> *You're rolling away.*
> *Roll into my mouth*
> *And you'll never get out!*

"Look at you," I said. "You were half-dead on the phone." The words were out before I could think better—you didn't reference death for the same reason you didn't lie in a hospital bed unless things were bad enough to be in a hospital.

"A boil on your tongue." He shook his head.

"Sorry."

We returned to the kitchen and cooked silently. I fried potatoes while he messed around with his salmon.

"How's everything with Alana?" he said. His idea of a conciliatory topic.

"The same," I said.

"I don't understand," he said. "I don't understand what your problem is."

"It's hard to explain."

"Is she barren?"

"What? No."

I wondered if there was a follow-up on his tongue—"Are you?"—but he would never risk inviting it to be true by mentioning it out loud. I had tried to explain truthfully many times why Alana and I struggled—this seemed more loving and respectful than a deflecting deception; besides, I wanted the understanding—but it made so little sense to someone of his mind that he assumed it was an elaborate lie. She was barren. Or I was gay. Or God only knew what he came up with but refrained from voicing out loud due to superstition. Sometimes it made me want to try to explain harder, smarter, better—the power was mine; I could do it. And sometimes it just made me want to be left alone.

"Five years together," he said. "Life isn't forever."

"Yes, I *understand*."

"I met your grandmother—"

"I've got it!" I snapped.

"How irritable you are," he tsked.

"No entrée?" I said through my teeth, trying to steer him away.

"You make what you know," he said. He looked over: "You know entrées?"

They didn't have the ingredients for the simple, hands-off things that I knew: roast sausages, roast pork chops. "What about a cabbage salad?" I said. "The way Oksana makes it—vinegar and a little sugar." He shrugged, and I went to the fridge.

When it was all ready, I offered to take it in, but he told me to go in the living room—as far from the bedroom's germs as I could. He was pretty germophobic himself, but he wanted to be the knight who brought in the food. The bedroom door opened, and Oksana called out a dull hello. "Queen for a day!" she yelled hoarsely, and we all laughed.

When he returned, he plopped down on the couch pillows, a shit-eating smile on his face. We all thought he took his privileges

for granted (who got a twenty-four-hour live-in home aide?), but he
was proud to have done that for her. "What do you want to know?"
he said.

"What do you mean?" I said.

"You keep asking questions. Navy tattoos, money on the side.
Ask. Ask what you want to know." He winked and gave me a
slanted smile. "I don't want you to think I'm a murderer. Just close
the window."

"It's a hundred degrees in here," I said. Starting in October, the
central heat went berserk. He had to keep the windows open all
winter.

"They can hear upstairs if the window's open," he said.

"You think they'll report you for stealing from a Minsk garden
seventy-five years ago?"

Finally, he was willing to talk—why was I ruining it? At some
point, I must've come to draw more pleasure from the anger I felt at
being denied information than from the prospect of finally getting
it—from getting to know the him who wasn't a bullshitter compli-
menting himself on his magnificence as a grandparent. The only
generosity I actually needed from him—his understanding—he
couldn't provide, and so I thought maybe we could cut a different
groove in the frozen soil beneath us. Certainly the alternative—
leaving each other's lives for good—felt impossible. The five
months we spent not speaking after Paris and Israel had been almost as hard for me as they'd been for him. But I was weary of
being publicly adored and privately deflected by him, like a child.
I was thirty.

It tormented me that I couldn't get him to crack, when I had
cracked so many who should have been harder (the Ivy League;
the Fulbright people; Carly K. next door in New Jersey). I wanted
to play him the way he played others. But I couldn't. Even though I
knew he was dying to brag. Either I wasn't good enough or he was
too good. (Or my grandmother too clearly visible shaking her head

no from heaven.) But then Oksana had gotten sick; he had made
soup for the woman who usually made soup for him; and something I hadn't been able to dislodge got dislodged. Defeated, I got
up and closed the window.

We spoke for several hours, the daylight turning to night outside. At some point, he reheated the *ukha*—good—and we slurped,
chasing with fried potatoes. A barracks meal. Our brains did not
work the same way. I asked him about navy tattoos and ended up
with a story about sixty-five mink stoles two decades later. Were
there, at that moment in New York City, two more different people
sitting across from each other in more intimate conversation?

Maybe it wasn't only feeding Oksana that had opened him up.
I'd been coming around more for a while now, and not even because I got to go home with one of Oksana's food bundles. Maybe I'd
crossed into some inside circle. Hell, we'd been at the stove together.
A day earlier, that would have seemed as likely as seeing him press
a hundred on a panhandler.

Once he started, there seemed no use in stopping. For the next
year, I came down once a week, often more, and this was what
we did. Finally we had something to do other than try to relate. I
gained ten pounds—"You've rounded a little, haven't you"—and I
wrote down a lot.

The concrete stadium seats from which he and I had cheered for
Dinamo Minsk on weekends—he had poured the concrete. As an
inmate of the old prison on Volodarskaya Street. He headed there
after he "turned off the lights" for a drunk who was taunting
him and his friends, on their way home from a dance club and
turned out in their finest—"Living well, kikes!" They had made
it through the war—out of three million Soviet Jews, only a few
hundred thousand survived, and a western city like Minsk, which
saw German paratroopers on the first day of the war, got the worst
of it—and felt light-headed with it. They went dancing every

night—at the Belarus movie theater, at the Officers' Club, in Gorky Park. Some finery—that night, Arkady had, under his jacket, a fake collar from a more expensive material.

He didn't stay at the prison long—his father bribed the judge on his case. But it was long enough to see the justice system for what it was—an old man who had taken home a bowl of oats from a government stable because his own horses had nothing to eat was sentenced to five years. The widow of a war veteran, a mother of seven, had pilfered, for trade, a pouch of tobacco from work. She got ten years.

Arkady went back in, however, when he broke a bottle of champagne over the head of another drunk slurring away from his table about the kikes having sat out the war in Uzbekistan. Unfortunately, the drunk was a colonel, this time Arkady got three years, and the envelope for the judge had to be fatter.

His younger brother kept up. One night, at a dance club called Ray of the Sun, two men started in with the usual. His brother took out his straight razor and took an eyeball clean out of one of them. Arkady hid him in the attic, but the police found him. Arkady gave the precinct commander two thousand rubles—a fairy-tale amount of money—and his brother went free. But the commander lied and had his brother picked up a second time.

Arkady had a friend named Lenny the Trombone. No one went by their real names—maybe because that made them less easy to find. ("Nicknames made the NKVD unhappy," as Nadezhda Mandelstam wrote about the KGB's precursor in the 1930s.) Arkady got Lenny to put on his marching-band epaulets, and himself found somewhere a moth-eaten war uniform. They rang the doorbell of Eyeball's family. Arkady stuck out and quickly withdrew a small laminated set of credentials—it was an old address book.

"Drop the case," Arkady, the "policeman," said. "Otherwise he goes before the judge, then prison, and two meals a day. Whereas you drop it and we'll teach him a lesson the hard way. An injury of his own, to remember."

The man and his wife were simple people, but not simple enough—they called the bluff and said, "Ten thousand." Arkady didn't have ten thousand—he had five. So that was what the judge got. And his brother got three years instead of ten.

During visiting hours at the jail, Arkady found a "warm" body among the guards and plied him with soccer tickets, high-end cognac, bags loaded with deficit food. The guard knew the steps to this dance; one night a month, he let Arkady's brother out for a family meal. But someone got wind of it, and brother and guard both were transferred to a penal colony in Siberia. They loaded bricks onto a barge in a river, ten thousand a shift. The penal settlement was full of Chechens, who used their work axes to chop the heads off anyone who spoke to them incorrectly. Dutifully, they delivered each head to the guards. So Arkady's brother kept quiet.

Because things became so bad for Jews after the war, many took advantage of how many records had been destroyed by reclassifying themselves as Belarusian in their passports. But then a decree went around saying that these had to be rooted out and turned back in. Arkady went around to what relatives and friends were left and collected their passports, then went to the precinct commander who had taken his money but then picked up his brother again. (No point holding grudges—it was a shifting alliance.) This time Arkady brought vodka—three bottles. Ostensibly, he had come with all the family passports like a tribal chief to make the reclassification easier. *But first let's drink.* And drink. By the end of the third bottle, the precinct commander didn't care who was a Jew and who Martian. (And maybe he felt a little guilty.) The price for these feats was Arkady staggering home blind with drink, night after night.

Arkady's difficulties with authority did not begin after the war. He had been expelled from the first grade. He didn't like going. Just didn't. Altogether, he managed six grades by the time the war ended his schooling forever. The angel brother was Aaron, the oldest. He was the handsomest; he lifted weights; he had a girlfriend. He'd finished high school and worked as an electrical engineer. His hands were always dirty with smudge, but he loved the work, and it had prestige—electricity was new. When the war started and Aaron was called up, Arkady "accidentally" dumped a vat of boiling water on Aaron's feet at the steam baths. But that delayed Aaron's conscription by only three weeks. Then Arkady got the idea to chop off one of Aaron's pinkies. In 1941—when you still had to be able-bodied to serve—this would have been enough to keep Aaron in the rear. Arkady got close several times, a butcher knife in his hand, but he never managed it, and Aaron, none the wiser, went off to fight.

They'd all gotten out of Minsk on the first day of the war. The radio had said to remain, but they knew enough not to listen. Arkady's father saddled his horses, they piled all they could into his cart, and they clopped off, nearly two hundred miles, to a settlement from which they managed to get on a train to a dispersal point deeper inside Russia. From there they were sent 1,200 miles to a village in an autonomous republic of Turkic people just north of Kazakhstan. These had never seen Jews before. "Where are your horns?" one of the villagers asked Arkady, without ill will. But the Jews were good workers, and the village needed bodies after an entire clan had vanished into the army. Even the women were good workers—an aunt of Arkady's had hauled twenty-kilo bags of potatoes from the Minsk market on her own shoulder. One time, a vendor had been rude to her and she smashed him so hard he "sat down on his ass."

By 1943, Arkady was up for the draft. A girl at the village council had been going around with a friend of his, so he went to her and came out with a new identity card that said he'd been born in 1927, not 1926, which saved him from the draft for a year. He would abide by that falsehood until his late eighties, nearly thirty years into his life in Brooklyn—he didn't like talking about it even when the window was closed—when it melted away in service of his desire to see himself make it to ninety. So he wasn't eleven days younger than my grandmother. He was 354 days older.

Even with the new document, he wasn't going to take chances. Aaron was gone, and his father had been recruited for a munitions factory in the Urals—half the family men was enough. Every week during harvest season, two boys delivered the village's grain to a regional center sixty miles away—all grain was requisitioned by the government. Arkady used one of their horses; in the town, he boarded a train for Uzbekistan, to which a great deal of the European part of the Soviet Union had been evacuated. He didn't board it—he didn't have a ruble to his name. He slipped into a compartment just above the wheels.

Once the train got going, he clambered out and switched to the roof. When the train stopped and passengers stepped out to stretch their legs, he swung down into their compartments to pilfer the poor food they carried: usually carrots or beets. This went on for eleven days, and with each one the weather got warmer.

> Those days, when all the railroad stations and piers in the country were besieged by sullen, grimy mobs who had to wait for weeks on end to buy a ticket. . . . All over the riverbank, charcoal fires were glowing in pits dug in the sand where they were making a stew for their children. The grown-ups chewed crusts of bread which they carried with them in bags—bread was still rationed at that time and they had stored up these iron reserves for the journey.

Nadezhda Mandelstam wrote that about her voyage east into internal exile with her husband in 1934. The scene was similar in Tashkent, the capital of Uzbekistan, when Arkady arrived there. The Soviet wartime evacuation effort had only one logistical model, that of all the forced deportations that had become a regular part of Soviet life in the 1930s.

Few evacuees had ever seen a place like Tashkent. Upon arrival, a more poetic observer than Arkady felt "as if the ground was covered with white snow and pieces of ice burned against the gleaming hot sun. In fact it was salt." The women were covered by flowing black garments. Donkeys pulled carts with wheels the size of a person. On every corner, Arkady saw teahouses and peddlers pulling flatbreads out of outdoor ovens. He was inside a fairy tale.

It was also unbearably hot. The endless dust turned to mud after a rain. There was nowhere to live. And some things were quite familiar: The same hierarchy that kept elites well supplied in Moscow and Leningrad had reestablished itself here; for the rest, there was nothing. The city was a black market. Fortunately, how that worked was familiar to Arkady, too.

He went to the bazaar, picked a corner, and watched. Soon he saw what he wanted. They pretended to be lame or deficient so no one would pay them attention, including the military personnel sweeping the city for draft-worthy bodies. Then the razor would come out and he'd see them slice through the bottom of a purse or a pants pocket. It took no more than a second. The one Arkady decided to approach was banging a stick at the pavement in front of him.

"You're a pincher," Arkady said. "I want to join in."

"I'm a blind man, little son," the man said.

"You're as blind as I am," Arkady said. He walked away and came back ten minutes later with two wallets. That changed the "blind" man's mind.

There was a safe house overseen by a boss mother. What you stole you brought there, where it was divided equally, an authority system that, perhaps for the first and last time in his life, Arkady abided—when he came across a nice pair of velvet pants, he kept them for himself only after checking with the boss mother. His adopted disability was incontinence. He stumbled around with soaked pants, then found something worth taking and took it.

Though they had left much behind, evacuees often brought with them what was most dear. Thanks to people like my grandfather, they soon parted with it. Nadezhda Mandelstam—who also fled there during the war—lost her ration of fish, and I sometimes wonder if my grandfather took it. Probably not—he had his eyes on bigger things. Also, he was a gentleman—he didn't take food from women.

Arkady was less concerned about the police than about the draft, which by now was conscripting without discernment. It was time to give in. Arkady said a rueful goodbye to his unexpected fairy tale—in regular Soviet life, one usually discovered a place so far away only against one's will—and found a train home. This time, he paid for a sleeping berth. Now he had enough money to buy every seat on the train.

He came home to joy and despair. Joy from his mother on seeing him, and the bundles of bills hidden around his body; despair exactly one day later, when Arkady did not recognize the emaciated man knocking on the door as his father. The wide-shouldered man who had hauled safes on his back had turned into a skeleton, the skin on his bones like ill-fitting clothes. The munitions workers had had to work all-day shifts, but there was almost no food; he had been discharged as a hopeless case. At the door, his father wept. Finally recognizing him, Arkady wept, too.

Soon, worse news arrived: Aaron, Arkady's older brother, was dead. A reconnaissance man on the 3rd Baltic Front, he had gone after a "tongue," a German soldier who'd (be made to) talk. On the way back, they came under artillery fire, which sheared off Aaron's leg; he died from the blood loss. He had served alongside the men from the clan whose conscription in 1941 had emptied out the village where Arkady's family had settled. "We . . . gave each other our word that we would write to the other's parents if something unlucky befell us," one of them wrote in a letter to Aaron's parents.

The 3rd Baltic Front existed for less than six months in 1944, long enough to kill 43,000 Soviet soldiers and injure 150,000 more. In 1941, a Soviet soldier survived, on average, twenty-four hours. By 1944 that number was higher, maybe several weeks. (Arkady had almost certainly saved his own life by delaying his draft by a year.) Aaron had been drafted at the very start of the war and had survived more than three years. He was killed two months after Minsk had been liberated; one month shy of victory on the 3rd Baltic; less than a year before the Soviet flag rose over the Reichstag; and on the same day that, forty-four years later, we left Minsk for good.

It was Arkady's turn, but he got lucky. He was assigned to a torpedo carrier in the Black Sea, off the coast of Crimea, already liberated. He finagled an assignment as a radio operator, a position that required additional training time in the rear. By the time he reported for duty, the war was nearly over. On the ship, it was more or less as it had been in first grade. He'd vanish to go dancing with girls on shore. When he came back, they sent him to solitary for three days. By the time he emerged, he was light-headed enough to sway in the wind.

Then he got five solitaries in a row. His mother had sent him money, but the sailor in the mail slot said nothing had come. Arkady checked with the main mail station, which confirmed that it had come; so the sailor had taken it. When Arkady went back, the sailor said, "You'll do without it, kike." This time Arkady returned with a two-kilo dumbbell and mauled the guy so badly he got fifteen days. Eventually, his superiors got sick of him and discharged him early. (He'd gotten his navy tattoos voluntarily, though mostly to fit in. But he didn't want his grandson thinking he was the kind

of person who liked getting tattoos—in the Soviet Union, low-
lifes got tattoos—so he pretended he had been "grabbed," that is,
hazed.)

It was 1947. Minsk had been reduced to nearly nothing; German POWs were building it back. He hadn't seen his parents in
three years. His father, always reticent, now said almost nothing.
Periodically, he stole out to the backyard with a small photo of
Aaron and wept wordlessly into it. Arkady's mother's hair had gone
entirely white. Arkady started seeing a girl whose father was in
charge of the city's alcohol distribution—in other words, the right
kind of family to be attached to. But then, at a dance, a neighborhood girl asked for his help. An army officer had been courting
her all night, and she needed help getting away without insulting him. Arkady went to the officer—they knew each other from
the neighborhood also—clapped an arm around his shoulder, and
thanked him for taking care of "his girl" while he talked business
with some friends. The officer blanched—Arkady had boxed before the war and, in any case, wasn't someone you wanted to argue
with—blurted out an apology, and fled. The girl was an orphan, a
single dress to her name, but Arkady found himself forgetting the
alcohol heiress.

Arkady and Sofia's wedding drew only fifteen guests; Arkady's
side alone had lost more than a hundred people in the war. Arkady
wore the fake collar. But for Sofia he had bought an expensive blue
dress. Arkady's mother wouldn't forgive him. Sofia lived with them
now, he said—she did more housework than anyone. *You had no
right to do it without asking us*, his mother said. Before the war,
she'd been a saleswoman in a food shop: She gabbed all day, struck
deals on the side, and spent the income just as freely. After Aaron's
death, however, she had altered. But the Jewish parents of Minsk
almost never welcomed new family members without suspicion.
Even though my grandparents suffered from this, they gave my
father his own taste of it thirty years later.

Fine, Arkady said to his mother—*we'll move out and eat on our own.* And sometimes, they didn't. They needed money; lots of it. In this hunger, Arkady couldn't have had a readier partner.

From his barber's chair at the salon by the train terminal, Arkady could see them through his window, his old tribe—the barber worked with a straight razor, and so did the pickpockets. There wasn't a surname among them. Nikola the Lisp, Shurik the Elephant, Vovka the Mongol. Ivan and a Half because he was tall. Misha the Whisper because he spoke quietly. Zhorik the Professor because he thieved with a surgeon's precision. Zhorik's wife was even more deft—she could slice open a purse with a single flick of her wrist. Sometimes they worked in tandem. She went around with a doll that opened and closed its eyes and said "Mama!"—a novelty at the time. He would liberate the distracted, laughing passerby from his wallet.

Others had other tricks. The Gypsy women who told fortunes paid confederates to accost them in view of unwitting marks and go on about the miracles they had performed on their wayward husbands, ailing parents, barren sisters, lame sons. There wasn't a woman at that terminal who didn't suffer from one of those problems, and they submitted to the Gypsy women in droves. While their eyes were closed, they lost their money and jewelry, if not their problems.

The pickpockets rose early—they had to catch the morning rush at the terminal. By the time the barbershop opened, they had enough to pay for a hundred hot-towel shaves. Arkady took goods as payment and fed them a liquid breakfast in the break room (cognac and vodka). This he traded with the commerce coming off the night trains—that was how the city got its food in those years, and the people transporting it always needed freshening up in the morning. These goods Arkady swapped later with regular customers who lived "to the left," the Russian version of "under

the table." In this way, a morning's bracelet or crate of grapes became, by nightfall, a profitable acquaintance with the chairman of
a collective farm that raised minks. My grandparents had such confederates at the food depots that supplied only the political people,
at the clothing stores, in hospitals (God forbid), at the offices that
dispensed vouchers for vacations in state sanatoriums. And that's
why we lived well.

That wasn't only why—Arkady fenced cars and carpets; peddled
special tables with compartments that hid foreign currency, handy
during searches; smuggled gold. The lattermost almost ended it—
the smuggling ring had five men in it; the other four were arrested
but, even under threat of execution, did not give up his name (and
executed they were). Not out of nobility—they knew they would
gain nothing other than sending a fifth man to his death. The KGB
was on Arkady's tail after that for a while. They even sat him down
for a basement interrogation. Lack of evidence hardly made the
KGB pause, but this time they let him go.

What if they hadn't? What if he had not forged his identity
card in 1941? What if his father, who was a POW in World War I,
had remained in Germany, as some Russian POWs did, and my
grandfather had been born a German Jew instead of a Belarusian
one? Would he have managed to escape the concentration camps,
too? I want to imagine he would have—his nose smelled ten
steps ahead. Where would he have fled to? South America? South
Africa? Palestine? As he talked that first night, I thought about
the alternate lives—German, Italian, Argentinean, Israeli—that
could have been mine. In that humble Brooklyn living room, they
couldn't have seemed more exotic. Perhaps I fell into that reverie
because the way he spoke about Minsk—"After they kicked me
out of first grade, I went to the school on Myasnitskaya Street,
right below the prison on Volodarskaya, and then sometimes I
would go for a walk on Respublikanskaya"—made me realize in
a sharp way just how native, how "his," Minsk had been, a sense

of belonging I'd never found in New York, no matter how fluently I navigated it, no matter that I was welcomed in it so much more than he had been in Minsk.

When I returned home the night I found him cooking for Oksana, I looked in my books for mentions of *ukha*. It wasn't even a fish soup to begin with, nine hundred years ago—*ukha* comes from *ukho* ("ear"), and that's what went in, along with lips, innards, and anything else that was soft. (Whatever it was, it made soup—on Russian tables, spoons predated forks by four hundred years.) It became a fish broth later, maybe because meat was proscribed for religious reasons more than half the year, but the broth didn't have to be clear until the nineteenth century, when the French said so. It turned out that the Pokhlebkins were just repeating the French, and it was my grandfather, who took his country for all it was worth, whose method happened to be honoring the original Russian way.

UKHA—HIS AND HERS

Time: 1 hour each   Serves: 6–8

Two nearly identical recipes, with quite different outcomes. The salmon, though meatier, should produce an impossibly delicate, almost refreshing broth in Arkady's version—if it comes out right, you'll want to sip it cold. The pike, in Oksana's, though tender, lends a stronger taste. (The salmon is also less bony.) The short boiling time means your vegetables should stay firm and flavorful—this is also the reason to cook the carrot whole and dice it only at the end. No Russian would think of eating ukha *anything other than piping hot, but there's no reason this soup can't bring the temperature down on a hot day.*

HIS

1 large carrot, peeled	1½ pounds salmon steak
1 medium onion, peeled	Kosher salt, to taste
2 celery stalks, diced	3 garlic cloves, halved
4 Idaho potatoes, peeled, 2 diced and 2 left whole	½ bunch parsley, chopped

1. Bring 10 cups of well-salted water to a boil and throw in the carrot, onion, celery, and potatoes. Return to a boil, lower the heat to medium, cover most of the way, and let cook for 20 minutes.

2. In the meantime, rinse the salmon and pat dry. Using a sharp knife, cut into 2-inch pieces. This will expose some bones; pull them out with your fingers or tweezers. Season with salt and set aside.

3. When the water and vegetables have been going for 20 minutes, lower the heat to the lowest setting and add the salmon and the garlic cloves. With the lid slightly ajar, cook for about 30 minutes, until the salmon looks done.

4. Remove and dispose of the onion. Remove and dice the carrot, and return it to the broth. Remove the two whole potatoes, mash them, and return the mass to the broth, stirring it in gently. Taste for salt and crown with the fresh parsley.

HERS

1 parsley root, peeled, with greens (or substitute 1 parsnip)	1 medium-size (about 1 pound) pike, or similar fish
1 large carrot, peeled	Kosher salt, to taste
1 medium onion, peeled	3 garlic cloves, halved
3 Idaho potatoes, peeled and diced	1/2 bunch parsley, chopped

Sources: You'll be able to find wild pike online from retailers such as Citarella .com; workable substitutions are walleye, branzino, and porgy, in order of preference. Pike is quite bony, so unless you enjoy picking out bones the way a Slavic person does, you might fish the pieces out after cooking and enjoy the pike mainly as a flavoring agent.

1. Bring 10 cups of well-salted water to a boil and throw in the parsley root, carrot, onion, and potatoes. Return to a boil, lower the heat to medium, cover most of the way, and let cook for 20 minutes.

2. In the meantime, rinse the pike, snip off the fins and tail (scissors are handy), cut off the head, and cut up the rest into 1½-inch pieces. Season with salt and set aside.

3. When the water and vegetables have been going for 20 minutes, lower the heat to the lowest setting and add the pike and the garlic cloves. With the lid slightly ajar, cook for 20–30 minutes, until the pike looks done.

4. Remove the parsley root, dispose of the wilted greens, cut the root into disks, and return the disks to the broth. Remove and dice the carrot and return to the broth. Remove and discard the onion. Taste for salt and crown with the fresh parsley.

✤

2009

✢

> People talk about growing up Jewish in Brooklyn . . . and they
> always dwell on the dark side. . . . It makes for good drama,
> makes good writing, and it makes good intellects. . . . Well, [in
> Los Angeles] we didn't have nothing to do with all that—no
> dark side, none of that struggle—everything was just a flow.
> —ROBERT IRWIN

It had seemed like a good idea. There was a place where the sun shone all the time. Where you did not have to walk around with your insides coiled up the way you did in New York. New York, where there was always a surcharge if you didn't look carefully, where the radio always reported "more traffic than usual"—did it still qualify as the usual if always there was more?—where, except for two weeks in spring and two weeks in fall, you lived in an inferno of wet heat or slush and spitting rain; where everyone was always so busy and rushed. There was a place, only two hours by plane, where they didn't rush (in fact, they were exasperatingly slow); where, outside of high summer, it was always like those four magic weeks in New York; where there were fewer people and cars; where it was no less expensive, but here the turquoise ocean glimmered all around. The anniversary of our arrival in the States had just passed; my grandfather's birthday was approaching. I had been saving, and my gift would be five plane tickets. I was going to fly us all—Oksana, too—for three days to South Beach. "All" did not mean Alana; she and I were on a "break." These had become more regular than the relationship itself. Even if we were together, I had as hard a time imagining her wanting to spend a weekend somewhere with me as with my family.

"I'm surprised you're so interested in the date," my mother had said, meaning the occasion for the trip.

"It's the day we came here," I said.

She shrugged. "None of the other children think of it. Or the adults, really."

She was right—I'd never paid attention to the date. I'd always envied people with generations behind them in America—all that compound achievement. Encountering someone like that was like setting eyes on a beautiful person, a rush of dopamine followed by regret and wobbliness at not possessing the same. Even those boys and girls who had emigrated from the USSR at my age, and even later, had made perfectly serene American landings, struggling with neither side of themselves. Perhaps that's why they felt no need to mark the day they'd arrived.

That year, however, it occurred to me that we'd spent a generation's worth of years in America. Not an actual generation, because I was past thirty and all but single, but it felt like there was a little root in the soil, and I wanted to celebrate. Celebrate that and celebrate actually wanting to go on vacation with my family.

"What if we went somewhere?" I had said to my mother on the phone. I had fought a long but delicate war to work us down from several phone calls a day to several a week, and so many of our conversations at this time began with her exclamation "And look who it is!" But eventually, we got onto a straight road. Was there somewhere she wanted to go? She and my father had nearly never used their vacations in the country where they actually lived.

"Anywhere you want," she said. "As long as we're together."

After we hung up, I ordered the guidebooks. Mexico, I proposed to her several days later—warm, inexpensive, rich culture, good food. "I don't know," she said. "Isn't it dangerous?" Los Angeles,

I offered next. "Isn't it far for him to fly?" (There was only one "him.") Arizona? "Maybe, maybe," she said, not meaning it, and I didn't bother asking why. Then she said: "You don't want to go to Chicago?" I stared through the phone darkly, the desire for time together draining away. All along she'd known what she wanted; she felt she owed a visit to my uncle and aunt in Chicago. (Owed. She didn't want to go.) But she had wanted to be accommodating. "Miami," I said through clenched teeth. "Warm, and safe, and close enough he won't flip out."

At least she really wanted to go somewhere. Nearly every time I visited, my grandfather slapped the table and said, "You remember Paris and Israel? What a trip! Let's go somewhere. I'm paying for it." Suicidally, I agreed and lost myself in trip research. Italy. Or back to Minsk. Or more Israel. Eventually I would bring him the options, planned down to the airport transfers.

"I don't know," he would say. "What do you think? Let's say something goes wrong. I don't want to ruin your vacation."

He wasn't going anywhere.

I never learned my lesson.

He said it again about Miami. I looked him in the eye and said, "You're going."

"Mama's going?" he said.

"Everyone."

"She doesn't like flying," he said hopefully.

"She said she doesn't mind it this time, because we're all going together. If the plane goes down, we don't have to feel bad about not being together."

He didn't get my joke.

My father had other questions. How would we reach the airport? Would we drive or take a taxi? If we drove, where would we park? How much would that cost? He had to work his graveyard shift, in Manhattan, before we flew off; my mother was in New Jersey; I was on the Lower East Side; and Oksana and my grandfather were in Brooklyn—how would everyone meet? What was the weather in Miami? What if we didn't make the flight? What if there was an issue with the off-site parking? What if there was a problem finding each other after his shift? How would he get home a day earlier than everyone? (He had to work on Sunday.) What if that flight was delayed? What if the original flight was delayed? What should he say to his boss? How much earlier should he ask his morning change-up to come? What if it snowed the night before we were supposed to go? What if it was raining when we met? What if the weather was bad in Miami? What if the hotel was no good? Where would we eat?

Maybe he'd always been like this. I noticed it only as a teenager. He wanted to know everything in advance. I spent a lot of time trying to understand why. (Asking him would get me nothing—as with his own father, for whom I was named, I could ask all the questions I wanted, but the answers I'd get would be like water slipping through fingers.) Mistakes cost more in this country; maybe that was why. Or maybe he felt less in control here. Maybe it was the Soviet resistance to spontaneity. I never found out. But it always fell to me to organize things, so if anything went awry, I got the glare, the weary shake of the head at my naïveté for thinking it could all go well.

At 6:49 a.m. on the appointed morning, my forehead wet with worry—I'd told him we would be there at 6:45—I slammed to a halt outside the Upper East Side apartment building where he worked. I was lucky—he didn't emerge for three more minutes. He was steaming, but about the morning guy, who'd promised to come at 6:45 but came at 6:50. I thought about pointing out that the man was doing my father a favor by starting early at all—the doormen tended to trade minutes with the precision of Olympic timekeeping devices—but instead thanked him silently for saving my ass.

It was not snowing. It was not raining. There was no traffic. The GPS worked. The off-site parking had no line, and my registration was recognized by the system. Then the shuttle to take us to our terminal showed up right away. I watched my father's forehead un-pucker, his shoulders unclasp. He slapped me high five. "Gays on their way to Miami!" he yelled. He'd heard somewhere that South Beach was a gay mecca. I lost my temper and yelled at him. A bad atmosphere descended. He shook his head; I was such an irritable person.

I sent them all to the security line and went to the restroom to compose myself. When I returned, my grandfather was at the metal detector, his pants around his knees, half of New York streaming by.

"Pull up your pants!" I hissed at him.

"Again, they're fucking with me!" he said. "Take off your shoes! Take off your belt!"

"Everyone has to take off their shoes!"

"So why are they checking my bag and not that fatso's?"

I watched the TSA agent pull out of my grandfather's bag a tube of toothpaste the size of a log; apparently, no wisdom had been gained on that front since he and I had gone to Paris and Israel. (Then again, he hadn't flown anywhere since.) His toiletries were so large, he needed an I ♥ NEW YORK bag to fit them. Again, I had told him—a Ziploc. *Small* Ziploc. The one with the twist tie? No, a fucking *Ziploc*—with a zipper.

Everything got confiscated. I thought he would spit at the agent. Then he made his pivot. "Big deal," he sneered at the agent, thank-fully in Russian. "I got a thousand more where that came from. Brush your teeth, asshole."

They—again, it didn't matter who *they*; the *they* who held all the power—oppressed him on the airplane as well. With his half globe of a belly, he barely fit in his seat, but every time he snapped off his seat belt or reclined, the flight attendant re-cinched him and brought his seat back to straight. She did it less patiently the second time, and quite impatiently the third.

"I'm sweating," he said. "Something's wrong."

"Nothing is wrong," I said.

He mopped his forehead with fanfare. "It's so hot here."

"Soon we'll be in the stratosphere," I said. "It's minus a hundred up there."

"I don't know what's happening."

I spun open his ventilation knob. He brought his palm up to it and winced theatrically from the effort. "I don't feel anything. It's broken. I don't feel anything." Surreptitiously, he reclined his seat once again.

My father leaned forward. "Hey, American, don't you know they're going to take you off the plane if you recline before we take off? So calm down. What? They're going to take you off the plane, that's right. And what's with you—it's hot?—take off your sweater."

"New York doesn't know it's sitting on a world of gasoline," my grandfather said. He called my father "the Kerosene Man." As in—he poured fuel on fire. That was their routine as long as I'd known them. My father needled him; my grandfather flared his nostrils to show he was smelling the kerosene. Nearly forty years of hostile intimacy had dissolved their earlier animus into the casual derision of a long marriage.

My mother closed her eyes. Oksana was trying not to intrude on our madness by focusing on the flight safety brochure.

Up in the air, my grandfather believed the sweating had increased. His eyes searched the ceiling—for God, or more ventilation knobs. "Pa, Pa—look at me," my mother tried to distract him. But he didn't want to be distracted. He was busy feeling out the encroaching doom. Was he about to faint? Was his blood pressure spiking? The measuring device was up in the luggage compartment—he berated himself for allowing it to be stored so far away. And was that a headache? Were his fingers going numb? I made myself consider the possibility that he wasn't exaggerating. Then I was responsible—I had forced him to go.

I turned to my father. "Can you tell me why everything has to be a certain way with you? Like this morning. It's impossible to know everything in advance."

He shrugged. "I like things to be a certain way," he said. "For example, the closet doors. If they're just a little open, I have to stop and close them."

"Why?"

"That's what makes me feel good."

"But why?"

"I just told you why."

"You told me the symptom. I'm asking about the cause."

"I just want to close the doors—it's neater that way."

"But another person wouldn't care."

"Well, I care."

"And Mom has to care, or she'll hear from you," I said.

I wondered if my father was secretly repelled by his gusher of a son. Secretly, because he would never admit it to himself. About this he was equally reticent. If you thought about it, even my grandfather, all secrets, was better known to me, and even before he had decided to talk. My father was a less noticeable cipher.

"What do you do?" he said.

"I close them, too," I said.

His eyebrows rose, by way of asking, *So? What's your problem?*

"Except I want to stop," I said.

My mother leaned forward. "Can we talk about something else, please?"

"How's the patient over there?" my father said.

The patient seemed fine—Oksana was "tying up" his ears with talk. He even laughed once. Oksana's carry-on began disgorging tinfoiled sandwiches, passed across the row hand-to-hand like relief supplies after an earthquake. We occupied the row all the way across, so we were nicely shielded from skeptical noses and eyes; also, having four other bodies palming tinfoil next to me made it easier. I was too worn down to worry much about it, in any case.

Above the clouds, it had been eye-hurtingly blue, but we descended into a gray gauze. I so badly wanted it to be azure down below. I wanted them to see the place in all its splendor. I got a compromise—the sky was a bruised blue, but there was sun. The water was turquoise beyond turquoise. The triple band—the sky, the water, the gold of the sand—looked rapturous from above. My mother exhaled. "My God," she said. "Everything is so within reach."

"What was the last time they put paint on these buildings?" my grandfather said, turning his nose at the bright but weathered exteriors of lower Collins Avenue.

A homeless man, shirtless and giddy, weaved past us, his unpared nails clutching a supermarket cart of possessions. He was hollering into his beard and gave us a great toothless grin as he sailed past. "The great attribute of any major American city!" my father exclaimed.

At the Cuban restaurant where I nearly wept the first time I tasted the oxtail, it began before anyone had started the food. Sandwiches got torn and mashed onto other plates, rice and beans spooned and flung, the roast pork and onions hacked and scooped over.

"I don't want it!" my mother was hollering. "How many times do I have to say it?"

"Just take it! Why won't you take it?"

"I'm trying not to eat bread!"

"So eat this fish. Let me give you some of this fish."

"I'm happy with what I ordered. That's why I ordered it."

"Just try the fish!"

The blocking was as aggressive as the sharing. No one who needed to give actually wanted anything from another. Except when they did. Then they said: "Is that good?" Then you had to offer it up. Then they'd protest and decline. Then you'd insist. And then, to accommodate you, they'd take some. But you could save them the charade by just mashing it onto their plates.

Only Oksana wasn't shoving and flinging—she took whatever was forced upon her without protest, piling it to the side; made another pile of her own food for anyone who wanted to try it; and ate contentedly from what was left in the moated middle.

No one could find any fault with the Standard hotel. I'd chosen it because it was on the quiet side of South Beach, facing Biscayne Bay rather than the ocean, away from everything that had upset them about Collins and Ocean Drive. There was a marble hammam, and a mazelike lawn of hideaways with hammocks and fire pits. The infinity pool looked like it ran right into the bay. The bay looked bottle green, or periwinkle, or even slate gray, depending on when you looked. The sun beginning to set, the sky was streaked with violet, dull gold, and snapdragon pink; across the bay, distant studs of shimmering light on the mainland melded with the blue lanterns of the restaurant deck, the canvas of its umbrellas snapping in the light wind. Thankfully, the rooms were tiny, and into this setback our group's members could channel the expectations of disappointment that built up in their chests and demanded release.

"Why can't he pack his own toothpaste?" I said. My mother and I were floating in the pool, relieved to be away from the men, who were scouring the grounds for new marvels and problems. Oksana was unpacking and changing for dinner. "The KGB he could outmaneuver, but choose his own pants—"

"You have to understand, he spent his whole life looking over his shoulder," she said.

"I know about all that."

"Not the KGB," she said. "Your grandmother. What she went through made her . . . She was very loving. To me and to you. But she could be very hard. If the three of us went to a café, I was allowed to order whatever I wanted, but not him. They had to economize—no money was ever enough. She was the boss. I think he forgot how to do things for himself."

"We're all like that," I said. "About money, I mean. Even me."

"Do you mind if we just swim and relax?" she said. "This is heaven."

I destroyed heaven, because I proposed a drink at the in-house restaurant before going to dinner. The five of us were gathered around the drink menu like criminals reading our sentence. For a cocktail, we would be penalized sixteen dollars. For a beer only eight, but none among us drank beer; the proof was too low. And a cocktail diluted the point of the exercise—what about a straight shot? There was no column for shots, so I had to call over the server, Björn Borgian in his white shorts and polo. Shots were also sixteen dollars. Glumly, I translated for my grandfather and Oksana. My mother's eyes bore into me: I couldn't say eight?

"We can't bring in our own bottle?" my grandfather said.

"They don't allow it," I said. "How are they supposed to make money?"

"By fleecing us, how," he said. "Give the guy a twenty and he'll allow it."

"And you think his boss won't notice a giant bottle of something they don't have behind the bar?" The Standard didn't carry Metaxa, the Greek botanical of choice back home.

"Oh, if only I had the English," he tsked.

"How convenient that you don't," I said.

"Okay, guys!" my mother said.

Grimly, we ordered shots of the brown liquor that seemed to best resemble Metaxa. They arrived in snifters, which had the unfortunate effect of spreading out the liquor and making it seem like the glasses held almost nothing. We toasted to good times and capitalism, and they all wet the edges of their tongues on their nectars. They had to make this shit last. To show my derision, I grabbed my bourbon with the intention of downing it all in one go, but instead I knocked over the glass, spilling between ten and thirteen dollars' worth of bourbon. My father and grandfather stared at me with something between bafflement and disgust. If only they registered the other— they were missing a rare chance for kinship. I was glad it was dark; I was crimson.

"It's for luck to spill," Oksana tried.

"I'm starving," my mother said.

The restaurant was called Talula. Inside, it was autumn—dark-colored wood, candles, potpourri, chestnuts, pinecones, and Norah Jones. I'd eaten there twice, and though the courtyard had strung-up lights and a canopy of trees rustling in the breeze, it was more informal, so I'd requested the red leather banquette inside, a ledge of old photos over our heads. Only now I was looking at the menu through their eyes, and it made the Standard seem fairly priced by comparison. Fortune had smiled, and my father had forgotten his glasses; he had to ask me the prices. All I had to do was divide them in half. But I couldn't.

"I guess someone won't be drinking wine tonight!" he declared.

"Do you want to just go somewhere else?" I said.

He opened his hand in the direction of the staff: *And what will they think?*

"They'll be fine," I said. No one had come to the table in ten minutes anyway. The warm service, neither starchy nor fawning, had been one of the reasons the prices had seemed worth it on my previous visit, but I was chagrined to discover that the restaurant had a large party in the courtyard consuming its attention. "Want to?"

He shrugged. Like me with my grandfather, he wanted to bitch, not get his way.

"It's expensive, but maybe it's good," my mother tried. "Let's just decide what we want."

I started translating the menu to Oksana and my grandfather. I had folded—I was halving each price. I sold my grandfather on "chicken with mashed potatoes, vegetables, and a piece of bread"—my translation of the "Pan Roasted Ashley Farms Organic Chicken," served with "maple-whipped sweet potato, slow roasted brussels sprouts, house smoked tasso ham, cast iron skillet cornbread, and sage-bourbon brown butter."

Then we began waiting. Those of us who dared order a drink had long finished it and did not dare order another. Ten minutes passed, then ten more. Then twenty.

"You know," my mother said into the silence, "I recently learned that when people look at a boy and a girl dancing, it's actually the boy they look at, not the girl. And I always thought it was the girl." She turned to me. "What do you think?"

I stared at her, dumbfounded. "I don't know," I said. "I don't think there's a rule."

"I think I hear them killing your chicken, heh," my father said, looking at my grandfather. My grandfather shrugged and pursed his lips in a confederate gesture: *Must be a king's feast if it's taking this long.* Oksana would have made ten dinners in the time that had passed. He didn't mind kerosene as long as it was targeting somebody else.

"One day after the war," he said, "my mother sent me to the market for a chicken. I'm on my way home, this beauty in my hand, and I pass by my friend's house. His mother's in the doorway—ancient woman. Says: 'Sweet child, how much did you pay for that chicken?' I say half what I really paid—let her be impressed. Then she says: 'I'm an old lady, weak . . . Sell it to me. And then run back to the market with your young legs and get yourself another.' What could I do? I had to give it to her. At half price. I paid price and a half for chicken that day."

We all laughed, grateful for the reprieve.

"In that place, food was everything," he said.

"We were well trained by Communism!" my father said, rolling his head toward the kitchen. "We know how to put up with tough situations!"

No one said anything now.

Several minutes later, he said, "Thank God I had a tough childhood with wooden spoons—I can put up with a little doing without!"

Silence.

At last, the food arrived. I closed my eyes and listened to my father say it. "Ah, look at that," he said to my grandfather. "They didn't even give you the whole chicken."

"Very good, very good," my grandfather said, not meaning it. He hadn't tried it yet—he was busy tearing off a leg to deposit on Oksana's plate. Seeing this, Oksana stopped chewing and began sawing off a piece of duck to put on the edge of her plate. She had to saw—it was tough. And thirty-eight dollars.

"I would share my pasta," my father said—cavatelli with broccoli rabe, house-made Italian sausage, garlic, and Fontina—"if it wasn't hard as a brick."

"You have to know how to order," my grandfather winked. I'd offered him the pasta dish my father had gotten, but he thought "macaroni with frankfurter" sounded boring.

"How's your hundred-dollar entrée, Grandpa?" the Kerosene Man shot back. "Good thing kindergarten in Minsk got me used to small portions." He was pointing at the toy-size skillet in which my grandfather's corn bread had arrived. Not the right kind of playfulness for this table.

"Why don't you send it back?" I said to my father. "You sent the fish back at the Cuban place." And asked for a cleaner set of utensils. And a cleaner drinking glass. He shrugged in that way again. He would send the dish back in a simple place, but he was too shy to here.

I tried to study the old photos on the ledge above us—a credible distraction—and drifted away. When I came back, my father was talking about mysterious stones in Africa—he had heard something on the radio. Did I have more information?

I tried to make the adjustments. If he said, "I just saw a great movie, the one with the blond woman, the one who was the prosecutor in the other movie," I had to think about brunettes who'd recently played judges.

"Machu Picchu?" I said.

But the waiter had walked up to ask about dessert. My father said he wanted a "cre-PAY."

"Crepe," I said, almost inaudibly, after the waiter departed.

"Cre-PAY?" he shouted. "Grandpa, you want to get a cre-PAY?"

My mother pushed out her chair and glared at my father. "I need to talk to you."

"Oh, calm down," he said.

"Right now—I need to talk to you. Come outside with me, please."

"I'm not going anywhere. Can't say a word to a person."

She stood up and ran out. I followed her. Outside, in the velvety breeze so painfully at odds with the doings inside, I put my arm around her. She'd worn a festive yellow blouse.

"You're no better than him, sitting there like someone died," she said. "Why can't you ignore him? Just let him be who he is."

"But I can't be who I am," I said. "I've got to be the adult."

"I wish I had a cigarette," she said. Then my shy, self-conscious mother accosted a man on the sidewalk and made him give her a cigarette.

When we returned, I tried to revive the conversation about Machu Picchu.

"What's that?" my father said.

When the bill came, no one fought me for it.

"You understand, he would pay it if the meal was good," my mother said to me quietly.

Back at the hotel, I complained to the front desk (to anticipate the others' displeasure? Because fifteen hours in their proximity had reinfected me with it?): I had called before dinner for fresh toiletries; housekeeping had left us with the previous guests' half-used shampoo. ("For three hundred dollars a night . . .") Someone called back a moment later to apologize—would we like an upgrade?

I turned to my father—the three men were sharing a room. "Do we want an upgrade?"

"Hm?" His face hung loose—the lips apart, the eyes puckered—as it did when he didn't understand. "What's that?"

"It's when they move you to a bigger room."

"Why?"

"Just—because. Do we?"

He shrugged. Something like that, I would have to decide.

"No," I told the front desk. "Just bring fresh shampoo."

There had been spilled cognac on the terrace of the Standard; organic chicken with seasonal fare at Talula; gelato on Lincoln Road, the night alive with its glitter and thrum; and an open-mouthed tour of the Delano, even Oksana gasping at Philippe Starck's wonder. It all paled next to the designer shampoo Standard housekeeping finally brought. "Mmmm," Mr. Pharmacy growled softly, palming the bottles. "Nice shampoo, nice."

We decided to finish the night in one of the hotel's lawn hide-aways, where wicker chairs had been set up around enormous terra-cotta pots with burning logs. My father, who, because of his graveyard shift, hadn't slept in thirty-six hours, begged off, and I was relieved. Before I could follow my mother and grandfather into the nook, Oksana beckoned me over.

"Is there a liquor store nearby?" she said.

"I think so," I said. "Yeah, sure."

She held out thirty dollars. "I'm asking for a favor," she said. "You know what I mean."

They did have Metaxa at the liquor store on Alton Road, and I even found two lemons—the Metaxa chaser of choice. The drinking cups came from the free water stand in the lobby; the plastic knife for the lemons Oksana had saved from the airport. We passed around the bottle, then hid it in a plastic bag between the wicker chairs, like hoboes with three-hundred-dollar-a-night rooms. The wind occasionally flattened the flame, but the log must have been treated, and it sprang back.

"So, Arkady," Oksana said, turning to my grandfather. The wicker chairs were deep, and, sunk in his, he looked like a giant baby. "How long since you measured your blood pressure?"

He slapped his knee. "How do you like that—I forgot all about it." Oksana opened her hands to say, *See?*

"But the dark day is looming," my mother, a little tipsy, said.

She meant that Oksana was about to take her annual two months of home leave. For my grandfather, it got worse with each trip. Sometimes the home-care agency sent God knows whom; my grandfather found one of his replacement aides splayed on the floor after having single-handedly emptied a rather select bottle of Armagnac I'd brought him from France. Most, however, were fine people whose only sin was that they weren't Oksana.

The previous year had brought an enormous Georgian with hairy shoulders. I knew they were hairy because he wouldn't wear anything other than an A-shirt, though even that was perennially soaked by sweat. "You're doing that wrong," my grandfather kept saying to him. "And you're full of shit, too." (I tried to visit more when Oksana was away, and the Georgian kept trying out on me, an emissary from "America," various entrepreneurial schemes: a Georgian-yogurt operation, a contraption to make tomatoes easier to grow out of a window.) Unfortunately, he came from Georgia, where rudeness to elders wasn't permitted, so this bear had to suffer the fox's insults in silence. He tried to ingratiate himself: At the cemetery, where my grandfather went every week to visit my grandmother's grave, the base of which was always flecked with dried grass from the groundskeepers' mowing, the man crawled around the burial plot like a cursed rhino, wiping and nicking while trying to avoid trampling the ground.

My grandfather's funereal pallor lifted only when the phone rang—it might be Oksana. He answered her questions about his health in infinitesimal detail, then asked about each of her children and relatives (a curiosity he rarely extended to my mother's life). Once I walked in on him counseling Oksana's son on his romantic predicaments. ("Buy her perfume and flowers. And another bouquet for her best friend.") A mournful tally closed every phone call: "Only five weeks till you're back." "Only two weeks till you're back." "Just several days and you're back."

"Speaking of," Oksana said now.

"Please don't say you're moving back for good," my mother said.

"No, no," she laughed. "My sister Nadia." She turned to me. "Do you remember? You were there when I wrote the daughter—"

"Of the man she used to know," I said. I looked at my grandfather. He knew already.

"My sister did call him a week later—for his birthday. They kept talking. And they saw each other when she went home for leave."

My mother and I waited intently.

"They're getting married!" she said. "*She's* moving back home." We broke out in cheers, and raised another round.

We had less than a third of the bottle left; no point in saving it. We skipped my grandfather—he couldn't handle what he used to, and besides, he was snoring in his wicker bassinet.

A laughing party—heels clicking the stone walkway, the flick of a lighter, the sound of Spanish—passed the small opening in our hideaway, and my warm head swelled with a new thought. New York had a larger, more diverse array of immigrants than Miami, but they lived on the margins. For the most part, New York was still run by white Anglo people. Whereas here even the "white" people were ethnic—an American city run by immigrants. That must have been part of why I liked coming here: immigrants in charge (though, critically, non-Russians). But why had I made my family come to Miami, if I was the one who felt good there? I hated them for not understanding me, but I wouldn't leave them alone, either.

I didn't think I could explain this to the others, so I just reached out to meet the cups waiting for me. We drank in unison, hissed from the burn, and chased with lemon slices. I stuck out a hand and high-fived the women—perhaps I had crossed the line to drunk. Though the trip had been a resolute failure, this moment was just as certainly a reprieve. Everything I had wanted to happen at Puerto Sagua, the Cuban place, at the Standard, at Talula had not—but it was happening here. They couldn't feel it there with me, but I could feel it here with them. They were blessed because they had the peace of knowing where they belonged; cursed because they lived in the other side's country. I was blessed because, unlike them, I was fluent not only in American life, but our life, too. This wasn't a birthright—I had been moving away from all of it quite effectively for some time. But then Oksana started looking after my grandfather, and cooking when we came over, and suddenly I found myself with more stomach for the family gatherings—in both senses. Her tables were the sublime distraction that allowed the old, well-grooved grievances to occasionally make room for something else. Now, sweetly warm from the fire and four shots of Metaxa, I felt a tremendous love for her, a huge gratitude. It started as a lark in my head, but when I turned to her, it came out as flatly and soberly as if I'd mulled it for weeks. I asked her whether, some year when she went to Ukraine, I could come with.

CHAPTER 12

2013

What to cook when you're going back home

✛

Borscht, let's be honest, can be only so good.
—MARCUS SAMUELSSON, *Yes, Chef*

Question: How do you know you've left the First World?
Answer: A queue will transform into a mad bum rush as soon as the window from which the product in question is being dispensed has, due to mysterious forces, finally opened.

This was the situation at the Moscow airport, where the plane Oksana and I were taking to Kiev was finally boarding—after a three-hour deicing delay at JFK had forced us to miss our earlier connection to Kiev; after the Moscow terminals refused to display the gate of our Kiev flight until the last minute, though we had waited for ten hours; until that last minute was revealed as quite an early minute by the inexplicable wait at the boarding gate.

Before I left New York, my frugality had warred against the exploitation of airport concessions. I'd carefully worked down the contents of my fridge until what remained was an unholy trinity that fit into no other meal: a pork sausage, a grapefruit, a beer. Like many such unintended encounters, the result was delightful: The sausage, roasted on a rack set above the evaporating beer, was sweet and hoppy; the grapefruit, quickly charred in a pan, tangy and improbably crunchy. So satisfying that I ate it on the spot, without thinking ahead to the wait at JFK, which became three hours longer due to the delay.

At some point, it occurred to me to ask Oksana whether she'd brought any food to the airport—sandwiches, maybe. She looked at me like an imbecile: She had made *six* sandwiches. And the only reason she hadn't made eight sandwiches was that the replacement aide said that was a ridiculous number of sandwiches to make.

There were no greens or vegetables hanging out the sides of the first sandwich I unwrapped. The bread wasn't even toasted. "What's in these?" I said. She nodded wordlessly—*Try and you'll see*. I made out four ingredients—ham, cheese, butter, and more butter. "That's really good," I said, still chewing. She only laughed. The bread was so fresh that its lack of toasting, I had to concede—I was a dedicated toaster—made the sandwich better.

The Ukrainian airline had gone under, and Oksana and I had been forced to repurchase our trip to Kiev via Moscow and Aeroflot, which had amenities such as seatback televisions. Sighting them, Oksana, who usually flew the Ukrainian airline, pursed her lips in the way that, for a person from my end of the world, meant *I can't find fault with this no matter how hard I try*. Aeroflot was subsidized by the Russian government, so it had the least expensive connections all over the world: Our airplane, in addition to Russian men in pointy shoes, zippered sweaters worn over bare chests, and thin leather jackets, had Hasidic Jews praying in the aisles (they were making a pilgrimage to the Ukrainian birthplace of a religious figure, or going on to Israel); Central Asians in headscarves (women) and gold (men); Turks; and whoever else had the fortune or misfortune to live south and east of Moscow. Though Aeroflot plied us with some of the best food I'd had aboard an airplane (even an ordinary tuna salad was tangy with a sweet-and-tart relish), I had found enough hunger during the ten-hour flight from New York to Moscow to sneak another Oksana sandwich. But no one on the plane looked at me oddly—everyone was busy unwrapping tinfoil of his own.

Now, at the gate for Moscow–Kiev, we watched travelers to

Tehran, at the next gate, board their flight in a patient, single-file queue. We had waited so long by the unmanned boarding desk, after having been summoned so urgently to it, that we had seen the Iranians replace patient, single-file Lebanese bound for Beirut. But as soon as our desk was activated by the wide-cravatted gentleman selected by Aeroflot to serve as our dictator for the next hour, the entire population-to-be of Moscow–Kiev Aeroflot 103 sprang from its seats and surged toward the desk, cutting ahead of those who had stood in line patiently for forty-five minutes.

The Ukrainian revolution wouldn't take place for another six months, the annexation of Crimea for six after that. In March 2013, there was nothing eventful about a flight from Moscow to Kiev. At the Kiev airport, we were made to fill out entry forms that no one collected and, though we had had to circle Kiev for an extra thirty minutes because of "all the air traffic heading in," stood in line with the passengers of only one other flight. It was of worshippers from Tel Aviv, including a radiantly beautiful Sephardic girl in religious vestments of a cutting elegance, her pimpled teenager husband, and a sage with a promethean beard, its strands gathered into eggy coils. A middle-aged Ukrainian couple staged a protest against the expedited treatment being received by a very large Hasidic family, while "we, who would walk through in a minute, are being made to wait." The possibility of ethnic slurs hung in the air but didn't materialize.

It was at this point that an animal was slaughtered somewhere in the arrivals hall. Well, no—who knew the provenance of the foul scent that suddenly settled on every inch of the terminal. It was heavy with ammonia, some combination of expired existence, unhygienic living, and bad decision-making about floor cleaners. It hung hard over passport control, over the baggage claim, the arrivals hall. The airport staff made a big show of holding their noses to demonstrate that this kind of thing did *not* happen all the time as they walked around doing apparently nothing at all.

In the arrivals hall, men slept across seats, awaiting flights or recovering from a night on the town. One man, as I passed him, sprang awake and began to hiss—*kss, kss, kss.* I thought I was finally witnessing the first instance of the fabled Ukrainian anti-Semitism my mother had so strenuously warned me about, but then I realized that the man was trying to summon a feral cat roaming the hall.

I didn't care. I was giddy with anticipation. I recognized all of it. Walking down the Bowery shortly before I left, I'd come upon a drunk shouting from the middle of the sidewalk. As I got closer, I realized it was a rhyme, and a Russian rhyme at that, though I didn't know it. He was finishing the fourth line of a stanza—a cigarette making orange trails around his head as he declaimed, his knees bent as if he couldn't hold himself upright—but then abruptly fell silent. He'd forgotten what rhymed the fourth line with the third. As I passed him, a word that did—wrong or right, I didn't know—floated up into my head, and I shouted it at him. His creased, bloated face collapsed into a child's surprise, and I couldn't help smiling.

An hour later, at the Kiev train terminal, where Oksana and I waited to board a fifteen-hour train to her hometown of Ivano-Frankovsk—we had missed the direct—I handed the oval-shaped grandmother at the entrance to the men's bathroom three hryvnia for the 2.50-hryvnia entry ($0.37 instead of $0.31). She didn't have exact change: Did I have half a hryvnia, so she could give me back one hryvnia?

"You can just take it all," I said. She seemed perplexed, then aggrieved that I would treat money so carelessly. When I got back to the main hall, I got the right change and, feigning incontinence, returned to the bathrooms. Only this time she would accept nothing more than two hryvnia, making up for the earlier overpayment, and in my effort to get the right change to make up for *that*, I now had too much for *this*. The old woman stared at me with anger and pity. Just then someone else showed up, she got the right change, and finally, miraculously, all was settled between us. Our train was not until 3:30 a.m., hours away, but I intended to keep it in at all costs until then, because I did not wish to meet her again, and in the great halls of the main Kiev train terminal I could find no other bathroom.

As I went back and forth, I realized they were all staring at me. All of them—the swaddled old grandmothers, with their crates emptied of berries and mushrooms, waiting for the 4:00 a.m. back to their prehistoric villages; the exasperated ticket vendors asked to do nothing more than vend tickets; the mob men stalking the halls in their dubious clothes. They were fair-haired, fair-eyed, fair-skinned; I was not.

At 2:00 a.m., Oksana and I filed into the only dining establishment whose doors remained open, a pizzeria with cheap plastic tables and a Depeche Mode remix album on the stereo. The salad ingredients slept in the same small stainless-steel containers where a Subway kept its banana peppers and triangles of cheese, though here an ancient woman in a bandanna was hand-mixing a fresh vat of dough. Against all expectation, the sleeping vegetables were impossibly fresh—the feta may have been the creamiest I'd ever had, and the pizza bianca had no reason to be that good, as they say. The stereo murmured about waiting for the night to fall. The Depeche Mode was fake, but the food was real. There was even a sign on the wall that said NO GMOS. There's nothing as forgiving as a traveler's hunger—and yet.

I slept for nine of the fifteen hours we spent on the train. (Miraculously, it kept to the scheduled fifteen, perhaps because it was not physically possible to go any slower.) When I was awake, the train attendant attacked with tea served in those silver glass holders. Oksana tried to press forty hryvnia ($5.00) on him; he smiled shyly into his mustache and took only twenty. I ate the last of Oksana's sandwiches somewhere in western Ukraine and rolled into

Ivano-Frankovsk famished. The lesson was clear: Always make
eight.

Arriving at Oksana's apartment, I saw the yield of her fanatical
Brooklyn frugality—she had a recently renovated three-bedroom
apartment that stood empty while she was in the States, her son Misha another in the same building. There was even a country house.
These were luxuries in that regional city; probably no other family
in Oksana's building—twenty-eight adjoining nine-story columns
in varying stages of advance and retreat, like crooked teeth, fronted
by a yard of homely cars, barren trees, and a massive field of snow
that sparkled indigo in the evening—had anything comparable.
She was the Arkady of her city—I wondered if the other residents
admired or resented her for it.

Inside Oksana's apartment, the Soviet period lived on—thick
rugs; lace window curtains; wood-paneled cases with books, china,
and religious icons; velour couches; porcelain and wood figurines of
country shacks, elderly burghers, and unicorns; plants that Misha
had neglected; and, on every wall, wallpaper. The small kitchen
table was soon laid with plates: Oksana fried onions and potatoes
in butter, untwined a cured pork loin Misha had bought, chopped
fresh cucumbers and tomatoes, and set out a grainy mustard. Then
the Zhan-Zhak cognac ("the spirit of France"). I was starving and
bit my tongue. The food was as remarkable as the view outside the
window was not.

Blurry with travel and drink, eventually I was dispatched to the
guest room—Oksana, possessed of some supernatural energy (she
hadn't slept on the train) or simply the adrenaline of reaching home
after a year away, would clean up. Before I collapsed, I looked out
the window, past the concrete balcony where Oksana kept a "winter garden" that survived even Misha's neglect: enormous tracts of
empty, snow-covered ground that eventually dead-ended in squat,

Soviet-era residential construction. It looked like what I'd imagined one of those industrial Siberian cities would—factories, housing blocks, boundless snow. Only the ocher brick and gold cross of a cathedral broke up the view. And yet, for some reason, it didn't depress me. Maybe because at least it didn't resemble the many places around the world—New York, Berlin, Mexico City—parts of which had come to seem interchangeable. Or maybe because it was familiar—a place where a little went a long way, where people knew lack and valued things in a different way when they had them. Even if this lack sometimes also made them primitive and crude, and though I knew they would kill—sometimes literally—to live where and how I did. Maybe I could feel what I felt only because I knew I could leave.

I hadn't been back to this part of the world in thirteen years—I thought I'd never be back. In 2000, high on Turgenev and all the Russian literature I was reading in college, I'd listened to no one, not even my terror—my mother had all but laid herself across the doorstep—and gone to Moscow for ten weeks for an internship at the U.S. embassy. Smell is the only sense that bypasses the thalamus and goes straight to the cortex, so that scents absorbed early become magnetic whether they're appealing or not. So you couldn't say whether the escalator lubricant in the Moscow metro—the same they were using in Minsk when we left—smelled good or bad; but it did smell, ineluctably, like home. That was all I could say—otherwise, the experience defied language. Even the light fell across a doorway from a sconce differently than in America, and this way of falling was the home way. In my best American moments, I had not experienced this kind of completeness: every part of oneself in alignment.

But that turned out to be only part of the story. My own was also no longer my own. Constantly, I was singled out as a Jew. Addressed without a fraction of the civility, even if empty, I'd come to take for granted in America. I was embarrassed by the way people around me blamed America for all their problems, then copied everything about it. I took a night train to Minsk and found the apartment building in which I'd grown up. The yard where I spent so much time, that I recalled being as vast as an ancient wood—as the world itself—appeared tiny. I came back to the States a week early. My parents gloated. That experience began my drift away from the Russian part of me. South Brooklyn made it easy.

But since then I'd made my way back to south Brooklyn. They were medieval and maimed, my people—you couldn't take them anywhere. But I wasn't as ashamed of this as I used to be. I was like that myself.

I wondered often whether the end of my relationship with Alana, eighteen months earlier, had released me into an acceptance of that. The thought had occurred to me only recently, because I had only recently emerged from the pall that set in when she ended it, in the fall of 2011. By then we had taken so many "breaks" that one had to be in epic denial to be surprised that this was finally it. But I had wanted so badly for us to succeed, and we had found reason to come back from so many breaks, that I didn't believe it was possible. I pleaded with her to reconsider. She burst into tears, but resisted.

The loss was made worse by the fact that she quickly met someone else. I went to my couch with a bottle of Tito's and a carton of American Spirits. We still mattered to each other and, every several months, came together to try to shift to a friendship. Each time, we dissolved into recriminations. A year after we split, she moved in with her boyfriend in Brooklyn, a borough I'd urged on her but which she had refused with all the fervor of a girl whose first love was Manhattan. I moved, too—back to the couch.

And yet, I kept reaching out to her. Why? Because I refused to accept the truth, my friends said. But I couldn't believe that our kindredness was a fraud. (Also, simply, I missed her.) I felt helpless—

when I didn't feel crazy. I was thirty-four. I was supposed to be figuring my life out.

One day shortly before I went to Ukraine, in the midst of yet another argument, I said, "What if we never talk about the past again?" She said, "I'm in." The desire had been expressed on a thousand occasions. But this time, for unknown reasons, it kept. Where we had looked for divergence, we became loving. Desperately grateful for the reprieve, we became fiercely protective of it. Again, we were doing the one thing that we always did so well: talk. One of the things I loved most about her having become available to me once more, this was when, perhaps not coincidentally, I finally fell out of love with her.

I woke less than five hours later, my head burning but my eyes unable to close. It was 4 a.m. I tried to write in a notebook, the crisp linen sheets under me twisting—Ukraine did not do fitted sheets. Then I saw a shelf of light under the door. I opened it to find Oksana in the kitchen, trying to be as quiet as I'd been trying to be in the bedroom. Probably, she had woken not from jet lag, but a long list of tasks. Later that morning, there would be a church service—her mother had passed away a year before—after which the mourners would come to her living room. Her in-laws were due from their smaller town, 150 miles away, with reinforcements from their farm, but Oksana would have to make most of the dishes. She already had several recipes clipped to small clothes hangers hung over the kitchen cabinet knobs; she did it that way in Brooklyn as well.

"*Zavtrak?*" she said, by way of greeting.

Though the previous night's meal was still with me when I'd woken, suddenly I was hungry. "*Zavtrak,*" I said.

She was about to ask whether one veal sausage or two, then answered herself. When they were done, she dropped two eggs into the runoff, which started to sizzle and pop. I hadn't heard that sound in years. Everyone I knew cooked their eggs in a careful amount of oil, and I saw my grandfather, and her, only in the evenings—I hadn't listened to eggs *frying* in a long time.

It came upon me in a hazy, swollen, jet-lagged rush that I was in a cramped kitchen in regional Ukraine in the middle of the night with a woman who had, through the years, come to feel more and more like family, but that was in Brooklyn, once a week. We were in Ivano-Frankovsk, in the darkness, with no one else in this three-bedroom apartment.

"Are you happy to be home?" I blurted out, afraid of the silence. It was 4:45 a.m.—more sparkling efforts at conversation would have to await the instant coffee for which Oksana was boiling the water.

She half turned back to me, half nodded, half smiled. "Yes, of course—it's home." She waited. "But something's missing. I keep thinking about Brooklyn. But when I'm in Brooklyn, I want to be here."

"So you've become one of us," I said. I climbed into the semicircular banquette that surrounded the small kitchen table. "I envy my parents—they're so far away from American life, they don't have to ask themselves do they belong. They know they don't, but it's a firm answer, and that makes life easier, actually."

She nodded, her back to me. "Last year, I was heartbroken—my mother died so quickly I couldn't come in time. But it's a good thing. Here, if you don't have money to bribe your way to a good doctor, you better hope to die quickly." She fell silent, pushing the eggs around with a spatula. Finished, she deposited them and the sausages onto a plate, wedged a piece of buttered bread into the pile, filled my coffee with white sugar and milk, and set it all down before me.

"And you?" I said through a mouthful. I hadn't seen her eat since we left JFK.

She banged the kitchen table absentmindedly with a knuckle. "When I was a little girl, I slept on a table exactly like this one.

We'd scraped together enough to move into the city, but the apartment was so little, I had to sleep on the kitchen table."

"Did you roll off?" I said.

"Probably," she sighed. "Otherwise, I would've made better decisions."

"After we came to America," I said, "I barricaded myself in bed every night with all the chairs from the kitchen, backs in."

"You were playing?" she said.

"I don't know. I had the same dream over and over—this big forest at dusk, gray and green. And a castle in ruins, open walls, the wind coming through. No people. Over and over." It occurred to me that in the novel I was trying to write, everything always happened at dusk.

"Sure, that happens," she said in that vague, banal way she resorted to sometimes. Its best version was some kind of proverb, its worst this flattening of what I'd offered into nothing.

"I think it was about—all of a sudden, I had to do everything for us," I said. "All the time, I lived in terror I'd get something wrong, and it would be the end. The end of what? No one specified. And the ripped-up house—I guess that's obvious."

"You're so hard on them," she said. "I'm sorry—it's none of my business."

"No, it's okay," I said. I wanted us to keep speaking. Even if she didn't agree, it felt different to speak about it with her than with my parents or friends. My parents were my blood but didn't understand, and my friends understood but weren't my blood.

"I admire you for the way you live your life," Oksana said. "You try to make something happen. You have to continue doing that at all costs." She stared past me, the spatula still in her hand. "Parents want something to brag about."

"By that logic," I said, "only someone who isn't family can accept the truth about you."

"You're right," she said. "There are probably things Misha needs to hear that he can hear only from somebody else." She sighed. "What to do? How to live?" This was one of the proverb responses. It was as far as Oksana went in showing her worries. If she was feeling playful, she said, "And what will be, we'll see." Or: "Let's keep thinking—because there's plenty to think about." Or: "I don't know what will be, but I know what is, and I know what used to." But when she was upset, she said, "What to do? How to live?"

At the sink, she was scrubbing the grease from the frying pan. She said, "I was on Facebook before we left. I came across a young man, from here in Ukraine. He had thrombosis in his legs. And they amputated them. That's the kind of country we have. If you have thrombosis, they amputate your legs. His wife left him and took their child. He moved in with his parents and started sewing icons from beads to make money for prostheses. I don't know what came over me. I wrote him and asked for his phone number. We spoke. And you can see—he's one of the good ones. A nice boy, hasn't drunk himself half to death. I sent him two hundred dollars." A woman who walked to save the bus fare had sent this stranger *two hundred dollars*. I listened to dishes clanking in her hands. "Let Misha sweep the street if that's what it comes to," she went on. "Just let him do it in one piece." She was briefly silent. "You two were born the same month, did you know that? Same year, same month." She said no more, and I wondered how she meant it: She saw me as a surrogate son and wished me as well as she wished him? Or "Lucky you, unlucky him," with all the resentment such unfairness surely conjured?

She turned off the water. "Talk, talk, talk," she said, "and I've got two dozen people coming for lunch." She was wearing an expression that said: *Nothing is different, the world is shit, but I still have to do this, and I might as well wear a smile while I do.* "I should have made the borshch last night, it's better on the second day. I just couldn't stand up another minute. I cooked the beets, at least. It helps them keep their color. Beets saved Chernobyl, you know. Their roots go really deep, and there's less radiation down there. Beets and potatoes both. Beans, buckwheat—the roots are too shallow."

"How did you learn to cook?" I said.

"When we were in the village, my grandmother cooked for weddings," she said. "In the city, my mother worked three shifts, so my sister and I divided the house. I got the kitchen. My father was home for lunch every day, but he only had a little time, so I learned to be quick. Dumplings, soup, cornmeal in sour cream. It's no mystery. You just do it over and over."

I could cook only from recipes, and with regular enough failure to keep my hands humble. And God help me if I understood how a sauce came together, or how exactly one got all that rich liquid out of a soup made from water. I asked if I could make the borshch with her.

"The borshch? Quit it—go rest!"

"I'd like to. I don't understand how the water becomes borshch."

She squinted at me, as if at an idiot. "Fine. I'll boil—you get the vegetables."

While I peeled and cubed, she diced onion and grated carrot. Periodically, she called out to ask if I didn't want to drop it and go rest after all. But I liked being there and doing that with her. It was only when I noticed that she had already fried the onions and was about to add carrots—I had just dropped the vegetables into the water, after it had boiled again and again—that it occurred to me that she was politely trying to get rid of me. I was slowing her down. First I had invited myself into her home, and now I would fuck with her cooking. How much would I like it if another set of hands offered to write my novel with me? Not very much.

Shame is a powerful stimulant. You fall apart, or you start moving faster. Oksana was only finishing the carrots when I had the beets skinned, diced, and ready; a tablespoon of tomato paste ready to add to her onions and carrots; two garlic cloves pressed to finish the mixture; the spices—bay leaf, coriander—set out and ready; and the remaining ingredients—sugar, vinegar, salt, dill, and more garlic—lined up in a kind of *mise en place*.

"It never occurred to me to have all of it ready and waiting like that," she said. She didn't seem to be saying it out of politeness.

By the time the sun rose, a large enamel pot of burgundy-colored borshch was "breathing" on the stove, and I knew how water becomes borshch. They say Russian astronauts eat borshch for breakfast, as my grandmother Faina had—one American doctor who spent half a year in orbit with Russians nearly went mad from it—and Oksana and I, having passed a somewhat otherworldly morning of our own, followed their example. Oksana kept reminding me it would taste better later, once it had had some hours to sit. Then this Jew dressed for church.

Inside the church, a crowd of mourners watched from a distance as a priest chanted commemorative liturgy before two ritual tables, one laid with buckets of white flowers and a gold cross with a pinned Christ, the other heaped with loaves of *kalach*, a ritual bread—its circular shape stood for eternity, its three braids for the Holy Trinity, et cetera.

I had always remained untouched by the rituals the living performed for the dead; it was like running after an airplane that had already lifted off. My grandfather visited my grandmother's grave every week, chanting some kind of DIY prayer in Yiddish (addressed to her, not God). I made myself go, too, but felt nothing, and had to force up my most vulnerable memories, sometimes having nothing to do with her, so that tears would come. At the front of the church, the priest said something that made most of the attending fall to their knees. I took it as my cue, and slipped out. I needed a very large infusion of very strong coffee. It was only 9 a.m., but I felt as if I'd already lived most of a day. I'd made a vat of borshch already, for God's sake.

It was March—cold, but blindingly bright. I spotted a small grocery across the road—it looked like one of those slatted wooden shacks from a Slavic fairy tale that might sprout chicken legs and hop off. Inside, I found the same supermarket scene Oksana must have left nearly a decade before: women in uniform aprons and paper-boat hats behind glass vitrines offering meats and cheeses, baked goods, desserts, grains, and breads. The walls had an odd, sickly green color, but the ceilings were tall and the windows wide, so that, despite the odds, the place exuded an air of threadbare grandeur.

"Do you have coffee?" I said in Russian. "Not packaged—right now." In parts of western Ukraine, they refused to answer you if you spoke Russian. Ivano-Frankovsk, Oksana's hometown, was deep in the west, but not so far that they didn't tolerate it. (It was Ivano-Frankivsk in Ukrainian, and I made sure to at least call it that.)

"Yes, of course," the young woman behind one of the counters said gravely. I must have looked different enough, and not many different-looking people made it this way. Maybe I was an inspector. She pointed to a press-button machine. I looked at her helplessly. I meant by this only that I'd hoped for something less prefabricated, but she mistook it for a plea for help, emerged from behind her counter, and bustled around the coffee station until I had in my hand an espresso's worth of instant coffee in a tiny ribbed cup. She was pretty in that tentative Eastern European way—soft cheekbones, soft jaw.

"Might you potentially . . . have bigger cups?" I said.

"Just if you want one of ours," the woman said, pointing weakly at her counter and, presumably, a little private station behind it.

Was she joking? Then again, she'd used the formal version of "you." Then again, Russians did that sometimes, to accentuate the ridicule. Then again, I wasn't in Russia. I made myself stop my tailspin: I would make do. Then I took five little plastic cups from their column and pressed the button once into each of them. These six would cost less than half a cup of drip coffee back home. ("Back home"—the meaning switched depending on where I found myself.) By now, the entire staff and all the patrons were watching me. Did these people not drink coffee? When I was finished dumping into my cuplets white sugar from a clay jar of the kind you would have found in somebody's home, the saleswoman materialized with a piece of cardboard I could use as a tray.

"We have little tables in the back," she said, pointing around the corner of the rear of the store.

"But no trays," I said, trying for a joke, but she only nodded gravely again. "Usually, no one . . ." she started, and pointed at my preemie sextuplets. She straightened. "Maybe you want a pastry?" she said. "We baked them this morning."

"I'm watching my figure," I said. This time I got a fearful smile out of her. Those words had not emerged out of a Ukrainian man's mouth in the country's millennium of existence.

On reaching, alongside me, the plywood tables in the back room, the young saleswoman seemed reluctant to abandon the American who'd surely taken a wrong turn: This was where people drank before going to work. But it was a peaceable bunch. The solitary men smoked and pulled silently on their fifths of cheap vodka; an older couple of radish-nosed alcoholics cursed amiably at their cards while they worked on a bottle—I recognized proudly—of Zhan-Zhak. Everyone cast me a long look, then turned back to their liquids. I looked down at mine. With my cardboard tray of six cups of sugar slightly diluted by small spewings of coffee, I must have seemed no less odd to them than they did to me. "Come back!" the young saleswoman waved in huge semicircles at me when I made my way out. In retrospect, it seemed clear that she'd been sincere the whole time. Or maybe she was just relieved to be rid of me.

I decided not to return to the church. Doing so would force Oksana to mind me instead of the service. I wandered without aim—an unfamiliar experience, my hours divided strictly back home. Before long, I'd made it to the city center, a holdover from the Hapsburgs. First the city was Polish. Then, when Poland was partitioned, it became Austro-Hungarian. When Austro-Hungary dissolved, it became Polish again. After World War II, it became Soviet. Possessed of nearly four hundred years of history, Ivano-Frankovsk was starting only its third decade as a Ukrainian city, much as the rest of the country it belonged to had spent most of the past thousand years ruled by others: the Mongols; the Poles, who sapped the proto-Ukrainians of their brightest and most skilled through assimilation and persecution, much as the Poles themselves would be by Russians and Soviets; then Muscovy, which took over in 1654 and didn't let go until 1991.

Everyone around me seemed lost in thought. The bundled woman in high boots striding past a teal-colored building. The aproned woman flinging sheets in the second-floor window of a laundry operation—I peered at her from the sidewalk for minutes, but she never noticed. The young man in the window of a boxy yellow city bus—he was close enough for me to make out his green eyes, an aquiline nose, and cheeks rosed up by the cold. But he didn't see me. As in a fairy tale, I was invisible.

What if I'd never left, like Oksana's son, like the young man on the bus? Would I be married and a father by my early twenties, like most of the men here, or was my untraditional living—untraditional by Oksana's judgment, at least—an intrinsic quality, and would it be my destiny anywhere? If the latter, what kind of outcast would it have made me in Minsk? Or would it have been rubbed out of me the way it had been rubbed out of my father?

I came around to a makeshift outdoor book stall—dozens of books with foxed, yellowed edges, organized neatly on a pair of tables that looked like they could go at any moment. Their peddler wore the

mismatched uniform of this part of the world—a leather driving
cap; a shirt with weak collars peeking out over a ratty sweater
festooned with rhombuses in five colors; trousers once meant for
a more festive occasion, even if ill-advisedly so; and thick shoes
ready for snow. There were two pairs of socks wedged into them,
I knew without checking. And I knew without seeing inside his
mouth that he didn't have all his teeth. And he probably had a
limp, from a war injury or bad local medicine. I knew all this as I
knew what preoccupied the people I'd seen on my walk: The laun-
drywoman was thinking about her daughter's husband's drinking; the young man about having to return to a home he shared
with too many people; all of them about living in a country run
by crooks and having to work much harder than was fair; about
having to leave Ukraine to make money—if they could manage
to get out.

The books were in both Ukrainian and Russian, but the man
was speaking the latter. I pretended to flip through a volume of
Hemingway—though Russian has an "h" sound, it becomes "g" in
translation from another language: Gemingway, Gitler, gomosek-
sual, Alzgeimer (ahlts-GAY-mer)—but it was a decoy; I was savoring the sound of the man's talking. I'd been speaking only Russian
since Oksana and I left JFK, and, to my delight, it was loosening despite thirteen years of my not having used it exclusively. He spoke
with erudition mixed with the plainest village expression, and a
small dictionary's worth of word-free sounds and gestures, to me
instantly comprehensible but so difficult to transliterate.

"Aficionado?" I heard in my ear. I came out of my reverie to find
him standing next to me. He was pointing at the Hemingway. I
wasn't an aficionado. But I wasn't sure what would work here—the
truth, or politeness.

"*Sukhovaty,*" I said, finally. "A bit dry."

"Sin to eat dry meat," the man nodded and moved away. He

did have a limp. He came back with a detective novel by a Russian writer. "Moist as a swamp," he said, pressing it on me.

"Thank you, no," I said, smiling and shaking my head.

He picked up the Hemingway and knocked its hard edge into my chest. "Then we must lubricate. *Teplenkogo ne zhelayete?*" ("You don't wish for something a bit warm?") He had said "you don't wish" rather than "you don't want," its courtliness an honoring of his visitor, though by virtue of its archaism it carried a faint note of ridicule, too. He had reduced "warm" to a diminutive—it was all but law if you were talking about food or drink. And he meant drink. There was an unmarked bottle amid a forest of cheap plastic bags under the book table. He scrubbed at two plastic thimbles with a rag that seemed like it could only make them dirtier. Seeing my expression, he said, "Alcohol kills all germs." Then, in open view, he filled the thimbles to the brim—the liquid was clear, like vodka—and touched the edge of his to mine gingerly. "To the friendship of the nations," he made the old Soviet toast, and threw his firewater into his mouth. I did the same. It burned my throat, but then seemed to go up rather than down, heat rising into my brain. His teeth were as crooked and gray as the columns of Oksana's apartment building. For lack of a chaser, he sniffed his sleeve as I'd been taught only gauche people did, then stuffed one fist into his flank and leaned the other on his precarious table. Miraculously, it remained standing. "Where from?" he demanded.

I wondered whether to deploy the saving answer of all Americans on sensitive ground: Canada. "America," I said, chancing the truth. I braced for the next question—"Jew?"—but he only made one of those untranslatable sounds—*gaw-gaw-gaw*, like a long-necked bird disturbed by intruders. It meant something like "A prized guest is among us!"

"I'm from here," I clarified. "Not here—but close."

"Well, fuck, we're all . . ." he started to say, then just shook his head, pulled out a pack of cheap cigarettes, offered me one, then withdrew them before I could reply—"No, you're a healthy American"—and lit one for himself. He smoked silently for a minute, undisturbed by the silence, sucking again on the cigarette before he'd exhaled the previous drag. He took care to blow the smoke away from me. "Read, young man, read," he said finally, pushing the Hemingway into me. "Young people don't read enough anymore." I reached for my wallet, but he only held out a finger to say no.

Part of it was the home brew, but as I walked on, I was filled with a warm feeling—for the man, for the people around me. Why? I had been expecting insult from him only a moment before. The relief of not hearing it? In her eloquent, knowing survey of Ukraine, the British journalist Anna Reid writes about the different kind of person visitors across history have encountered in Ukraine as opposed to Russia. It was in what would become Ukraine, not Russia, that Slavic Orthodoxy was born. The Vikings came to trade, intermarried—Waldemar became Volodymyr—and brought Christianity back from their encounters with Byzantium. (Volodymyr, the ruler responsible for the conversion to monotheism in 988, bid out the contract to all the religions, but Muslim teetotaling would not work, for "drinking is the joy of the Russes," and neither would the Jewish and Muslim objections to pork.) Christianity gained a high-end recruit: The Kievans, as they were known, constituted one of those advanced civilizations—the Aztecs, the Abbasids—now lost to history: They didn't allow corporal punishment, maintained courtly manners, and, in general, were "more unified, happier, stronger and more civilised than France herself," as a French observer wrote.

This glory soon came to an end, for the old, tiresome reasons: first, infighting; then the Mongols, who turned Kievan Rus back a thousand years and left it to languish while the more northern lands that would become Russia persisted because the Golden

Horde allowed the local princes to govern on its behalf. Perhaps this was fortune, of a kind. Later, visitors kept seeing a difference in the inheritance. In the middle of the seventeenth century, an Orthodox cleric from Aleppo reported that "anyone wishing to shorten his life by five or ten years should go to Muscovy." The monasteries there forbade laughter, religion police inspected the faithful for proper devotion, imbibers were exiled to Siberia, and users of tobacco got death. The cleric, a user of tobacco, wrote that "during those two years spent in Muscovy a padlock had been set on our hearts." Ukraine's sins—mosquito infestations, interminable religious services—seemed mild by comparison; its inhabitants "were to us boon companions and fellows like ourselves."

Nearly three hundred years later, Robert Byron, the great British travel writer, found in Moscow "a stifling air—how stifling I only realised on reaching Kiev, which preserves in some indefinable way its old university tradition of the humanities and allows one to breathe normally again." John Steinbeck, traveling around the USSR with Robert Capa after World War II: "Everyone had told us it would be different once we got outside Moscow, that the sternness and tenseness would not exist. And this was true . . . the people in Kiev did not seem to have the dead weariness of the Moscow people. They did not slouch when they walked, their shoulders were back, and they laughed in the streets." And this was after Ukraine spent the 1930s enduring a Moscow-manufactured famine that starved millions, while millions more, most of them middle-class farmers, were forcibly collectivized, killed, or deported to the Far East; and then, in the 1940s, World War II. Steinbeck thought the Ukrainian women were more attractive, too.

But what did I share with these people? Was it that I felt more at home with their sorrow than with all the diversion I had in the States? In coming back to the places that reared me, I could never reconcile with the feeling that here were grown men and women living, if not like animals—the competition for limited resources,

the readiness for violence—then like children of bad parents; like
people dependent on usually unaccountable forces; like people
without much of their own. But that helplessness coexisted with a
ferocious aptitude for survival that dwarfed that of any "indepen-
dent," "self-directed," and well-appointed life I knew in New York.

That was the true resourcefulness of my father and grandfather—
in very different ways, they knew how to do whatever it took. I
had never been tested—a privilege, but also a corner of myself
roped off in darkness. My elders wanted me to never have to know
how to be so resourceful, but in removing the "have to," they'd
thrown out the "to be," too. My grandfather managed to withhold
his secrets until well after I'd been shaped as a person. And my
father had been sending me and my questions away from the time
I was a child asking what he was up to on the stepladder from
which he always did his painting. They'd won—I was so much
not like them—and they'd lost, for the same reason. But for all
the American blessings I'd reaped, I couldn't make myself come
around to my new country. America was like a person who had
given gifts of great generosity—support where others wished to
knock down, protection where others wished to attack, opportu-
nity where others wished to deny—and my heart was beyond full
with gratitude. But it wasn't love. Try as I might, I could not make
myself fall in love.

Maybe I recognized something in Ivano-Frankovsk because it
had barely changed in two decades of freedom, the same reason
my grandfather felt so at home with Oksana: Here, they remained
Soviet creatures. (They did in Belarus, too, but I had no one there
anymore.) Having savaged for so long all that remained Soviet,
the detection of my own lingering Soviet self, like a bad spot
picked up on an X-ray, was bracing. In one thought, I was implacably American; in the next, irredeemably Soviet. I felt hopelessly
sundered.

But it wasn't as if I wished to live here. Perhaps the only way for me to be in Belarus was to be in Ukraine, but even here I could feel close to the people around me only as a visitor; if I came any nearer, the connection would dissolve. It didn't exist outside that fleeting, precarious moment. Meanwhile, if the Ukrainians around me had American passports, they would probably settle into American lives as self-accepting and unruffled as those I observed in south Brooklyn, whereas when I returned there, it would be to the old emotionally stateless solitude. My nation was neither old Soviet territory nor America. It wasn't on the map, had no place to gather in numbers. It was among those who couldn't, for whatever reason, ease into an answer. Sometimes one met a kinsman or kinswoman, in life or in the pages of a book, and one tried to create them between the pages of one's own writing. But that was as good as it got. It had never occurred to me that these pieces could be enough. All my attention had previously been on recovering the wholeness that had been mine until nine. Anywhere would have done. But it had to be wholeness.

It was cold, and I decided to find a place to warm up. Down an alley, past an only-in-that-part-of-the-world congregation—boxy sedan, one man in a black leather jacket, another with a man purse and trousers bunching over his pointy-toed shoes, a young girl all in pink prancing around the trunk, and a third man dressed either like Elvis or merely like himself, in a nearly fluorescent cream suit over a high-collared shirt of silk periwinkle—I found a belowground bar called Bunker. The hour—late morning—hardly precluded the presence of tipplers, but Bunker was polished and themed, the kind of nod to upscale clientele that kept away career drinkers. My only companions were three businessmen in suits that shone brighter than the lamps. They huddled over a huge Dell laptop, an early lunch and shot glasses around them.

Behind them was an engraved map of the territory in western

Ukraine controlled in 1944 by the Ukrainian Insurgent Army (UPA), which welcomed the Nazis as deliverers from Soviet rule. The bar, I realized, was made to look like a UPA bunker. Historians differ about the degree to which the UPA and other nationalist groups participated in the mass murder of Jews. But the city I was visiting, in which virtually no Jews continued to live, had been more than 60 percent Jewish in 1941. Its location on the railway line west to Poland, in whose death camps so much of European Jewry perished, made Ivano-Frankovsk the spout through which Ukrainian—and non-Ukrainian—Jewry was funneled. Sixty or seventy thousand died in the city itself; the rest were sent to the camps. (Ukraine lost 60 percent of its Jews, 1.5 million out of 2.5 million, a comparatively fortunate ratio. Poland lost more than 90 percent of its 3.5 million.)

Oksana's mother had seen it herself; she'd told her daughter about it. I'd asked Oksana once, back in Brooklyn, if she'd known any Jews. She named several distant acquaintances—a fellow counterwoman at the supermarket, the man at the recycling depot—but she also understood the drift of my question. "We were ordinary people," she said. "We weren't nationalists or the opposite. We went with the flow. No one talked about the war." I wondered what all this came to in practice—whether, if she had heard someone at her supermarket say what my grandfather had heard ("Quit pawing that bread with your grubby Jewish fingers"), she would have spoken up in his defense or remained silent. I was afraid to ask. There was no reason to be—she wouldn't answer me the wrong way. This truth was lost, too.

In all my walking that day, I didn't see a single commemoration. Many people in the West make the mistake of interpreting this as evidence of active anti-Semitism. But it doesn't feel that way when you're there. The citizens of Ivano-Frankovsk were guilty of doing nothing to commemorate the extent of specifically Jewish murder during the war. But they had been unable to do so during the Soviet period, when the required emphasis was on overall Soviet suffering; often, to save their children the trouble, the older people didn't pass on the information that Oksana's mother valued enough to pass on to her. And now, with more freedom, the focus was on Ukrainian aspirations and Ukrainian losses. Was this anti-Semitism? If so, it was passive. It took a great deal of consciousness, humanity, and education—and, perhaps, prosperity—to become the kind of person who wished to commemorate outside the tribe simply because it was the truth. The people I saw in Ukraine seemed to overflow with humanity. The consciousness seemed to have been whipped out of many of them. And the education was often withheld. All the same, how could I feel so at home among people who ignored—and had aided—a genocide that took hundreds of relatives and left me an extended family of fewer than a dozen?

I returned to Oksana's with frozen feet. She greeted me with the same reprimand and relief that must have greeted my father after he took too long on his first shopping trip in Vienna. She couldn't scold me like her own child, but she also wouldn't scold Misha if he were late and didn't call—I required special attention. Nothing mattered more than looking after one's own, at the expense of others if needed—unless one of those others was placed in one's formal care, in which case appearances took over, and a whole dinner could burn if it meant the guest was well looked after. Or so it was in my family. That Oksana was not part of it, no matter her ubiquity and closeness with us, meant that sometimes I was more polite to her than to even my own, and that sometimes I could be more honest. It wasn't a bad bargain. I thought of the way she and my father had never moved on from addressing each other by the formal "you," now understanding it in a new way. There were things better than closeness. Her status created boundaries in a family that had none. "What am I supposed to do with you, tell me?" she chided me indulgently now, and steered me to the dining table.

There, finally, I met Misha, her son and my birthday doppelganger, loping and sweet. It felt odd to—I knew things his mother felt about him that he didn't. Just as Oksana knew things about my parents that they didn't. Just as Misha surely carried information that they, and I, didn't about Oksana's experiences in New York.

With Tanya, Oksana's daughter, I tried to ingratiate myself by praising her mother's cooking. "My mother's cooking is no different or better than any other Ukrainian housewife's," she said curtly. My eyes "climbed my forehead" as I continued to pump her hand absentmindedly in the American way. Then I understood: She thought I was going to try to take advantage in some way. Entice Oksana into opening a café and make off with the profits—the only thing she could imagine, especially from a foreigner with all the power. Not even: Entice Oksana into opening a café—into just taking a chance. The Soviet way still prevailed here. To avoid trouble, avoid sticking your neck out in service to unguaranteed things.

I felt a prisoner's hunger. Oksana had made rabbit in sour cream, ribs with pickled cabbage, a radish salad, pickled watermelon, and a waiting table of cakes and profiteroles "Ukrainian style." An empty chair had in front of it a vodka-filled shot glass covered with a piece of black bread—a commemorative spot for Oksana's mother. The in-laws had arrived from their town with gifts from the village: canned river fish, canned zucchini, tomatoes marinated and brined. Also a five-gallon plastic drum of spring water that I belatedly discovered to contain not spring water but moonshine, and a huge jar of beet juice that had been fermenting for more than a week. A boy with jug ears and big teeth, some still finding their way, and a girl with a polite, serious look sat at the adults' table, but

Tanya's youngest had set herself up with an iPad inside a suitcase Oksana had dragged from the States. Flattery or the truth, all present praised the borshch to which I'd contributed, and drank to the honorary new Ukrainian at the table.

My contribution had been decidedly limited, but I felt a swelling, embarrassing pride all the same. It was different cooking for others—I understood why frying potatoes for Oksana made my grandfather so expansive (even if he probably didn't). Even though I'd tried to paint many walls and replace many faucets, I would never be the painter, builder, and craftsman my father was. But cooking supplied something of the same sense of . . . I couldn't pin down the word for it. Sitting at a writing chair, I used a part of myself that couldn't feel more essential, and the fulfillment of that, even when the writing was going badly, had no comparison. So it was a surprise to realize that wasn't enough. I needed to use my body. Was that because my elders had not really been mind people—safe haulers, furniture builders, haircutters, wall painters—and so there was an invisible birthright of physical labor I had failed to fulfill? Or was it simply that most boys had been less comprehensively kept from physical labor as boys, and so weren't as restless?

"In Moscow," the food writer Alexander Genis has written, "they say that the Ukrainian kitchen differs from the Russian like twins separated at birth. Having grown up without its older brother, [the Ukrainian kitchen] has taken on a lot of foreign influence." This is in keeping with the historical attitude of Russia toward Ukraine as "the little brother," on such vivid display in recent years in Crimea and eastern Ukraine. In Russian jokes, Ukrainians are the hicks, both capricious and self-inflating in their exasperating insistence on independence. But it's the Ukrainian countryside that always fed the Soviet Union. ("On business trips," as Genis points out, "Ukrainian delicacies were

the most effective form of bribery with hotel administrators.")
And it had fed Russia in the lean 1990s, when all was chaos after
the collapse of the Soviet Union. At Expo 67, in Montreal, it was
Ukrainian borshch (and Georgian kebabs) that represented the
Soviet Union. "In Kiev," Genis writes, "they fully agree with [the
Moscow] thesis—if you invert it completely."

I was not set free from the memorial table until I was dazed
from all I'd eaten and drunk. The sun was out in a late-day surge, so
I begged to go outside and try to waddle it off. In another sign of my
acceptance, I was told to round up the children and take them with
me; three bedrooms or not, children in confined spaces, like dogs,
needed occasional airing. I looked at Tanya for final confirmation,
but she didn't seem to object. The ill wind of first meeting—the
mandatory suspicion upon encounter with something unknown—
had seemingly passed.

Outside, the sun was so bright off the knee-high snow that I
couldn't open my eyes. That meant I had a hard time keeping track
of the children, but my hopeless stumbling around in the snow
was comic enough that I knew they were close by their hysterical
laughter. The broad, open smiles they wear in the photograph
I have of our outing—open-mouthed, glowing, those shambolic
teeth—feel endangered, because in just several years they will
begin to live in the world that put such different expressions on
the faces of the people I'd seen walking through town that day.
As their giggles echoed around the scraggly, barren winter trees
all around us, I understood in a different way why the first thing
I felt from Tanya was wariness; why Oksana had gone halfway
around the world to earn money even if it meant being mute and
alone; why, all those years ago, my parents had wished so badly to
shelter and save me.

OKSANA'S BORSHCH (V)

Time: 1 hour, 10 minutes   Serves: 8

The beet must not lose its color.
—Oksana

3 medium beets
12 cups water
3 medium Idaho potatoes, peeled
and cubed
1 medium parsnip, peeled and
sliced into disks, the larger
slices halved
1/4 head cabbage, roughly
chopped
1 jalapeño, seeded and minced
1 1/2 tablespoons kosher salt, plus
additional to taste
3 tablespoons vegetable oil

1 medium onion, chopped
2 large carrots, peeled and grated
1 heaping tablespoon tomato
paste
4 large garlic cloves, put through
a garlic press and divided
1 1/2 teaspoons ground coriander
1 1/2 teaspoons curry powder
2 tablespoons white vinegar or
lemon juice
1 teaspoon sugar
1 bunch dill, chopped
sour cream to taste (optional)

THE DAY BEFORE:

1. Cover the beets with water and bring to a boil in a pot with the lid mostly on. Boil until a small knife goes through easily. (About an hour— you may have to top up the water now and then.) Leave the skin on and refrigerate. This step helps the beet keep its color and not blanch when it's cooking the next day.

THE DAY OF:

1. Bring the 12 cups of water to a boil, then lower the heat to medium and add the potatoes, parsnip, cabbage, jalapeño, and 1 tablespoon of the salt. Cover, with the lid slightly ajar, and cook for 30 minutes.

2. Meanwhile, heat the oil in a sauté pan over medium heat. Add the onion and cook until golden brown. Add the carrots and sauté until fully cooked. Add the tomato paste and half the pressed garlic and cook for another minute. Set aside.

3. Peel the beets under running water—the skin should come off in your hands—and cut them into small pieces.

AFTER THE SOUP HAS BEEN GOING FOR 30 MINUTES:

1. Add the coriander and curry. (Oksana always adds them toward the end, so their flavor keeps.) When I asked her what a Ukrainian might think of curry in her borshch, she said, "We're Americans, aren't we?"

2. Add the onion mixture to the soup, deglazing the pan with a little water and adding that to the soup as well. Add the beets and the remaining ½ tablespoon salt and turn the heat down to low.

3. Check the taste. Does the soup need salt? For a little acid, add the vinegar or lemon juice. (Oksana uses vinegar.) Add the sugar, the remaining garlic, and a generous helping of the dill.

4. Taste again. At this stage, Oksana usually adds a little more salt—"The day after it's made, borshch always tastes like it needs salt."

5. Turn the heat to high; at the first sign of boiling, shut it off or the beets will start to lose color.

Leave for the next day—the flavor will concentrate overnight. When reheating, reheat only what will be served, as repeated boiling will blanch the beets. Serve with a dollop of sour cream.

✦

BANOSH (POLENTA) WITH MUSHROOMS AND SHEEP'S MILK FETA (V)

Time: 25 minutes   Serves: 4

Banosh comes from the Carpathians, the prettiest unknown mountains in Europe and home to the Hutsuls, pastoral highlanders who still take their sheep flocks to high pasture for summer grazing. Banosh was their bacon and beans. Cornmeal traveled easily, and the sheep were right there—summer was a good time for milk production, the lambs just having been born—as were the porcini. By Hutsul tradition, the men had to cook all sheep-related dishes, including banosh, which had to be prepared in a cast-iron pot over an open fire so the dish would be "impregnated" with smoke. (It's nice when men take over the kitchen, but you see how they start talking among themselves.)

Banosh was an autumn dish in Oksana's household. "After we got the wild mushrooms from the woods," she says, "I threaded a thick, sturdy needle with fat yarn and then ran it through the mushrooms, one by one. You hang it over the stove, cover gently with cheesecloth so the flies don't get at it, and after 2–3 days of cooking one thing or another, you'll have dried mushrooms."

If you can find dried porcini, as in the recipe for **Cabbage Vareniki (Dumplings) with Wild Mushroom Gravy,** *use the same amount (around 1.5 ounces dried) and soak them in hot water, as that recipe specifies. Otherwise, ordinary button mushrooms will do—this dish packs plenty of flavor.*

1¼ cups milk	Ground coriander, to taste
2 cups sour cream	Curry powder, to taste
⅔ cup fine cornmeal	Paprika, to taste
Kosher salt, to taste	1 clove garlic, put through a
Sugar, to taste	garlic press
1 tablespoon vegetable oil	Handful of chopped dill
8 ounces mushrooms, sliced	Sheep's milk feta cheese, for
1 bay leaf	serving

POLENTA

1. Combine the milk and the sour cream in a large pot, stir until the sour cream has blended with the milk, and heat over medium heat until boiling, stirring frequently to prevent scorching.

2. Lower to a simmer—"it needs to breathe"—and pour in the cornmeal little by little, stirring as you go, to prevent clumping. (Oksana insists that only a wooden stirring spoon is right for the task, per Hutsul tradition, but a whisk does the job fine, too, in addition to giving the mixture more fluffiness.) Cook, stirring, until quite thick, 10–15 minutes. Season to taste with salt and sugar.

MUSHROOMS

1. Heat the oil in a sauté pan over medium-high heat. Add the mushrooms, bay leaf, and salt to taste and sauté until the mushrooms have let off their liquid and it has evaporated. Add the coriander, curry, and paprika (the piquancy of the paprika works well with the sweetness of the mushrooms) and sauté until the mushrooms are browned.

2. Stir in the garlic, and sprinkle with dill.

3. Serve the mushrooms over the polenta and crumble some feta on top.

Skip the feta and mushrooms and you have a fine breakfast base. The tang of the sour cream also begs for the sweetness of something like pork, so consider topping with your favorite cut. Or just buy extra rib tips when you're making **Braised Rib Tips with Pickled Cabbage** *(recipe follows).*

✤

BRAISED RIB TIPS WITH PICKLED CABBAGE

Time: 1 hour, 30 minutes　　Serves: 6

½ cup vegetable oil
2 pounds pork rib tips
1 large onion, chopped
1 pound sauerkraut
½ pound fresh cabbage, roughly
　shredded (optional)

12 pitted prunes, chopped
3 garlic cloves, put through a
　garlic press
½ bunch dill, chopped
2 tablespoons chopped parsley

Note: If the sauerkraut is too sour for your taste, rinse it under cold water or add the ½ pound of fresh cabbage. As for the rib tips—the triangular ends that come off spare ribs if a butcher is trying to make the ribs more neatly rectangular—Oksana uses them because they are inexpensive and tasty; other cuts work well, too.

1. Heat the oil in a deep cooking pot over medium heat. Add the rib tips, cover, and cook, stirring occasionally, until browned, 10 to 15 minutes.

2. Turn the heat to low and cook for another 20 minutes, covered, stirring once in a while to make sure they're not sticking.

3. Add the onion to the pork. Raise the heat to medium-low and cook the onion for 10 minutes.

4. Add the sauerkraut/cabbage to the pork and onion. Oksana doesn't mix the ingredients at first. (The liquid from the cabbage should help things along.) Cover and keep at medium-low heat. After 5–10 minutes, gently mix the contents. Cover and cook for another 20 minutes. No salt or pepper necessary—the dish is getting all the flavoring it needs from its ingredients.

5. Add the prunes, garlic, dill, and parsley and cook for 5 minutes more.

✤

"SAND" CAKE (COCOA-LEMON LAYER CAKE) (V)

Time: 45 minutes   Serves: 12

The "sand" in the name of this "special-occasion" cake refers only to the Ukrainian word for the way shortbread pastry sheets crumble—not the texture you'll have in your mouth! After the filling soaks in, you'll be reminded that it's not so far from Ukraine to Vienna: It's a delicate and airy improvement on any slice of Napoleon cake you've ever had.

¼ cup flour	¼ cup lemon juice
1 tablespoon cocoa powder	2 teaspoons vanilla extract
2 cups milk, divided	6 prebaked shortbread pastry
¾ cup sugar	sheets (approximately 9 by 7
¾ cup butter	inches)

Note: Shortbread pastry sheets—pesochnye korzhi (peh-SOTCH-knee-yeah kor-ZHI)—are commonly available in Eastern European food markets, but if there isn't one near you, make them yourself using the recipe below. They should have the consistency of butter cookies—shortbread—rather than pie crusts.

Note: The milk mixture will take a while to cool after step 4, so you may wish to schedule something else to use up the time.

1. Whisk together the flour and cocoa powder. Whisk in 1 cup of the milk until smooth. Doing all this in a graduated measuring cup with a pour spout will make step 3 easy.

2. In a small pot, bring the remaining 1 cup of milk to a boil.

3. When the milk comes to a boil, reduce the heat so it doesn't scald, and pour in the flour mixture slowly, in a thin stream.

4. While continuously stirring with a wooden spoon, turn up the heat and bring the mixture to a boil. Lower the temperature and simmer for 2 minutes, making sure to keep on stirring.

5. Remove from the heat and let cool completely to room temperature. You can accelerate the cooling by placing the pot in a wider container filled with ice water.

6. Using an electric mixer or a food processor, cream the sugar and butter until fluffy. Slowly mix in the lemon juice and vanilla.

7. Once the thickened milk has cooled, add it to the butter mixture one tablespoon at a time, using the mixer.

Note: Acid like lemon juice can cause dairy to separate, but if you see clumping, don't worry—it won't affect the taste or be visible in the final result.

8. Crumble one of the pastry sheets using a rolling pin. Spread the rest out on a countertop. Reserve some of the filling for covering the sides of the cake, and divide the rest among the pastry sheets. (Or "go with God," as Oksana says—eyeball how much is right for each sheet as you go without first spreading them out.) Spread the filling almost to the edge of each layer, stack the layers one on top of the other, and coat the sides with filling using a spatula. Then cover the uppermost layer and sides with the crumbs from the crushed sheet.

Note: The cake needs to sit so it can soak up the filling and won't crumble when you cut into it. Overnight is best. Oksana "puts it on the balcony, and by the morning it's ready."

✢

PESOCHNYE KORZHI

Time: 2 hours (including 1-hour wait)   Makes: 6 rounds

2 sticks (1 cup) butter, softened
1 cup confectioners' sugar
1 egg yolk
1 whole egg

2 cups flour
½ teaspoon baking powder
1 pinch salt

1. Using an electric mixer or a food processor, cream the butter and confectioners' sugar until smooth.

2. Add the yolk and mix until fully incorporated, then add the whole egg and mix until smooth.

3. In a separate bowl, whisk together the flour, baking powder, and salt. Beat into the butter mixture with a wooden spoon. Depending on the size of the eggs, you may need more or less flour. The result should be soft and a little sticky.

4. Wrap the dough in plastic wrap and leave in the fridge for an hour.

5. Preheat the oven to 350 degrees.

6. Divide the dough into 6 pieces. Roll each one into a thin disk between sheets of parchment paper.

7. Cut around the edges of each pastry disk to make a smooth edge. Circles work as well as rectangles; if so, each one should be uniform in diameter (about 7 inches).

8. Divide among 2 baking sheets, with the bottom parchment intact. Place on the middle oven rack and bake until the edges become golden, approximately 15 minutes, switching the position of the baking sheets halfway through.

✣

PART III

CHAPTER 13

January 2015

What to cook in the dark

✤

Outside, a soft snow lined the railings of the balcony. I went out there several times a day to smoke. I ate little—food hadn't lost its taste, but hunger was rare—though cigarettes were as delicious as a good meal. I wasn't hungry, for the first time in my life. Wasn't thinking about what I would eat, how I'd cook it, where I'd get the best ingredients for the least money. I was dazed by how much time that left unclaimed. I felt spectral. The cigarettes helped. I inhaled; the orange end lit up and ate a little paper; I still existed.

I was in a friend's apartment because I'd rented mine out to make extra money—I had been supposed to go to Mexico for a month. It took me two hours to leave bed in the morning, so a trip abroad seemed unimaginable. But people said I should go, try to distract myself.

People were full of well-meaning counsel. Most of it was about finding ways to think about anything other than what I was feeling while presumably, behind the curtain, it made its slow way off the stage. "Time," they said. "You'll get better," they said. These comments made it hard to believe they were paying attention. So I doubled down on my disability—in my impairment, I performed a greater impairment, like my grandfather pissing himself to get out of the draft. I wanted people to say something like "It's very bad, isn't it," or "There's nothing I can say that'll help you, so why

don't we just sit here, I'll hold your hand, and if you'd like to weep
into my shoulder, that would be fine." But I didn't have the self-
understanding to ask for that, so I just wished someone would catch
my frequency. I became so despondent that I told an old friend—he
called me almost every day, though with platitudes—I couldn't see
him again. Another friend had said it: "You'll never have the same
friends again."

I was destroyed for a reason men are not supposed to be destroyed, or at least show it: love that had failed (again). Outwardly,
Amy (not her name), the woman with whom I'd fallen in love two
years earlier, in 2013, could not have been less like me—her people
could have come over on the *Mayflower*. But we found the other so
interesting that we spoke for hours—three hours, five hours, six
hours. We read the same kinds of books, and hoped to find the same
things in them. We looked at the world with the same doubtful,
laughing eye. She was neither neurotic nor repressed; was deeply
connected to her feelings but not owned by them—something people often lay claim to but rarely carry off. Certainly I didn't have it,
but she didn't mind the intensity.

When she and I met, two years after the end of my relationship with Alana, I was dating with the terrified industry of a late
bloomer starting a second career. Nothing worked. With American
women, I felt Russian; with Russian women, American; with Jews
of either nationality, like a heathen.

I was as interested in one among them, Yvonne (not her name),
as I'd been in any of the hundred women I'd met. She had com-
pleted the Camino de Santiago, the five-hundred-mile religious
walk across northern Spain. She had worked with orphans in Ro-
mania. She was well read, conscientious, so pretty. But only she said
something I'll never forget.

Yvonne was skeptical and guarded, as many New York women
have reasons to be, so I'd set to melting her brick wall, as I had
with so many others. I spent hours crafting e-mails balanced be-

tween wit, sincerity, and intelligence. When we went out, I worked so hard to get her to laugh that you would have been forgiven, were you at the next table, for assuming here was someone doing a dry run of his stand-up routine.

Eventually, my fever eased enough for her to get to say some things, too. When she did, I didn't feel any of the connection I'd been certain was there. She was, indeed, smart, interesting, and accomplished—but it wasn't the kind of chemical match that makes you unable to sleep. Feeling like a madman, I began to back out. Yvonne became upset, and wrote this message: "You looked at me like I was a refrigerator and you just couldn't put your finger on what you wanted to take. Like you have some craving for some feeling that you can't identify. And then instead of discerning it, you eat whatever is there until you're sick and too exhausted and full to want anything more."

It wasn't Yvonne I was interested in. It was in not being alone. Most people mourn the end of an eight-year-relationship, and many would choose sealing the wound through serial dating over figuring out what had caused it. But with me, it was an addiction. Being with Alana from twenty-four—the age I moved away from my parents—to thirty-two had concealed it. So had the fact that, whereas it was I, the single child, whom my parents wished to keep near, it wasn't them I was desperate to have close but, in a person's experience of intimacy, their reincarnation: a romantic partner. A reasonable thing—unless it caused problems. And it did, though it wasn't until Yvonne's message that the real reason—the addiction, which had until then worn the camouflage of a blameless desire to meet someone—became impossible to ignore. An evening alone at home without prospects harbored something unbearable—I couldn't focus, didn't eat, just paced the apartment. I didn't need to sleep with someone—it was enough, simply, for there to be a person in the mix. But that I needed. It turned out I was as incapable of being alone as any of my elders.

The discovery of all this was as surreal as realizing that as an American adult seventy years after the war, my grandmother dead for a decade, I devoured food with the same desperation she had in 1945. The hungers came from the same place, the trauma-derived mother-hunger that won't give you a moment to wonder if you're really hungry underneath all that worry. Unless, somehow, you free yourself of the worry—of the mother-hunger itself. But how? The hunger and the worry—they're home.

Yvonne's judgment was like discovering that an illness I thought I'd survived by distancing myself from my family had actually entered the bone long before, and so I carried it still, in ever-metastasizing ways. I met Amy before I grasped the solution, but after I realized there was a problem. Meeting her held out the magnificent possibility that maybe there wasn't, like the doctor calling to say you were accidentally read someone else's results and you were fine after all.

I did go to Mexico. I set my alarm for two hours earlier than I needed. The first hour to keep pressing the snooze button—it was only while I slept that I didn't feel pain; contrary to expectation, my dreams were mostly untroubled—the second to work on leaving the bed. I tried to will it. I imagined myself separating from the useless body on the bed; the cover turning back; my feet touching the floor. Perhaps this would be the day I would want some breakfast. I made deals—I would count to twenty, and then. I would count to fifty, and then. But the floor was cold, the kitchen far away, and the comforter thick and warm. I wanted its weight. It reminded me I was there, because hours went by during which my mind was elsewhere, and when it returned, I couldn't say where it had gone.

In bed, I would sit up. Then slide back down. Turn over and rise on all fours, like a dog, hoping it would serve as a prelude to liftoff, but then my arms would collapse and I would fall prostrate. Every part of my body worked—certain parts of this frozen house were quite thick with action—but I couldn't fire the neurons that would make them work all at once. Sometimes, in my chest, I felt an anthill—very small things crawled around in there and droned. Sometimes a stone; sometimes wire-like lines inflamed by rough touch. I saw this inflammation mapped as if on an MRI. When my mind wasn't blank, it was the opposite: I kept hearing my mother intone, in Russian, "Oh, it feels very bad, very bad." Had she ever uttered those words? The apparition-mother quaked, held herself in her arms, rocked back and forth—none of these gestures like my mother's—and said, over and over, "Oh, it feels very bad, very bad." Other than that, I kept hearing a voice say, in Russian, "And what is your name?" "And what is your name?" "And what is your name?" "And what is your name?" "And what is your name?" Sometimes it sounded as if the voice was saying it to mean "And who do you think you are?" and sometimes just informationally.

I had spent the preceding twenty-five years in a frenzy of productivity. Every morning, I mapped out my days to the quarter hour. I took pride in my efficiency. I was out of bed as soon as the alarm clock went off. The two-minute increments of loose time in line at the supermarket that others used to check social media, I used to read two more pages. I was a good machine. This is where you would expect to hear all the costs—*the great human mess does not submit to such formulas; he was efficient, but without friends or lovers or pastimes*; et cetera. But none of this was true. When factors outside my control interfered, I adjusted. I made time for friends and lovers and much else. I just always had my eye on the clock. The one real cost was that I couldn't allow things to take their own time rather than mine.

In that bed in which I spent hours every morning trying to rise, my horror as my eyes crossed the clock was proportional to each quarter-hour increment that passed without action.

I did make it up the morning of the Mexico trip. I managed to put some things in a suitcase. (Maybe I was getting better?) My frugality didn't permit me to take a taxi to the airport, so I bounced on subways for nearly two hours. I hardly noticed the time—mind-vacating paralysis makes the downside of frugality easier to ignore. At the Aeroméxico gate, I made no effort to dry the tears that dropped from my eyes; I couldn't summon the usual energy to think about what the people around me would think. The gate agent who scanned my ticket neither smiled nor looked away. For this I was grateful. It was a non-American person's reaction. She did not wish to cheer me nor pretend it wasn't happening.

From the Cancún airport, I rode for two hours to the spot on the northern shore of the Yucatán from which ferries departed to the island where I was heading, for a friend's wedding. Then I took the ferry. The island did not allow vehicles—it had no paved roads, only sand—and a golf cart delivered me to my humble hotel. Recent rains had turned every walkway to mud. I had dinner. I smoked half a pack of cigarettes. I slept—sleep was the most welcome part of the day. When I woke up, I hired one of the golf carts to take me to the ferry dock. I got on the next one back to the mainland. There, I hired an expensive car—even my frugality had fallen away—to take me back to Cancún, and then I paid Aeroméxico a lot of money to put me on the last flight of the day back to New York. I was back under the thick down comforter before midnight.

In Andrew Solomon's lucid, compassionate, and frightening book *The Noonday Demon*, the account of the onset of his first episode of severe depression goes on for many pages; his approached incrementally and without linearity, like an ambivalent love interest.

Mine seems to have been many years in the making, but when the time came, it happened in no more than several hours, like that cliché about losing money gradually and then all at once.

My connection with Amy felt so singular that it obscured the moral degradation of what we were doing, something neither of us had ever imagined we could. She was married. With children, to a good, talented man with whom the original passion had turned into something less peaked—an old, familiar story. After a year and a half, I finally managed to break it off. Two weeks later, I received a message from Amy saying she would leave her husband.

For the next month, my heart felt like a balloon filled with too much. Because Amy was, short of a miracle, past childbearing age, I would be giving up the chance to have children of my own, which I very much wanted, and committing myself to a city I'd wanted to leave for a long time. It all seemed worth it. For once, I'd let go of all my unreasonable expectations in order to live in the real world, glorious and imperfect, with all the other normal people. This prospect filled me with relief rather than fear. I took comfort in the symmetry with Alana's experience: The man she had met, whom she was about to marry, was also older, and had children from a previous marriage.

But Amy did not leave. Her husband, ears finally open after years of distracted nodding, came to and said all the right things. It was December, an unhelpful month. I had gone to a country home borrowed from friends to try to finish my second novel, so I was surrounded by silence and snow. After receiving the news, I was overcome by a terrible feeling—feverish, queasy, cold; dead and bursting at once. My chest was slowly filling with the drone that would be its unleaving presence for months. I lay down on the living room couch and did not get up until the next morning. I did not get up even then. Who knows if I would have plummeted in this way had my intense disappointment after the end of my relationship with Alana not started me on the descent. But I did.

After two days without food or even the coffee without which life had previously seemed unimaginable, I realized I was incapacitated and reluctantly called my parents, who came and brought me back to New Jersey, as my place was already rented—I kicked myself out whenever I could to make a little money to live. I spent the next week in bed or smoking on the balcony in my father's warm jacket, watching the reservoir in front of their apartment building freeze over. I read through Graham Greene, his books the right combination of bleakness and beauty. Grief is devouring, but if it makes room for the self-centeredness of self-pity, sometimes the world feels like everything it's saying, it's saying about you.

> Shut-eye's the answer to all, isn't it. . . .
> Saturday came and passed, then Sunday began its long
>   course. . . .
> For it only deepened my sense of being without parentage.

My parents made my bed, and fed me, and even made themselves say nothing when I smoked on the balcony, though I knew my father would throw out the jacket after I left. But they couldn't hide their terror—"It's been a week, shouldn't you pull yourself together?" my father said—nor my mother restrain her desire to keep having explained to her, over and over, what had happened and why. I called the friend with the empty apartment and, on a frozen January day, moved under her comforter. Her apartment building happened to sit across from mine, rendering my exile cruelly comic, and surely metaphorical, too: I was only one hundred yards from home, but could come no closer. The restraining order was against myself.

The Mexico trip laid me out for three days. As a snowstorm piled up outside, dampening further the already dampened sound of the world, I stayed under the comforter and read Andrew Solomon's book. It had a sick urgency; in the pages of his clear-eyed and deeply empathetic story, I was seeing myself as I couldn't in the eyes of some friends. But the more I recognized, the more afraid I became.

> That vital sense of purpose that is the opposite of depression. . . . Grief is a humble angel who leaves you with strong, clear thoughts and a sense of your own depth. Depression is a demon who leaves you appalled. . . . Racked by this thing no one else seemed to be able to see. . . . Every second of being alive hurt me. . . . You cannot gain pleasure from anything.

That was the first five pages. The book had 443.

On the fourth day, I became so afraid that I sprang out of bed, as if to prove to myself that our stories weren't alike, that I was getting better. I was cold. I was cold all the time, even though my friend's high-rise heated wantonly. Pacing the small living room, I felt as dizzy, feverish, and chilled as if I didn't have the comforter wrapped around me, its tips "cleaning the floor," as the Russian went. (In my haze, I heard my dead grandmother say, "Take care, the tips are cleaning the floor.") I stopped and gazed out the wide windows—late on a weekday morning, the world at work, there was a man pacing the living room in T-shirt, boxers, and a massive down comforter, its tips cleaning the floor. I sat down on my friend's sectional (she was of Russian descent, and less ambivalent about it than me, which meant that her living room was incomplete without a sectional sofa) and dialed my grandfather. I knew my parents wouldn't have said anything about my situation to him; whether to Oksana, I wasn't sure. I pleaded for her to pick up, but his voice came on and I had to go through ten minutes about whether I had all the shampoo and toothpaste I needed. Finally, he gave her the phone.

"Can I come cook with you?" I blurted out. I was about to mention the borshch in Ivano-Frankovsk to reassure her it didn't have to go badly, but before I could, she said, "Yes. When? Tomorrow?"

"Today?" I said. "Right now?"

"Come right now."

Yes, they had told her.

I hadn't left the apartment in days, and I'd just signed up to travel an hour each way. I dressed myself, then sat back down on the sofa, already sweaty and spent. According to Russian superstition, a person must sit down before a long trip—his or her last peace for a while. I sat there so long I collected enough luck for ten trips. Does the luck still accrue if you don't go on the trip? I stood and went outside.

Watching cars flood down the street, I was overcome by a monstrous new feeling—if I stepped forward, the pain would end, as it did when I went to sleep, only that this sleep would go on forever. I stood, frozen; the light changed, then changed again. I remained on the curb not because I was remembering all the people who loved me, or thinking of all the books I wanted to write, or because my grandmother had fought so hard to remain alive. Because I was in shock. Every day, I awoke with a hope: *Perhaps today I'll get better.* But I was getting worse. Tears in my eyes, I backed away from the curb and took the far side of the sidewalk, just in case. Once I was in the subway, the long ride was welcome. For an hour, I didn't have to do anything.

On the ten-block walk from the subway to my grandfather's, I practiced smiling. Like a wrestler before a match, I flexed my shoulders, rolled my neck, pursed my lips, raised my eyebrows.

I made myself utter phrases such as "No, nothing new on the love front" and conjured scent-deflecting jokes such as "You offer me shampoo one more time and you owe me twenty dollars." And then I was there, in the glazed, sweet-smelling heat of their apartment.

For some reason, my grandfather looked different. Maybe it only seemed so to my addled brain, but he was stepping more gingerly than I recalled, the television was louder than usual, and he seemed content to sit in front of it even after I'd come. He may have been exaggerating the first; my stricken ears may have been exaggerating the second; but appearances would go last, and I knew he wouldn't permit himself to reveal greater interest in a Russian game show than in his grandson unless some mental levee had given. Or had he gotten very old at some point? Had Oksana's pampering made it less visible? Had I not noticed because I now saw him so frequently that the shift was too incremental to grasp?

It was as if my own sunken-eyed grayness, like a perverse borrowing from a magical-realist novel, was suddenly his. I hadn't thought of it since, but several nights before, I had dreamed of him. He was under a Soviet blanket—the duvet cover opened through a rhombus in the middle, not a slit down a side—and smiling too hard, the gold aflame in his teeth. He was supplicating, not joyful. "Please, no, why, there's no need," he kept saying. Begging, in a way I'd never heard him beg. Whom would he permit himself to beg but death?

"What are we making?" Oksana said.

I swiveled around the kitchen, but nothing cohered in my mind.

"Fried pork belly with stuffed dumplings in a mushroom gravy. Fritters with strawberry jam for dessert." She put her hand on her waist. "How does that sound?"

"Like a heart attack," I said and smiled one of the smiles I'd practiced.

"Well, it's not time for salads," she said, looking me over.

Not trusting myself to remain steady, and remembering that a cook prefers minimal intervention, I hid behind my phone camera. If Oksana would cook and narrate, I would chronicle. She stripped the hide from the pork belly, pressing her fingers into it as she went. "They didn't burn the hair off this pig," she said. "They used some kind of chemical. If this was a properly raised pig, this hide would peel off like a sticker." The phone rang in the living room.

"Arkady, I'm not home!" she yelled out. "I'm not here."

"Fine, fine," he said as he shuffled toward the phone.

Now she was pawing the belly—"If this was my pig, raised on milk, believe me, this belly would feel like a cloud. But I'll have to add a little water to this after I sear it, or it'll be tough." I smiled weakly behind the phone. She was "tying up" my ears.

"Oksana!" the shout came from the living room. "It's for you!"

She and I exchanged the same look, and I laughed an unpracticed laugh. He appeared in the kitchen doorway, the belly entering first. "You two will be ready to hang out a shingle soon," he said. He pulled a wad of twenties out of a pocket. "First reservation is mine." He nodded toward his water glass in the living room. "I hope this establishment will pour something stronger." He had stopped drinking completely because of his prostate.

Just then, the tears I'd held back all morning flailed forward. They were about him, not me, though surely it all got mixed up on the way. To hide them, I put down my phone and clamped my hands around his neck. His body was an old baby's—the skin of his neck was smooth, and his hair was soft as feathers and boyishly cropped; my parents had just visited, and my father had given him a trim. My grandfather honked shyly, awkwardly—he wasn't used to this kind of endearment from me. Oksana watched us from the running sink.

The video of that afternoon doesn't clarify whether the film-maker's obtuse questions—

Oksana: And we let the cabbage boil until we know it's
    ready.
Filmmaker: And how do we know it's ready?
Oksana: Well, we try it.

Filmmaker: But how will the jam get inside the fritters?
Oksana: You slice them open with a knife.

—have to do with his culinary callowness or his disability. But the cook he's filming answers him patiently, even when she can't answer, which occurs twice. The first time it's because periodically, the film-maker tries to focus and ask things like how much flour, exactly, and how much sugar. The cook can't answer—she can eyeball-pour the right amount of flour, but she can't give you a number. How much salt? As much as feels right in the small of the palm.

The other difficulty occurs when the filmmaker asks why the recipe is this but not that. Why must the cabbage be boiled before it goes inside the dumplings? The cook stares, dumbfounded. "Are you going to make dumplings with raw potato as well?" she says.

"But the pickled cabbage is perfectly edible even without cook-ing, isn't it?" he says.

"I guess," she concedes. "But it's too crunchy." She shrugs again. "This is how my mother did it, and how my grandmother did it. This is how I know."

Eventually I got rid of the phone. The cabbage was ready by then, so I rolled out the dough Oksana had made, then rolled it back up, chopping the tube into two-inch cylinders that I flattened into vaguely circular receptacles for spoonfuls of cooked cabbage and caramelized onion. Then I tried to pleat them closed. This felt like a cross between rolling a cigarette and trying to make sure nothing would fall out of your taco. It requires a little dexterity in the best of times, and my manual elegance was at a low just then. But for no reason at all, I had a hand for it, and I pleated away like a maestro. Oksana managed to express her approval without those excessive exultations that make you feel like a child.

Cooking is making something where there was nothing. That something happens to keep you alive—you can eat raw cabbage, but not, indeed, raw potato. It is the literal opposite of the emptying out of depression. Only something so elemental could do it—because your emptying is elemental. For a minute, the pain is eclipsed by a vision of a resuscitated existence. During that minute, you rush to offer bargains (because you believe in deities now). Now you will treat unremarkable routine as the greatest of gifts. You will not wait for pain to remember that painlessness is a blessing. But then the good feeling slips away. It really is like an eclipse.

Oksana set the table, but I couldn't put any of it in my mouth, even though the scent would've woken a dead man. I said I'd eaten before coming, but she knew I was lying. I never ate enough before leaving home that I wouldn't be hungry all over again once I got there. To her, it didn't count unless you ate it, so she was upset until I told her I'd take some home.

My grandfather and I made something that afternoon, too. We stumbled onto a new way of being together. As always, he wanted me close, but, as always—our conversations about his life long complete—we had little to say to each other. It had never occurred to us that there was another person in the apartment I could come to see. Oksana and I would cook, and he would be in the next room, near but not across from or next to—finally, the right distance.

CABBAGE *VARENIKI* (DUMPLINGS)
WITH WILD MUSHROOM GRAVY (V)

Time: 2 hours   Serves: 6

Patsyuk opened his mouth, looked at the vareniki, *and opened his
mouth wider still. At that moment, a* varenik *popped out of the bowl,
splashed into the sour cream, turned over on the other side, leaped up,
and flew straight into his mouth. Patsyuk ate it up and opened his
mouth again, and another* varenik *went through the same performance.
The only trouble Patsyuk took was to munch it up and swallow it.*

—GOGOL, *"The Night Before Christmas"*

*If you want to see Ukrainians in August, head to the countryside—everyone's
picking mushrooms. "Quiet hunting," they call it. The prize is the humbly
named "white mushroom," but don't mistake it for the mild, button-like main-
stay of American supermarkets. The Ukrainian white mushroom is what the
French call cèpes, and the Italians porcini: nutty, creamy grandees whose sight
and aroma stir something Proustian in every European. In the States, they're
more commonly available in dried form, which you want anyway, as it's more
pungent than the fresh version.*

*This vegetarian dish shows up on many Ukrainian tables during Advent
(Saint Philip's Fast in Ukraine), when meat is proscribed. You won't miss it after
you taste the mushrooms in this gravy.*

*Note: It's worth making this dish in alternating steps, as below, since several
of the steps require somewhat lengthy cooking times and there might as well be
two things going at once.*

FILLING

1½ pounds sauerkraut	Kosher salt and black pepper, to
2 tablespoons vegetable oil, plus	taste
additional if necessary	3 garlic cloves, put through a
2 onions, diced	garlic press

MUSHROOM GRAVY

1½ ounces dried porcini	2 tablespoons vegetable oil
mushrooms (a bit over 1 cup)	1 onion, diced
1 medium carrot, diced	2–3 tablespoons flour
2 bay leaves	1–2 garlic cloves, put through a
10 whole peppercorns	garlic press
Kosher salt	

DOUGH

3$\frac{1}{2}$ cups flour	$\frac{1}{2}$ teaspoon salt
1 egg	$\frac{2}{3}$ cup warm water

TO FINISH

1 tablespoon vegetable oil	1 bunch fresh dill, chopped
2 garlic cloves, put through a garlic press	

FOR THE FILLING:

1. In a large pot, bring around 6 cups of unsalted water to a boil (sauerkraut is well salted). Add the sauerkraut with its juices. After returning to a boil, cover, lower the heat to medium, and simmer for about 20 minutes, or until soft. Drain. When the sauerkraut is cool enough to handle, squeeze out any remaining water. Transfer to a cutting board and chop finely.

2. While the sauerkraut is boiling, heat the oil in a large pan. Add the diced onions and sauté until golden brown. Salt to taste. Transfer half of the onions to a bowl and set aside for use later.

3. Add the chopped sauerkraut to the pan with the remaining onion and season to taste with salt and pepper. Stir in the garlic, adding oil if necessary. Sauté over medium-low heat to get rid of remaining moisture, about 15 minutes. Set aside to cool.

FOR THE GRAVY:

1. Cover the mushrooms with 2 cups of hot water and let soak for 20 minutes.

2. Remove the mushrooms from the liquid and rinse under running water to remove any grit. Strain the mushroom liquid through cheesecloth or a couple of paper towels lining a strainer and reserve. Finely chop the mushrooms.

3. In a medium pot, combine the mushrooms, their strained liquid, the carrot, bay leaves, peppercorns, and 2 cups water and bring to a boil. Season lightly with salt. Turn down to a simmer and cook uncovered for about 40 minutes, or until the mix has just a little liquid left. Season with salt to taste.

4. Meanwhile, heat the oil in a medium pan and sauté the last diced onion over medium-high heat until golden.

5. Lower the heat to medium, mix in the flour (add a third tablespoon if you want thicker gravy), and continue cooking until the flour has disappeared and the mixture is golden brown again. Add $\frac{1}{4}$ cup warm water, little by little, and mix vigorously with a wooden spoon in order to beat out any lumps.

6. As soon as the mushroom mixture has finished boiling down, stir it into the pan. The result should be semi-liquid—thicker than a soup, thinner than a stew. Stir in the garlic. Cover to keep warm.

FOR THE DOUGH:

1. While the onion and cabbage are getting to know each other, mix the flour, egg, salt, and water to create a soft dough. There are two ways to carve out the individual dumpling pockets you'll need. You can use your hands to roll the dough into one very long log, cut it into two-inch chunks, and roll each into a small coaster-size pocket-to-be (about 2 inches in diameter). You can also roll the original mass of dough into a giant pancake and carve pockets by pressing the rim of an upside-down glass into the dough. Bunch the excess dough, roll out, and repeat. Make sure the dough is thin enough to produce about 35 circles, each with a diameter of 2 inches.

TO FINISH:

1. Drop 1 teaspoon—no more—of the cabbage-and-onion mixture onto each dough circle and flatten with the back of the teaspoon. To close the dumpling: Cradling the dough from below, close the circle in half around the cabbage-and-onion mixture, pinching the now semicircular edge of the dumpling as flat as possible, so that the cabbage-onion mixture is bulged up in the middle. Now fold the edge over itself starting from one end, so that the semicircle ends up looking scalloped. (The dumpling should resemble a crescent moon with scalloped edges.) You may wish to sic the job on smaller people with more nimble fingers, a.k.a. children.

2. Fill a large pot midway with water and one teaspoon of the oil. Add salt and bring to a boil. When the water is boiling, drop in about half the dumplings. They will rise to the surface in a minute or two, and need 2 or 3 minutes more at the top—a total of 5 or so minutes. Scoop them out with a slotted spoon, getting rid of as much water as possible before dropping them into a shallow bowl. Toss with another teaspoon of the oil to prevent clumping.

3. Mix the last 2 garlic cloves into the caramelized onion that was set aside. Cover the dumplings with half of this mixture and mix gently. Add dill to taste.

4. Repeat for the remaining dumplings.

5. Reheat the gravy on low to medium heat if it needs it. Serve it over the dumplings.

✣

CHAPTER 14

March 2015

*What to cook when Oksana has finally
decided to teach you*

✤

Almost no ideas occurred to me during this time, which was frightening, because new ideas sometimes felt like the true currency in which I was paid for the work I had chosen. The barrenness felt so complete, I took it to mean that *this was the way things would be now*. All the American optimism I'd been working to cultivate within myself dissipated like so much illusion—*I had been the platitude peddler, I my own gullible audience*—and I reverted to the view, so familiar from my family life, that only a fool looked out onto desolation and thought, *Things will get better.* If you'd told me that the next day would bring a strange discoloration of the skin, or difficulty pronouncing words, I would have believed you. Even writing, which had saved me every other time, wouldn't come. I imagined myself accelerating toward blankness; sometimes I couldn't remember what I'd said a moment before.

But I had an idea on the subway home from my grandfather's. I nearly burst into tears in gratitude for it. It came to me while I was rewatching, on the subway, the video of Oksana talking about how she would have handled the pig that became the pork belly in her hands. When I got back to my friend's place, I brought up a list of farms around the city that accepted volunteers and, even though it was getting into evening, started calling.

On farms near New York, it's harder to give away labor than one might assume, even in the dead of winter: too many fried corporate

people on apprenticeships for a new life; semi-fried corporate people on sabbaticals; and yet-to-be-fried corporate people delivering
on their company's fervid commitment to social responsibility. (Of
course, there are a couple of people apprenticing to become farmers, too.) I called five or six farms before I heard back. The place
boarded horses, ran a small dairy herd, and grew vegetables over
four acres. Louise (not her name), the farm manager, who was as
welcoming as the other farmers were not, asked if I wanted to come
up that weekend and have a look for myself. That weekend? Suddenly it was all very real, the road there nearly three times as long
as the trip to my grandfather's. Yes, I said quickly, so it was out
before I could change my mind.

"What do you think?" Louise said after we'd finished walking
around. The sky was dove gray, small pleats of clouds that looked
like they were trying to decide whether to unpleat and let go. She
wore jean overalls and a plaid parka. "You want to do a little work?
See what it's like?"

I had worn nice clothes—corduroys, my good leather boots—
partly to make a good impression and partly to remind myself that
I owned something other than soft old jeans. I hadn't cooked my
own meals in a month. Had not managed a brisker pace than a
walk. Mostly out of gratitude for her time, I said yes. If you said
yes, things happened, though all of you wanted nothing to happen.
Louise brought out a jiggly, pliable rake, like the one I'd used to
scour the leaves off Signora Limona's yard all those years ago. She
pointed me to an enclosed paddock.

"All the horse poop from last fall that got frozen over is thaw-
ing," she said. "We'd want it anyway, but this stuff has been sitting
under snow collecting nutrients all winter long. It's super-manure
now. We didn't have time to get it in the fall before the ground
froze over, but messing up has its benefits." She extended the rake.
"See you later."

I must have looked a little horselike myself in that paddock, bucking at the frozen ground with my rake, great clouds of steam storming out of my mouth, time an abstraction. (The sky leaden, it was impossible to say how much had passed.) For once, I was covered with sweat from exertion rather than an impression of fever. In the end, an hour was all I could manage. I had done a fairly pathetic job, scraping together only several buckets' worth of manure. But my boots were covered with horseshit, as were my corduroys to the knee. It was scrapingly windy, my hands raw and chapped, and tears had been falling out of my face—from the cold, I was fairly sure—but now real tears came. I began wiping at my face with my shit-flecked sleeve, hoping that, just as no one had appeared in the previous hour—I could have been alone on that three hundred acres, alone on the whole good earth—no one would now.

Louise and I agreed I'd come for the weekend. I'd sleep in one of the stalls in the old stallion barn. When my grandfather heard that I was going to spend my weekends gathering shit and planting acres of seeds with my back bent like a peasant, some of the old energy reappeared in his voice. "Why would you do that?" he shouted into the phone, with a mix of shame, horror, and rage. His grandson had been taken in. Someone with more guile had preyed on an innocent boy. "We're worse than others?" he shouted. "Your labor's not worth anything? I paid people to get your mother out of that shit!" The extra effort took its toll, and he lapsed into a crestfallen silence. After all this time, like an insurgency biding its time, my father's way was winning, and after my father himself had so earnestly tried to suppress it. But my grandfather's animation was also that of a seer proved true. He had lived for so long imagining the collapse of what he'd managed to build that he began to want confirmation of that more than proof that he was worried for nothing. Here I was, handing it to him. Thanks to me, he was quaking with the perverse, erotic thrill of having one's fears confirmed.

On my first day, I worked a pickax to loosen some soil in a greenhouse for "the three sisters." Beans, which need a stalk to wind around, get planted between corn seeds that will become those stalks. The corn gets help keeping down weeds from squash, which flowers horizontally. And the squash gets the shade it needs from the corn leaves. (The cultivars had wondrous names—Gold of Bacau beans, Country Gentleman corn, Galeux d'Eysines squash.) It would be like the old Communist slogan—"From each according to his ability, to each according to his need"—and if the human hand could just stay mostly away, perhaps this communism could succeed. (Later in the season, I would notice two tomato plants that had intertwined as thickly as a tangle of hair. My fingers were in there unwinding before I knew what was happening. "They probably know far better than we do what to do," Louise called out as I broke one of the stems.)

The handle of the pickax soon tore through my work gloves, a nice blister forming in the seat of my palm. Periodically, something nauseating began to spin in my stomach and I'd have to pause and straighten myself. However, the ache in my hands eventually subsided to a dull burn, and the strain in my stomach eased as I learned to wield the pickax from the right part of my body. I swung, sank, pulled, and hefted, then switched to a rake; then fell to my knees to gather the mound in which I'd bury the seeds. When I was done, there were three long rows and I couldn't move. But my mind felt like water resting in a cool jug, exhausted into silence.

On Saturdays, I woke at 6 a.m.—animals summon a sense of responsibility that even one's own well-being does not, and I was out of bed before the clock turned 6:01—and by 9 a.m. I was a hundred miles away, rolling a punctured oil drum to make divots for plantings or coaxing milk from udders. At quitting time, I dragged myself like a ghost to the stallion barn, showered, and, feeling a measureless hunger, in one meal devoured more food than I had in the previous week. Physical labor—especially when food was involved—was a more effective emollient than rage. By the time

I drove home after another shift the next day, I felt as if I were returning from another country. As if I had a secret.

Farm life, at first, seemed ritualistic: You do the same thing every day, partly to maximize already thin profits, partly because of
natural facts—cows like to milk in the morning; when summer
comes, you hay in the late afternoon, after the grass has received
that day's nutrients but before it has sent them down to the root.
The humans fit in between: Chores start at 5:00 a.m.; you pause
at 7:30 a.m. for coffee and a plan for the day; 1:30 p.m. for fresh
bread slathered with whatever's at hand, whether peanut butter or
tuna salad or the cheese that the farm makes from the cows' milk;
a mind-vacated dinner at 8:00 p.m. Coming from a city where routine felt impossible, and where no authority greater than my own
directed my days, I found myself submitting eagerly to the impla-
cable requirements of cattle and grass.

But then, like the haze that burns off on a hot day, that impression dispersed. After enough weekends, it began to seem like
actually you could rely on very little routine. You didn't know if
the seeds in the garden would sprout, so you planted extras, except if they *all* sprouted, the plants would throttle one another.
One morning, after something spooked the cows on the way to the
milking barn and they dispersed wildly—my eyes filled with a
dozen near-tonners with horns that could go through armor—we
managed to get them back together, but not before the day's
schedule went to shit. And if we hadn't tarped that hay before the
rain started, it would have cost the farm twenty thousand dollars.
The notion of control was so laughable that, counterintuitively,
the anxiety fell away. I had never greeted failure and lack of control in this way.

And then *that* impression went away. Farm life *was* ritualistic. And it was improvisational, too. Brunhilde won't milk from
her hind left teat, and the calves don't help by gravitating to the
others, from which it's easier to suck. But the milk has to come

out—unmilked cows can develop mastitis, an inflammation of the mammary glands—and the farm needs that milk to go into a vat, where it will curdle after the addition of rennet and harden into a wheel, which, after aging, will head off to the farmers' market, where it will inspire exclamations about the agrarian life. The swollen sac that empties into Brunhilde's left hind teat bulges painfully.

So you wedge between her and Cordelia, off to the side there—cows kick back, not to the side—get your left hand on the teat, dodge the shit-caked tails swatting lazily to and fro, and squeeze. And—squeeze. Over and over. She doesn't like it when you squeeze with the whole hand, so you clamp your thumb and forefinger over the udder and pull without using the other fingers. That hurts her less. It hurts you more.

Her skin is warm and taut, eight hundred pounds of muscle. She looks like a bulb laid sideways. You give her a firm squeeze, then harder. It takes you a while to believe it, but they don't feel pain like we do. Brunhilde's chewing her cud and staring blankly at a calf lounging on the other side of the feeding trough. You don't know when you cross the line, at once absent and alert (if she kicks, you dodge). The muscles in your hand ache so badly you don't think you can squeeze again, so you switch hands, but Brunhilde likes the other way, so you go back, and, little by little, you disappear again. Every moment is identical.

One afternoon, I was in my rubber overalls, shoveling mounds of cow manure, turned soupy by urine, out of the milking barn, when my phone buzzed. It was my grandfather.

"So?" he said by way of greeting.

"I'm wearing a smock and it's covered in shit," I said. "But I feel good." I was referring to the story about his brother Aaron, who worked with motors. Though he revered Aaron, Arkady had refused to do the same work—he'd work in a barber's "clean smock," not a dirty one.

Now my grandfather issued a consignment of all mothers to an unspeakable fate—in Russian swearing, as in many things Russian, mothers are at the heart of things—and then said, giving up: "I don't understand anything." Then he became convulsed by a fit of terrible coughing and gave the phone to Oksana as my pleasure at needling him turned to regret. Then again, maybe he was faking the coughing—upset or not, he wouldn't want me to think he didn't want to talk to me anymore. The line was silent as I heard the muffled sound of Oksana ministering to him. His iron was low—every morning, she poured into him sixteen ounces of beet juiced with other vegetables. But when she got on the phone, she was laughing—he had issued some choice exclamations between sips of his throat-clearing tea—and her laugh was so infectious that I began laughing, too.

On weekdays, I took the subway down to Brooklyn, and on weekends I drove to the farm. In Oksana's kitchen, I figured out how chicken liver alchemizes into a crepe. When the time came to flip, Oksana "drew" around the edge of the crepe with a thin wooden skewer, as if she were crossing something out, until it began to separate from the pan; then, in a lightning motion, slid her fingers under the crepe and flipped it onto its backside. My tries tattered the crepes, which Oksana "darned" with more batter, and finally, ten crepes later or thirty, I flipped one without tearing. Then I tore five more. Then another the right way.

I learned to baby the rabbit in sour cream, tenderer than chicken and less forgiving of distraction, as well as the *banosh* the way the Italians did polenta. You had to mix in the cornmeal little by little while the dairy simmered—Oksana boiled the cornmeal in milk and sour cream, never water or stock—as it clumped otherwise, which I learned the hard way. I learned to curdle and heat milk until it became a bladder of farmer cheese dripping out its whey through a cheesecloth tied over the knob of a cabinet door; how to use the whey to make a more protein-rich bread; how to sear pucks of farmer cheese spiked with raisins and vanilla until you had breakfast. I learned patience for the pumpkin preserves—stir gently to avoid turning the cubes into puree, let cool for the runoff to thicken; repeat for two days. How to pleat dumplings and fry cauliflower florets so that half the batter did not remain stuck to the pan. To marinate the peppers Oksana made for my grandfather on their first day together. To pickle watermelon, brine tomatoes, and even make potato latkes the way my grandmother made them.

PUMPKIN PRESERVES (V)

Time: 30 minutes, plus 3–4 heating sessions of 20–25 minutes, with cooling periods in between

Ukraine reaches as far south as Provence—or used to, when it had Crimea—so the Mediterranean vegetables and fruit are in ample supply there: eggplant, melons, pumpkins. The lattermost show up in soups and preserves, and as oil infusions. With pumpkins, it's color that matters, not size—the brighter the orange, the riper and sweeter the pumpkin. There's something pleasingly koan-like about this recipe—extremely simple and subtle at once: The syrup has to thicken without turning the pumpkin and fruit cubes floating in it to mush.

2 pounds pumpkin	1 orange
1 lemon	2 pounds sugar

1. Peel the pumpkin and cut into small cubes—each piece no larger than a fingernail.

2. Deseed the lemon and the orange and cut (with the rinds intact) to the same size.

3. Combine pumpkin, lemon, and orange with the sugar. Stir gently. Leave overnight in the fridge, covered by a napkin or paper towel.

4. By the next day, the sugar will have interacted with the pumpkin, lemon, and orange to let off liquid. Bring the mixture to a boil, then immediately turn the heat down to medium-low and simmer for 15 minutes. Stir infrequently and gently—stirring breaks up the cubes and hastens their breakdown into paste, which means you will end up with jam instead of preserves.

5. Turn off the heat and let cool *completely*. The goal is to thicken the liquid (by full cooling) without turning the fruit and pumpkin cubes into puree (by stirring too hard).

6. Reheat the mixture the same way—bring to a boil, then let simmer for 15 minutes, stirring gently—until the liquid has turned viscous. Again, allow to cool completely.

Oksana reheats—and lets cool—the mixture three times, and ends up with a quart of preserves. Then the teapot gets filled and the tea biscuits come out.

Note: The sugar in the preserves will inhibit bacteria, so storage in a sterilized jar isn't required.

✢

SOUR CREAM−BRAISED RABBIT
WITH NEW POTATOES

Time: 1 hour   Serves: 4–6

New potatoes are sweeter and make a great counterbalance to the tang in the sour cream and the vinegar used to soak the rabbit.

1 medium rabbit (about 2 pounds), cut into 8 pieces	1 large onion, chopped
3 tablespoons white vinegar	1 large carrot, grated
$\frac{1}{4}$ cup vegetable oil	$1\frac{1}{2}$ cups sour cream
$1\frac{1}{2}$ teaspoons ground coriander	2 garlic cloves, put through a garlic press
1 teaspoon ground caraway	12 small new potatoes
Kosher salt and black pepper, to taste	Fresh dill, roughly chopped
	Fresh parsley, roughly chopped

Note: If rabbit is scarce where you are, substitute chicken parts.

1. Cover the rabbit with water and add the vinegar to remove gaminess. Let stand 2–3 hours.

2. Drain the water without rinsing the rabbit. Heat the oil in a medium-size nonstick pot over medium-high heat. Add the rabbit and sear for 3 minutes per side. Add the coriander, caraway, salt, and pepper, and cook for another minute on each side. Transfer the rabbit to a plate.

3. In the same pot, sauté the onion until golden brown. Then add the grated carrot and cook fully, adding salt to taste. Return the rabbit to the pan and cover with the sour cream, but no need to mix it in just yet; it will soak in. Turn the heat down to low, cover, and cook for 5 minutes.

4. Now, the sour cream having softened, mix all the ingredients gingerly. Add the pressed garlic and cover again.

5. While the rabbit is braising, boil the new potatoes—skin on—in salty water.

6. How much time the rabbit needs varies depending on age and toughness. Every 5–10 minutes, swish the liquid around carefully so the sour cream doesn't stick to the pot and burn, and test the rabbit with a fork. If you're low on liquid, add water, sour cream, or a mixture of the two. Taste the braising liquid from time to time to see if it needs salt, pepper, or spices. The rabbit should need no more than 30–40 minutes braising at low temperature.

7. When the rabbit is ready, add the dill and parsley, quarter the potatoes, and serve alongside each other or mixed.

✻

PICKLED WATERMELON (V)

Time: 30 minutes (and 2 days)   Serves: 40 Americans or 2 Ukrainians

The Ukrainian palate adores the contrast of tart and sweet, which shows up at its purest in recipes for pickled fruit. Sounds strange, perhaps, but biting into a cranberry fished out of a jar of pickled cabbage, or a pickled apple, in the dead of winter is the closest I've come to enjoying the services of a time machine. The watermelon in this recipe comes out sweet, garlicky, and earthy with dill all at once. Don't forget to drink the brine—especially after a hangover.

⅓ of a small (pinkie-size) jalapeño pepper, scissored into rings	1 tablespoon sugar
The cloves of 1 head of garlic, divided	1 medium watermelon (about 2 pounds), rind removed and flesh cut into 1-inch cubes
2 tablespoons kosher salt	1 bunch fresh dill

1. Cover the bottom of a nonreactive container with half of the dill and the jalapeño rings.

2. Slice 5 of the garlic cloves in half and toss those in as well. Add 4 cups of water and the salt and sugar.

3. Scatter the watermelon in the container. Put 2 of the garlic cloves through a garlic press and add. Scatter in the remaining garlic cloves. Mix gently with your hands to make sure the garlic, salt, and sugar are well distributed. The watermelon should be peeking out of the water. Over the next day, it will "give" its own liquid and submerge.

4. Cover with the rest of the dill.

5. Let stand unrefrigerated for a day, and then refrigerate for another day.

Keep refrigerated while you consume. It should keep for a week.

✦

When it became warmer, we cooked with what I hauled home from the farm, which was as much as I could load into my car. Oksana had never seen tomatoes in so many colors. She had never laid eyes on Swiss chard, which she hesitantly subbed for the sorrel in her sorrel borshch. She even tried some "leaf salads," though she went back to cucumbers, radishes, and tomatoes as soon as I left her alone.

She never brought up what had happened to me. Over the years, I'd become nearly as able to read her silence as my mother's— sometimes better, as there was none of the occluding anger that makes it so hard to agree to see what a mother wishes one to. But we also knew, without discussing it, that there was a point of intimacy past which we were too different to go. My family was too close, Americans kept too far, but she and I had found the right distance. I don't mean the ideal distance—just the right one.

Through a training institute, I found a psychoanalyst. He was as far north of my friend's apartment as Oksana and my grandfather were south. He was unfashionably Freudian and asked me for my dreams. I told him the one about my grandfather in bed, the gold teeth, the pleading.

"Gold," he repeated.

"Soviet dentistry," I said. "It's a long story."

"Tell me some words that rhyme with 'gold,'" he said.

"Cuckold," I blurted out.

He smiled and dipped his head affirmatively. "We'll have plenty to talk about." Then he said I should go to a psychopharmacologist to get medicine.

"Can't we just figure it out here?" I said.

"Don't negotiate with me," he said. "Tell me another dream."

"I don't remember any. They float up at odd times."

"Last night, for instance."

"It's not coherent."

"Try it," he said.

"I've got a heavy pack," I said. "I used to work as a hiking guide to make money to write—maybe it's that. And I'm walking a long way. I'm with a woman, my age. I don't know who she is. And we get to—a roadblock, I guess. It's a hole in the ground. And there's a man in it, a young man. He's got a thick beard. Dressed in a plaid shirt. And he says, 'No, you're not needed here.' And I say, 'But I've walked with this goddamn pack for how many miles.'"

He gave me a small smile. "We could spend a year on that dream."

The psychopharmacologist he sent me to knew everything about my condition and nothing about how to speak to someone who'd never taken antidepressants. But why should he have been able to see himself clearly? A writer is never more blinded than when writing a memoir. I just wanted desperately to feel myself in competent hands. I was afraid. Afraid of never again being like the person I'd been. (Even as I wished to shed so much of that person.) Afraid because I didn't know whether drugs would make things better or worse. The longer I delayed, the analyst had said, the more freely my ailment would surge through my neurons, detaching from its cause until it was an ever more permanent part of me. It already was. Just by having experienced it once, I was 50 percent likelier to experience it again.

I had been so frightened by what had happened, my understanding so limited and my faculties so impaired, that I found myself wishing, simply, to be able to turn to my parents and ask what I should do—not a wish I experienced often any longer, having had to answer not only my own questions, but theirs, for a long time. But I wanted it now. However, I knew they would become obsessed by the medicine—they thought even talk therapy was for degenerates—and, in their anxiety, unload on me their medically uninformed worst-scenario nightmares. Many parents couldn't understand their children—but these people didn't communicate with each other in six months as much as my family and I did in a week. I used to think that if I could just persuade them that risk brought reward, that things turned out okay now and then, I could be myself without confusing or hurting them. But their losses and shocks reached so far, they couldn't manage—didn't try—to let go of them. I couldn't save them. I'd have to be content with saving myself. The most frightening thing about that winter was that it often felt like it was too late even for that.

CHAPTER 15

What to cook for the family (meal)

✢

Misha, Sasha, Nikita." Seth pointed around the room, as if he were naming the three musketeers. "Misha is hot station, Sasha is cold, Nikita's the chef."

The previous year, a Russian restaurant called Moscow57 had opened near my apartment. Manhattan was full of Russian restaurants, both classics such as Russian Samovar and new arrivals such as Mari Vanna, but the main distinction, as I saw it, was in their flavors of kitsch—puffed-up nostalgia and arriviste vulgarity, respectively. And now places like these had set up shop on my walk to the subway. I had started taking the other side of the street.

I'd been too young to say no when my family packed off to places like the National, in Brighton Beach, for somebody's birthday, a pocket of salt in my oversize suit to ward off the evil eye. (Why did I need that if we were going to see friends? *Just do it.*) There, seated at banquet tables worthy of Rabelais, we gorged on sturgeon, quail, duck liver, and fried potatoes with morels and watched elaborate floor shows—dancing girls, costumes, smoke—stunned by the food and the spectacle. I had my "bar mitzvah" in one such place—the bar mitzvah portion consisting of a cake in the shape of a Torah scroll. I'd had enough for a lifetime.

But the depression meant that sometimes I didn't have the energy not only to do things but also to not do them. Something like spring had arrived, rainy and cold. One Sunday night, a friend and

I went through three rounds at a neighborhood bar and, gin in my head, I forgot to cross to the right side of Delancey Street when we walked past the restaurant. My friend was a Russian non-Russian like me, and we probably thought the same thing: Whatever affectation we'd find inside would at least share nothing with the studied scruffiness of a Lower East Side cocktail den circa 2015. Also, Russian food soaked up booze really well.

It was beautiful inside. Blood-red walls, soft light, decorative chaos: a pressed-tin ceiling, blocks of mirrors, photographs hung up with clothespins. And the menu was both familiar and not: *bliny*, but also cucumber-and-pomegranate salad; borshch, but also pistachio-and-fenugreek shrimp. The restaurant felt like nothing but itself, an elusive commodity in the city that has everything. To reach our table, we had to squeeze past a woman belting "Little Girl Blue" with help from a small band; when she finished, she introduced herself—Ellen, one of the owners, an American. (Her parents had run the Russian Tea Room, hence the food.) She took a swig of honey and returned to the mic. It was everything I'd always wanted to find in a Russian restaurant: warmth rather than pomp. The spring stayed rainy and cold—at the farm, I weeded and raked in two sweatshirts—but I started walking on the Moscow57 side of the street.

One night, I joked to Seth, one of Ellen's partners, that maybe they could take me on as a waiter. He understood: In the culture we shared, so much of it defined by hunger, the experience of bringing food to another could feel satisfying enough to redeem even the indignities of a waiting job in New York. Plus, I was good with people—or had been, once. I'd do it for free. "Serve?" Seth said. "You don't want to go in the kitchen?"

Now, standing in that kitchen, where I had made my leaden legs walk despite the dread that kept me up half the night, the cooks turned around to assess the flotsam before them. The shortish young man at the hot station was frying a wheelbarrow's worth of what smelled like mushrooms and onions. His hair was so translucently blond, it was a history lesson—the Vikings were here—and he was so lean and muscled that the veins stood out on his arms like blue cables. The young man at the cold station had hooded eyes and a limp body, and below a shapeless black T-shirt he wore what could only be described as capri pants. The tips of his fingers were burgundy from dicing beets. A small radio behind him pumped out trance, as awkward in that silence as a loud fart at a dinner party. Nikita, the chef, had a cherubic round face and more Viking hair, his sprouting from his head like a hedgehog's.

In the cast of their faces, the hue of their skin, the shape of their bodies, they were implacably *Russian*, obviously all recent arrivals, and not from the big cities. I was startled to realize that I was probably older than all of them. But for the rest of that spring, I would be their bitch, and that prospect made me lonesome and frightened, as if I'd wandered into an establishment I shouldn't have, on a street that wasn't for people like me, in a city where I should have been more careful.

But they didn't know that. They saw the same age disparity that I did, the non-Russian cast of my face and hue of my skin, the American clothes and posture, the thousand little things that allowed us to recognize a person as "one of ours"—or not—on any street in the world, and concluded that I was one of the potential investors for whom the kitchen staff were trotted out like horses getting their teeth checked at my grandfather's Minsk prewar bazaar.

"Boris is going to be interning in the kitchen," Seth said, correcting their impression. "He's a writer. Anyway, let's go, I already have someone at the bar."

I experienced a great wish to follow Seth back out to the front room. Sasha, Misha, and Nikita continued to stare at me.

"So, like what, you're writing a book?" Nikita said.

I shook my head. I thought about telling them the truth, but saying I was there to get my mind off heartbreak would have been like telling them I was transgender. I didn't have the energy for all that anyway. Every time I recounted my story to someone, I sank a little deeper into its mud. "Just—learning how to cook, I guess," I said. "I'll do anything you need."

"So, like, for free?" Nikita said, his sweet round face turning dark and confused.

I shrugged. His expression said, *Well, here's some kind of fucknut.* A practical person—a Russian person—would have been smart enough to pretend he was writing a book.

I went downstairs, changed into a cook's apron, parked myself at the prep station, and waited for instructions. But the instructions didn't come. By five, everyone was in the thick of prep, chopping salmon for tartare, making the pistachio-based sauce that went with the shrimp, and skewering sliced vegetables and cubes of lamb or chicken onto kebabs. But even tasks that a child could perform—resupply from the basement walk-in refrigerator, dicing vegetables—Nikita assigned to Misha or Sasha, even though they were doing something else, and I continued to stand there in my spotless whites like a wraith. I tried to wash some of the dishes piling up in the sink, but then the dishwasher showed up and I was relieved of that task as well. I was reminded of making borshch with Oksana—she had to make me feel like I was doing something, but that something had to minimize my involvement so I could screw up as little as possible. Huge smiles and nods of acknowledgment came my way every time someone passed me, but our interaction ended there.

At six, the ticket machine began to whir with new orders. "*Poshla khuyachina*," Misha sighed. "And the fuckness begins."

Misha, who was from Russia, didn't join the others for smoke breaks; he'd installed a pull-up bar over a doorframe in the basement and heaved himself up and down until he heard the order machine croak to life, whereupon he told the machine to go fuck its mother and reluctantly relinquished the bar. With swearing he was as profligate as he was chaste about the rest.

Sasha was different: Ukrainian, dark-haired, and he didn't curse at the order machine. I thought Sasha and I could be allies because his soft-spokenness meant he was the butt of the kitchen's vitriol. On my first evening, as I listened to Nikita haranguing him because it was almost seven and Sasha still hadn't finished a new round of a beets-and-herring nostalgia dish, I proposed to peel and dice some of the beets to help out.

"Nah, everything's normal," Sasha said phlegmatically as a bunched hand towel hit his face from the other side of the kitchen. "Well, what the fuck," he said matter-of-factly. If Misha was irritable and combative, Sasha moved as viscously as the dressing he dolloped onto the Esenguly salad (dates, Napa cabbage, carrots, orange slices, scallion, and pistachios; Nikita's grandparents came from Central Asia). But they all swore. They were united in swearing.

A restaurant kitchen is a place of great, joyous hate. Hate for the owners, who don't understand what the cooks need. Hate for the servers, who always show up at the wrong time. Hate for the diners, who have the temerity to actually order. And hate for one another—for Sasha, who never defended himself when Nikita and Misha flung insults and towels; for Misha, who seemed maniacally focused when it was busy and simply uptight the rest of the time; for Nikita, who failed to understand how lucky he was to have the sous-chefs he did. Only I didn't seem worth hating. I knew enough to know that a new body in a kitchen is welcomed by fire: You're abused and, if you last, you become family. I had feared, but expected, the abuse. What I didn't expect was that being the Writer would render me ineligible for it. I was steered clear of, and even that without hostility. Perhaps for the first time in the history of restaurant shifts, I spent ten hours without a bead of sweat forming anywhere on my body.

That night, instead of crashing to sleep the usual way, I stared at the ceiling. I had even more lead in my legs when I went back for my shift the next day. I was there at two, as I had been told to be; Sasha and Misha came at three (big, dutiful nods) and Nikita (firm handshake) at four. By five, the previous day was repeating itself. Then something occurred to me: Was I being avoided not because I was The Writer, but because I was A Russian who had become An American? Not because they imagined I could offer little, but because they didn't feel like *they could tell me what to do*? I was frightened of them. But they were frightened of me.

So I used the authority vested in me by the United States of America. On that second day, Nikita yelled at Sasha to get him peppers from the downstairs walk-in, even though Sasha was moated by mounds of cucumber and pomegranate seeds for the Shirazi salad (cucumbers, pomegranate seeds, grapes, honey, and hot pepper flakes, tossed with lime sesame oil). "*I* will get the peppers," I said loudly. No one said anything—didn't even look up. I turned around and sprinted down the stairs to the walk-in before anyone changed his mind. And when the machine spat out "potato pancakes," I'd watched Misha make them enough times—and made them enough times with Oksana—that I was upstairs with the ingredients (two potatoes, one onion, one egg) before he'd had a chance to get to it. I nodded at the bowl, which he understood correctly to mean *Okay?* He shrugged: *Why not.* And so I grated and mixed them before handing the batter to Misha, though I was trying so hard that I shredded my knuckles on the grater and had to finish the job one-handed while my left knuckles bled into my jeans pocket, where no one would notice. Next time, Misha didn't have to ask, and I didn't tear up my knuckles. I knew how to make quite a few of the dishes, in fact—I'd learned them from Oksana. So that when a borshch order came in and the vat of borshch in the walk-in was discovered to have been there too long to pass muster, I said: "I'll make the borshch."

"*Borshch umeyesh?*" Nikita said skeptically. "You can make borshch?"

"*Umeyu.*" "I can." (My heart beat madly all the same.)

"What else do you know how to make?"

"*Bliny,*" I said. "Yeast or no yeast."

"Honey cake?" he said.

"If you show me," I said.

"*Nu, tak, svoi chelovek,*" Nikita said, his face broadening into its giant-baby smile—"So, one of ours"—and my heart nearly flew out of its cage. That night, I soaked through my apron and the shirt underneath it before dinner rush had even gotten going.

Cooking food in a restaurant is not that different from cooking at home, except for the speed with which you must do it while minding a slew of other time-sensitive tasks, all in a very small, very hot kitchen. But that difference was my salvation. From 2:00 p.m. to midnight, my brain powered down to survival mode. Just as at the farm, the kitchen wasted my body but loaded my mind with a numb stillness. The restaurant entered the week's rotation: Wednesday and Thursday there, Monday and Friday with Oksana, the weekend at the farm, and one slow day I killed waiting for the others to start.

Soon I was assigned to the family meals for the staff at shift's end. It felt like a lovely, accurate term for people who were swearing at each other just moments ago, but who also shared an intimate duty. I joined the family in other ways: Nikita asked me to rewrite the menu; Sasha asked me to find him a bride; and when, one night, I greeted the first chirp of the ticket machine with a distracted "*Khuyachina!*"—Fuckness!—the entire kitchen (even Misha, who was last to let go of his suspicions of me) broke out in a roar of banging tongs, knives, and spatulas, the Haitian dishwasher staring at us with confusion and pity. No, Nikita and I probably wouldn't have much to say over a beer in the backyard of the new suburban house he had just so proudly bought in New Jersey in anticipation of his first child. But that moment, then—that, no one could deny us as equally true. You did not have to go all Russian or all American. You could pick and choose. Notably, the iPhone doesn't have an emoji for "chagrin," but all the same, I wrote Alana—she who had insisted on the validity of picking and choosing her Judaism all those years ago, to my fundamentalist condescension—and she had the graciousness to be happy for me.

I began to sleep deeply, but this wasn't the obliterating unconsciousness of before. Every night, my brain sent up dreams my analyst laconically announced we could spend a year taking apart. By then, like consecutive life sentences, we'd racked up enough year-worthy dreams to take us through two lifetimes. Maybe he kept forgetting that he'd already said that; he was no longer very young, and half our appointments began with his surprise at seeing me on the other side of his door. But the other half went well past the end mark without his resort to the false apology of "I'm afraid time's up." He was the only therapist I'd ever met who did not do it by the book, and even if, by his own admission, he had a liability—"I get parental," he said—arguably it was exactly the sin that I needed. (It was with him that I understood about Yvonne, about Amy.) A surrogate mother in the form of my grandfather's home aide; a surrogate father in my semi-senile analyst; and three demented stepsiblings in a hot Russian kitchen—I was finding my way to some kind of new home.

CHAPTER 16

May 2015

What to cook when your son is making a mistake

✦

The restaurant had music every night. On Thursday nights, the same young woman sang "Miss You" and "Valerie" and "Ooh La La," refitted for a lounge setting. She was dishearteningly attractive, and I wanted to be different about all that, so I just hid out in the kitchen and snuck looks through its porthole windows, though I wouldn't let anyone else take the trash out on Thursdays. (You had to walk through the restaurant, as there was no back entrance.)

Several months had passed since my lowest point: I could pound out two ten-hour shifts in the kitchen, then spend the weekend at the farm tearing up weeds using a manual antique Amish plow and crawling around for hours in the rising heat, planting two thousand lettuce heads. And the things that hadn't gone back to normal felt just as important: I was less garrulous, in that performative way I had been; my views on what made friendship friendship had changed and stayed that way.

As these blasts of self-illumination arrived, as often in the kitchen as in the analyst's office—and often in the kitchen as a delayed reaction to what had been discussed in the analyst's office, and vice versa—suddenly scales that had been up for decades fell away. I heard myself, in real time, trying to make Nikita laugh, though my heart wasn't in it; trying to get the analyst to agree; trying to be good at something I didn't care about.

It seemed important that, throughout this time, I had not thought of women. (*Other* women; Amy never left my thoughts.) Perhaps noticing the singer was progress—I was ready to meet someone new. Except that I was noticing her for the same old reasons—she was attractive, and therefore someone to impress. Even I had gained enough self-understanding to notice myself starting to perform in moments like these, to understand that being attracted to and being interested in someone—an elementary, obvious distinction that had taken an eternity for me to grasp—were different things. I hung in this ambivalence, taking the garbage out on Thursdays far more often than necessary and then scurrying back to the kitchen.

One Thursday, I wasted a bag-half-full garbage outing—she wasn't even in the dining room. But that was because she was outside, talking to Seth's partner. He called me over, and I made the approach that I always want to make to an attractive woman—in a cook's apron smeared with entrails and a garbage bag filled with a restaurant's worst.

"Boris, this is Cici," David said as fish carcasses rotted between us in the prematurely warm night. "You don't smoke, do you? Cici wants a cigarette."

"But you're a singer," I said, with all the tolerance for contradiction of one of my parents.

She pantomimed duress and said, "That kind of day."

Did I smoke? I'd smoked a thousand cigarettes in the previous three months. (Literally—ten a day, three hundred a month, a thousand a season.) And yet, in my misguided attempt to drop this habit because I was starting to feel better, just then I didn't have one.

"Wait," I said too loudly, dropped the garbage bag at David's and Cici's feet—she danced backward slightly to avoid it grazing the nose of her Hasbeens—and hurtled through the dining room, flinging the kitchen door open so hard that Misha had to dance backward, nearly into the deep fryer. He treated me to a particularly flaying Russian expression.

"Nikita," I said. "Cigarette. Can I have?"

Taking advantage of a slow night, Nikita was experimenting with a dish that involved, somehow, both egg whites and beer. He flung a pack of Parliaments at me. "Thought you were trying to quit, he-he," he said.

"Did I ever tell you my mother smokes Parliaments?" I said.

"He-he. Can I have two? The singer wants one." Instantly, I regretted my apparently unfixable inclination to tell these people only the truth.

"Ho!" he said. He turned to Sasha, who was disappointed with me for coming up with no leads on a bride. As an American, I was supposed to be omnipotent, and my failure to deliver love left him confused. "Sash, isn't it time for a smoke?" Nikita said. "Let's keep them company." I sped out of the kitchen to the sound of their laughter.

Parliaments smoke down too fast. If we had American Spirits, we could have spoken twice as long. But when we were through, she said she could wait for me at the bar if my shift ended soon. My shift was over, I said. Over, over, over. I could go to the bar now.

Her name was really Jessica—Cici was a stage name.

"Why do you need a stage name?" I said.

"Sometimes people want to stay in your life even when you're done singing to them," she said. "You know what I mean?"

I coughed evasively. No, I didn't, quite. My awareness of this person's difference reasserted itself: She was tall, blond, blue-eyed. She wore a country fedora, a ribbed tank top, pleated short-shorts, and those Hasbeens: the uniform of a nation—hipsters—whose citizens felt more foreign than a desiccated blue-hair on the Upper East Side. On what mother ship did they give out the uniforms?

All that blondness was not Scandinavian, but Irish. She said it sheepishly—the Irish in America embarrassed her. It was easy for them to bray about Ireland because they never got near the actual thing, whereas she'd spent part of every summer there for the past twenty years. I told her about what I'd felt in Ukraine—any closer and the connection would end. Any closer to Nikita, Misha, and Sasha, and the connection would end. Any closer to Oksana and the connection would end. But that didn't mean I couldn't have a connection at all. Something like that.

She owned a science fiction bookshop—she'd decided a long time before that she wouldn't try to make it in music. "I didn't want the heartache," she said. "And the humiliation. I don't mean rejection, though that, too. I mean the ways you have to degrade yourself just to get a hearing. Especially if you're a woman. I wanted to continue to love it."

I was ready to think of her decision as a failing of courage, but it occurred to me that you could also think of mine—to pursue writing at any cost—as masochistic. And yet, it would have been inconceivable to me to "write for the drawer," and not because I needed to post results on a scoreboard. I really did love it, and part of that love was reaching people—many people. I loved it so much that it had survived a great deal of rejection and humiliation. I told her so.

"Then that's remarkable," she said. "Then you're lucky and strong both."

"I guess so," I said.

She laughed and clinked my cranberry juice. Miraculously, my depression made me allergic to alcohol instead of the opposite, and I liked what I felt when I stayed sober through the kinds of experiences during which I used to drink.

"I'm trying to write a science fiction novel," I said. I wasn't even making that up. I'd never been drawn to the genre, partly because its typically far-off future settings conveniently owed nothing to the restrictions of the present. But what if a novel was set only fifteen years from now? What if things were different by only a little? What would that little consist of? That twist was enough to make me interested, but I knew nothing about the history I was up against.

"So you should come by the bookshop," she said. "I'll make you a reading list."

"Comrade Writer," Nikita yelled into the dining room, his sausagey arm holding open the door to the kitchen. I saw Misha and Sasha piled up at his side. "I'm sorry to report the cleaning crew for your station didn't make it today." Jessica and I exchanged the same smile. On the air of that vision, I mumbled an awkward goodbye and sailed off to the kitchen.

But there was no bookstore meeting. When I wrote the next day, Jessica didn't reply until after the day we'd agreed to meet, and with no explanation. During the next Thursday at the restaurant, I avoided the dining room and asked someone else to take out the garbage. I felt properly and deservingly singed.

We did drift into a conversation, again warm and rich, on another evening. I was about to say something about being stood up, but she had to go off to the airport for a friend's wedding. "I'm away for a week," she said. "I'll call when I get back. We'll make a plan." A week passed, then two, and three. I ignored her at the restaurant, but she greeted me with the same smile, as if nothing had happened. This sort of inhumanity in dating manifests so frequently in New York that you're the crank if you won't just accept it and move on. I couldn't, so I just avoided her.

Impossibly for midsummer in New York, the sun was soft and forgiving when I walked outside the bar one early evening in July. I had a good fog in my head—I had been nearly without alcohol for so long that two glasses of white wine, with a friend from out of town, were enough to make me forget all the guardrails. I took out my cell phone and pressed Jessica's name. "It's because it's a beautiful day," I said to no one, a normal thing in New York. I had never tried with someone a third time. After so many rings, it was time for voice mail, but then she answered.

"This is so strange," she said. "I never pick up my phone when I'm here. It's on silent for two weeks."

"But you heard it," I said.

"There's no service here, even," she said.

"Where are you?"

"I looked at it for some reason, and it started to ring. I might lose you, sorry. I'm in a fifteen-passenger van full of groceries."

"Where are you? Camping?"

"South Dakota," she said.

"I've been there," I said. I wasn't making that up, either. A meaningful part of my second novel was set there.

There was a short silence, but I was swimming too much in my head to fill it.

"I didn't call you like I'd promised," she said.

"Yes, I'd like to kill you about that," I said—affably, I hoped. But I was also grateful to her for bringing it up.

"But you're calling," she said.

"It's a beautiful day," I said. "I had an extra glass of wine. You're the beneficiary."

"If I lose you, I'm not hanging up, okay?"

"I've really been to South Dakota."

I walked to my apartment, my bike in one hand, the phone in the other. I didn't want to risk losing the connection in the elevator, so I leaned the bike against the fence of a basketball court, sat on a nearby bench, and jammed my earbuds in to keep out the subway clatter on the Williamsburg Bridge. New York's cruel law is: If you're on the platform, the train doesn't come. But if you're trying to conduct a conversation in which both the reception and feelings are tenuous, it arrives with maddening regularity.

But the South Dakota wires stayed strong. It took ninety minutes to get from Rapid City, the nearest town with big supermarkets, to the Pine Ridge Reservation, where Jessica was going, and it was near darkness by the time we clicked off. She was in South Dakota because she spent three weeks every summer as a counselor at a camp for Lakota kids. They went swimming and camping, hiking and rock climbing. I had to guess at some of what she'd said. I wondered if it was easier to start a relationship in quiet places.

The conversation stayed sweetly in my head, but I was mad at myself—I hadn't said another word about the ways she had flaked. I wasn't fearful of the confrontation—I wanted it, was good at it. But everything about the conversation had felt so fragile that my complaints seemed like a careless hand that would take the tablecloth with it. I went upstairs and wrote her a text: "Again we spoke for so long and so well. But I don't believe we will meet when you return. If I'm right, could you please release me from this sweet crush?"

She answered quickly: "It's not great for text. Can you talk again?"

"You ready?" she said when her voice was on the other end of the line. She had unpacked the groceries and was heading to a patch of roadway with reception. "I'm married."

"No," I said.

"Yes," she said.

"But you don't wear a ring," I said.

"Sometimes people don't wear rings," she said. "But I do."

"You don't," I insisted.

"It's a very thin band," she said. "You didn't see it."

"Fuck," I said. Had I really not looked? Or, God, had I looked and not seen it? But why had she spoken to me in that close way again and again? However, making people own up to such a thing if they've changed their minds . . . Here, too, you were supposed to shrug and move on.

"I know what you're thinking," she said. "Why did I speak to you that way?"

"Yes," I blurted out gratefully. "*Yes.*"

"Now you know why I flaked," she said. "For which I'm sorry. Those conversations weren't a lie. I just don't——"

"Know how to reconcile that with being married. Yes, I know all about it."

"How could you possibly know?" she said, less softly.

"I've been here before," I said. "It went differently, but I know the general score."

"So maybe you don't know everything already," she said, even less softly. "It's not a good marriage. It's been over for a long time. I just haven't figured out how to——"

I was silent. I knew what she meant, but I wanted to make her say it.

"I wanted to give it every chance that I could," she said. "It's very easy to talk to you that way. I'm unhappy at home. But ultimately, I have to go back there."

"And then flake."

"And then flake."

"Why not just speak directly from the beginning?"

"My ring is right there."

"Don't hide behind your ring. It's not my job to make sure you're available while you're sitting there acting like we're falling in love."

I'd overspoken, and the words hung, heavy and premature, between us.

"You're right, of course," she said. I was pretty sure she was referring to the hiding, not the falling, but I decided not to inquire. "I'm very confused. I'm sorry. I'm telling you now."

I stared out at the light fading over the traffic on the bridge. This was the moment to hang up—I had only one foot out of the hole where I'd spent the previous six months, and a second episode increased the likelihood of a third to 70 percent—but I was, finally, getting the truth.

"Can you tell me everything from the beginning, please," I said in a tone of voice that I hoped was neither forgiving nor hostile.

By the time we clicked off, it was dawn. She'd found a patch of ground with reception and walked it back and forth, a young woman alone on a desolate road at three in the morning. The moon was nearly full, bathing everything in a bluish light that made it less frightening. And then it really was day, at least for me in New York, and she had two hours of sleep before she had to fire up the camp stove for forty servings of oatmeal with heaps of butter and sugar. (At home the children got mainly commods—low-quality bulk supplied by the government—so the camp tried to provide better food, but the bridge between Cheetos and oatmeal was long.) A counselor who was supposed to be in charge of the food buy and prep had last-minute canceled, which was why Jessica had been shopping the previous day—was it the previous day?—and why she had to get up to cook.

I was too wound up to sleep, so I wandered the neighborhood, seeing it the way my father must have seen all those people heading to work when he was leaving his graveyard shift as a doorman. He had a secret as he peered at all those weary faces: He wasn't one of them. He was heading in the opposite direction, just as he liked it. I stepped into a coffee shop.

"Early start," the counterman said.

"Late finish," I said.

"Hope it was worth it," he said.

I went home and slept until it was time for my restaurant shift. Many New Yorkers live this life—a job in nightlife or restaurants, sleep past noon, start again. To me, they had always seemed as foreign as people who needed stage names for safety, but now I was one of them, just as our nerd fathers were transfigured into peanut-shelling street hawkers by the secondhand markets in Italy. The restaurant was blissfully quiet that night, and I begged off at nine. That was around the time Jessica told the kids their last stories—

they weren't supposed to sleep in her tent, but they were afraid to sleep in the open—wriggled out past their bodies, and went to Reception Road to try me. Again we spoke until dawn.

It was only after three days of this that I realized I had no bicycle. That first night, in my trance, I had forgotten it by the basketball court when I went upstairs to write my lovelorn text. It was a monstrosity, a Mongoose mountain bike too heavy for the city, but my ungentrified corner of the Lower East Side wasn't choosy. My parents never liked coming there.

We spoke again from nine to dawn the next night, and the next, until we had done it six or seven nights in a row, the effects of the sleeplessness covering everything with a glow that makes it hard to tell one thing from another. At a certain point I said, "Don't you think I should just come there?" And Jessica said, "I think you should."

"I'm going on a trip tomorrow," I said.

"Tomorrow?" my mother said. She put her glass of wine down. I had told them I needed to come over, and my father had spent the day cooking: pork roulade, Indian butter chicken, roast salmon in his shallot-and-white-wine sauce (all one meal). "Why didn't you say anything?" she said. "For a reading?"

I hadn't planned on lying, but a reading from one of my novels—that would've made a good excuse. Some years before, I had concealed from them a trip to Iraq by saying I was going to Turkey. When I was there, I happened to exchange e-mails with a reporter for a Russian-language newspaper in New York, who proposed an interview about what had brought me to Iraqi Kurdistan six months after the American invasion. Emerging into the terminal after landing at JFK from Istanbul—I was kind of telling the truth; the Kurdish airports were closed; you had to fly in and out of Turkey—I saw a woman who looked remarkably like my mother brandishing a copy of a Russian newspaper above her head like

John Cusack with that radio in *Say Anything*. Only the cold steel of a security barrier kept her from charging me to refit those hands around my neck.

"Denver," I said now. "Not a reading. Denver, and then I'm going to drive to South Dakota. I've—I've met someone," I said.

Instant sobriety.

"I know you're worried," I said. "She's written you a letter." I passed over my phone. I had told Jessica about Amy, and she had volunteered to write a letter to try to put my parents' minds at ease. I couldn't sit there while they read it, so I pretended I needed the bathroom. Risky move—my mother could end up scrolling through my photos, "just to see what you've been up to." My father had opened my mail until I was in my early twenties and I demanded he stop. But I couldn't sit there.

When I returned, they were staring at each other, the food untouched. That never happened.

"Did *you* write the letter?" my mother said.

"What? No."

"What are you going to do there?" My father crossed his arms and inverted his mouth, the way he did when he couldn't understand.

"Help?" I said. "It's a camp. I don't know."

"She lives in South Dakota? Where is that?"

"Out west. No, she lives in New York."

"You can't wait till she comes home?"

"I didn't want to lie to you," I said. "I want you to understand."

"If you want us to understand, don't tell us after it's set."

They had a point. I saw myself through their eyes. I was the most embarrassing kind of fool—the kind who deserved it this time. Why *couldn't* I wait till she came home? This option hadn't even occurred to me. All the progress I'd made, all the restraints I'd worked to erect—all blown away. Either I had met someone who made all that unnecessary, or I was making the same old mistake.

"If I have to pick you up off the floor again," my mother said, "first I will kill her and then I will kill you." She popped food into her mouth, drained her wine, and held out the glass like someone who was ready to have quite a bit more.

"This one isn't married, I hope," my father said.

"Oh, God," I said. "No."

"But what are you going to *do* there?" he said.

"I don't know," I said. "Cook?"

CHAPTER 17

July 2015

✦

The Denver airport is 350 miles from Custer State Park, in South Dakota. I drove past Cheyenne; Fort Laramie, where the U.S. government signed one of the many treaties it betrayed with the Lakota; and Hot Springs, South Dakota, from where I'd received a note about my first novel from a not-Jewish Anglo woman who filed claims for the Lakota. (The novel was about Holocaust reparations.) I thanked her in the darkness.

In daylight, I had been able to summon some marvel. Somehow, my hopefulness wasn't dead. My parents were the reason. I'd been raised in love, and now I couldn't stop believing in it. Of course, my family kept that love strictly for its own. But I didn't have my own family yet. Et cetera.

But then my father's question tolled in my mind: *You can't wait till she comes home?* Generally, my father worked to conceal his bafflement at the person I'd become—I could see through it, but he was trying—but this time he stared at me in open bewilderment. He was bewildered also because he knew he couldn't stop me. I'd known it for some time, but this may have been the moment he did. I knew that we would never discuss it.

Since virtually the day we'd arrived in America, more than twenty-five years before, I had helped him—found him the subway schedules that would get him back to the Port Authority bus terminal from the building where he worked as a doorman; planned his and my mother's vacations; found and bought him the things he needed on Amazon, all of which he wanted his son to keep doing instead of learning how to himself—but in asking me to slow down and find patience, *he* was being a parent, and a proper one. And the experience was so unrecognizable to me that I'd nodded absently through it, and here I was now on this ill-advised road in full darkness. His words beat like a shrill bell in my ears, like the refrains that hounded me when I was most ill: *You can't wait till she comes home? You can't wait till she comes home? You can't wait till she comes home?*

My upbringing seemed to have left me both repelled by and addicted to closeness: Alana and I had spent our eight years separating and getting back together every several months. Did that explain Amy, the married woman, then? I'd made sure to get together with someone who wasn't available? I pushed hard for a life together with Amy because I knew that's what you were supposed to want, but perhaps the distance we had was the right fit? Maybe all the distances I had been discovering—with where I'd come from, with Oksana, with my grandfather, with my kitchen mates—signaled not an acceptance of my self and how I could choose among its parts without having to be completely, perfectly anything, but an inability, simply, to come any closer. And was that inability some authentic self I had to accept, or a betrayal of some truer self that was better at intimacy and that I had to keep digging down to?

I felt an unfamiliar sympathy for my parents. I seemed unable to take good care of myself, but I wanted to take care of them. For all that I'd tried to disown, and had, I was their perfect alchemy: my father's mother's willfulness and preference of singing to socks full of cash, and my father's need for his own way, somewhere far from most people; my mother's side's obsession with good marks, appearances, lots of noise, and never having enough. By now I had stood in front of many rooms, my first novel in hand. They always asked why you became a writer. An impossible question, but my four-headed answer floated up easily. Immigration gave me a million stories. Learning a new language at nine rather than zero left me astonished by what words could do. Because my people never expressed negative feelings directly (not a bequest of our totalitarian surroundings, but because they wished, above all, to show love, and what kind of love was it, they thought, if you disagreed openly?), I had to learn how to listen for what was meant rather than said, becoming acutely observant. That same love, however, meant I was never discouraged from speaking. A table of adults would fall silent so I could ask, or say. That last was the key: A fellow immigrant writer friend with a nearly identical background had only the first three, and had to work much harder to find the courage to put words on a page. I owed to my elders the career that had given them such alarm.

I was feeling too much about my parents to handle a phone call to them, but I desperately wanted to hear a familiar voice. I hadn't seen another car in what felt like an hour, and now I was pinned between two ridges, violet in the weak moonlight, that seemed ready to come to life and enfold me as I swiped right and left on that mountain-pass road, proper for one car, not two.

My grandfather had been getting tired out earlier and earlier in the evening, and it was later in New York, but I decided to try. But when I tried the "big phone"—that was what he called the landline—no one answered. This meant that either something bad had happened or he and Oksana were out somewhere at ten in the evening. To my relief, he picked up the "little phone": They were outside the building, on the row of ratty foldout chairs that was out there all the time. When the weather was clement, various old people who wanted fresh air but couldn't walk far descended to Kibitz Row and kibitzed.

"Nothing good, nothing good," he said when I asked how he was. I saw myself turning around in the darkness, rushing back to the airport—whatever illness it was would be significant enough to overcome my self-sabotage, and I almost wished for it. But it wasn't his health—they had gone for a walk, and he had left his jacket in the Chinese café on Bay Parkway. Fuck the jacket, he had ten jackets—it's that there were two lottery tickets in it! These were going to be the ones—these! I thought about pointing out that it was his mania regarding the murderous power of drafts that made him wear a jacket in July in the first place, but I refrained. They walked to the Chinese café every day, ostensibly for exercise, but also for baked buns. He dunked them in tea and chewed on the mash like an infant. On the way back, he bought lottery tickets like an addict. He had become too old to hustle up neighborhood deals. For the first time in his life, he wasn't making money, and it had undone him.

The upsetting part was that it made this most generous of men ungenerous and suspicious. He and Oksana always split the cost of the lotto tickets so they could split the grand win when it finally came, but one time, she had scratched off the forms, said it was nothing, and thrown them away. But she didn't throw them away! They were winners—big winners! And she was secretly collecting the millions. So secretly, I said when he claimed this, that she couldn't stop cooking and cleaning for an old man? *What can I say*, he said. *She's devoted to me.*

Why was he outside at bedtime? The heat had died down, he said—you could breathe. I knew what he was doing—delaying the moment he had to turn on the A/C. Now he really did have to make it on his Social Security—he refused to take money from us; it was supposed to go the other way—and Con Edison rates did not take pity in the summer. My mother had come up with the fiction that the federal government reimbursed senior citizens for 50 percent of their cooling bills in the summer—she would give my grandfather the money and then get "reimbursed" when she sent in the bill—and it seemed like he bought it, but I knew he kept it off whenever he could, just in case. A liar knows lying.

For better or worse, speaking to my grandfather had made me forget my surroundings—I was next to him on that warm, dusty pavement outside his building—so that when he asked me where I was, I had to think a moment before I said "*Colorado.*" With him, you could be truthful, because Colorado, Calcutta, Kaliningrad— all were the same. I could have told him Colorado was next to New Jersey. The only thing he wanted to know was "what they had there." He meant, partly, what kind of natural formations— mountains? rivers? oceans?—so that he could curate his admonishments properly: *Be careful in that water—do not go deeper than the knee. Be careful with those forests—let other people go in them.* The second meaning was: Did they have unique, well-made liquors? Perhaps there was a good bottle I could buy to add to the fancy-liquor collection in the cabinet of his wall unit.

Having moved through our script—

Me: Okay, I won't go in the river.
Him: Who needs it? Don't do it.
Me: I'm telling you, *okay!*
Him: Let other people do it.
Me: For fuck's sake—I'm thirty-six years old!

—and the bad feeling without which we could not complete a conversation, I was safe to move on to Oksana.

"Hello, lover boy," she said.

"I see the grapevine is working efficiently," I said.

"We all want something to root for," she sighed.

"What do you think?" I asked her.

"If she is good, if she is kind . . ." she began. "The woman is what matters. If the woman is certain, then the man can have all the doubts he wants. She is the rock."

"Oksana!" I yelled before I could stop myself. "I want a life partner, not a servant!" This was the platitude side of her. The submitting side. It was the first time I'd raised my voice at her, and I felt instant regret, not least because maybe it was just carryover from talking to my grandfather. Then again, it wasn't a friendship until you had fought. Right?

"You're right, of course," she said without resentment. "I've lived for others for so long I wouldn't know how to do otherwise."

Sometimes, "submission" was just another word for acceptance. I did not have her submission, and I did not have her acceptance.

"If you had all the money in the world," I said in a conciliatory tone of voice, "and a week when you couldn't work, and you couldn't have contact with your kids—if the world froze, basically, and you had a satchel of cash in your hands—what would you do?"

There was a long pause. "I don't know," she said finally. "You know I'm proud of taking care of your grandfather. But so badly, I want a result. You know what I mean? A *result*. An outcome that affects lots of people. Let it be a café I own where I cook for people. Or I don't know what. But lots of people. I'm good at doing things fast, I'm organized, I can do a lot with a little. I want to leave some kind of trace, you know? And I know I never will. What it would take to do that—to have less time for my kids; to go without income for a time—I know I will never be able to do. It's a dream. That's okay. It's a dream."

First, I felt all the usual caretaking feelings. I would save her. We would open a café together. She would cook, and I'd be front of the house. I would put up the money so she didn't have to interrupt earnings. Et cetera. The next thought was: As they fantasize about an entrepreneurial life of exactly the sort you're living, they keep trying to fill you with fear about the foolhardiness of its worry and risk. The third thought was: I love you all so much, and I am so tired of you. I signed off in the family way that I had started to use with her after our trip to Ukraine—"a kiss for you"—and returned to the road, no longer at all like the road I was on before I had called them.

CHAPTER 18

What to cook for forty Lakota children

What to cook to turn a mistake into hope

✛

It was nearly midnight when I arrived at Custer State Park. My headlights swept up the drive Jessica had walked so many hours, and there she was, her shoulders drawn because of the chill. Over the phone, we were nearly in love, but the last time we'd seen each other, I'd spent the evening angrily avoiding her gaze. We'd been in the same room all of three or four times.

Everyone would wake up if I set up my tent in the main camping area, so we pitched it in some very tall grass near the road. Inside, it felt like a small boat in high water. "It's better in person," Jessica said, and fell asleep on my chest. I stayed awake, trying to think of what we'd said to each other all those nights on the phone. To my disbelief, I remembered very little. It was impossible to put on a show—to keep saying only things that would achieve the desired effect—for a week's worth of seven-hour phone calls, wasn't it? That kind of madness would have to be noticeable even if one's self-awareness wasn't very high, wouldn't it? Or had that falsehood grafted so fully onto whatever was underneath that they were indistinguishable?

What had been a star-dusted black bowl the night before revealed itself, in the sharp morning light, to be a field of tall grass on the edge of a lake scored with contrails of what looked like sun crystals. It was bright. After Jessica left, I counted to a hundred and followed her. A cluster of boy tents climbed up one side of a depression that kept camp protected from the weather, and a cluster of girl tents climbed up the other. One of the other counselors, thin with long hair, walked past me holding the fresh-ground coffee and raw sugar I'd brought in the hope of ingratiating myself, sat down by a camp stove, and clapped in anticipation of this improvement on the instant he'd been drinking. His gratitude didn't extend to acknowledging me.

There were children in the trees above him. A girl of ten or so, with high cheekbones, a round face, dark skin, and light brown hair that swung like its own curtain whenever she moved branches, and a boy, a little older.

"Loretta," the counselor called, digging in the grounds with a camping spoon. "You're going to fall into my coffee."

As if challenged, she yelled and leapt down to the ground from what seemed too high up the tree. Then she charged him, he began shouting "no, no, no," and she stopped just short of him and fell to the ground laughing.

"Loretta, for God's sake, go brush your teeth," he said.

Loretta got up and walked off, though for some reason she went into the boys' bathroom.

Though I stood next to them, I could have been invisible.

By a group of picnic tables enclosed by a semi-open log structure, Jessica was scooping yogurt into plastic Solo cups and sprinkling it with granola while a junior counselor cut up apples. She was as beautiful as she had seemed that night I dropped trash on her feet outside Moscow57. Other than that, I felt nothing clearly. The children were eyeing the row of Solo cups without great excitement.

"What about cereal?" a boy with short, spiky black hair said.

"You had cereal yesterday," Jessica said. "This is good, try it."

"Yogurt makes my head hurt," he said.

"Yogurt does not make your head hurt."

"It hurt my head yesterday, seriously," he said.

"You didn't *have* yogurt yesterday." She waved the yogurt tub— she had just opened it.

"It makes your head hurt 'cause there's nothing in there," another boy proposed.

"If there was nothing in there, it couldn't hurt," the first boy said. He nodded, as if, upon reflection, the logic checked out. A third boy—he had light brown hair that reached midway down his back, but he had the first boy's face and thick chest—came over and laid his arm protectively on his shoulder. They looked like two little refrigerators. They had to be brothers.

"What's he, your boyfriend?" the first boy said to Jessica, pointing to me.

"He's my *friend*," Jessica said. "He's from Russia. You know where that is?"

"You gonna teach me some Russian curses?" he said.

Curry favor by despoiling the youth, or take the high ground and miss a chance to establish a connection?

"*Va fangul*," I said.

"*Va fangul*," he said.

"And you've got to—you have to scrape your nails up your neck, sort of—like this."

He scraped skillfully. "*Va fangul*," he said to Jessica.

"*Wonderful*," she said.

One of the other senior counselors appeared, holding boxes of Frosted Flakes and Froot Loops. The kids began chanting: "Cereal! Cereal!" Deflated, Jessica stared at her. "Shit," the counselor said. "Sorry. I thought—"

While the children blew milk, pink from their cereals, at each other, Jessica and I set to making lunch for the road: She smeared Miracle Whip over limp slices of wheat, I wedged in one piece of turkey and one cheddar, and she wrapped in plastic. At one point I realized she was holding out bread and looking at me quizzically. I wasn't sure how long she'd been waiting.

"You all right?" she said.

"Yes," I said to her. "Of course."

"I know it's a lot," she said, motioning to the kids.

"No, it's not that."

"So what is it?"

"Nothing. Nothing."

I was saved from further interrogation by the approach of the lead counselor. She didn't introduce herself. Instead she said, "You're going to cook dinner for forty people?" I had gone through a phone interview and a background check, but for some reason I was feeling a wall of doubt from the counselors.

"Jessica said your cook canceled," I said neutrally.

"Well, we've got our hands full," she said.

"So that's all I mean," I said.

"I've got two hundred dollars left for food, and that's it," she said.

Forty people, two hundred dollars a meal—I could manage that.

"No, no," she said. "Two hundred total. Until the end." The end was three nights away. Presumably, the children were meant to eat dinner on all three of them.

"I see," I said.

Six chicken roasters, 5–6 pounds each

Two pork shoulders, 10 pounds each

Aluminum cooking trays (3)

Bell peppers

Tomato paste

Cilantro

Apple cider vinegar

Apples

Onions, 10 pounds

Kale (5 bunches)

Dijon mustard

Garlic

Parmigiano Reggiano

Lemons

Idaho russets, 5 pounds

Goat cheese, 2 large logs

Ground beef, 10 pounds

Carrots, 5 pounds

Bay leaves

Extra-virgin olive oil

Linguine, 10 pounds

Black Forest cake ~~(2)~~ (3)

I had come in at $193. None of it was organic, but some of it came from more or less nearby—California is a lot closer to South Dakota than to New York, though the same things cost more in South Dakota—and none of it was very terrible for you. Except the Black Forest cake. But I needed childproof insurance. The rest of the first dinner would be simple: roast chicken along with egg noodles, which I'd found in the camp larder, sexed up by a bath in the chicken fat. We had moved from a campground to a college in Rapid City, which had given us a kitchen with virtually no utensils, cooking implements, or serving plates, but I'd bought aluminum cooking trays, and the camp had its own pot to boil water. The only problem with the chicken recipe was that the high temperature—you cooked it at 450, for a crispy skin—invariably set off the smoke alarm, and there were no windows in the kitchen. I wondered what the Jewish prayer for competence was. I did the only thing I could think of: I sat down, as if to rest before a trip, as per Russian tradition. The only good thing about the cooking anxiety was that it covered up the other one.

I was grateful to have had a reason to absent myself, to do the food shopping. And now I planned to hide out in the kitchen making dinner until—until I didn't know what. Until night came and I could no longer delay speaking honestly. I was filled with apprehension.

Then I saw Jessica's face at the door, and instead of the joy I had flown and driven all this way to take hold of, I felt my stomach disappearing into my feet.

"You're okay on timing?" she said. "We're about to do showers. I'm afraid to ask what you think of all this."

"Why are the counselors so weird with me?" I blurted out.

"Weird? No. Everyone's just, you know. It's crazy."

"Honestly, I don't think anything," I said wearily, answering her previous question. She gazed at me, puzzled. I tried to correct the course: "I get it about the kids. I get why you come here."

"Thank you," she said cautiously. "It means a lot you see that."

"I'm not here for the kids," I said.

"I know," she said. "I was just—"

"I'm not explaining myself clearly." I breathed out heavily. It was like listening to someone else speak. "This was the next step in the seduction," I said. "A romantic grand gesture. No one else would do such a thing. It would play well. Et cetera."

"Oh," she said, her face changing. "I see."

"I try in the wrong way," I said. "It's hard to explain. I should have waited till you came home. You're married. I bet he has no idea you're not here alone." I looked at her. "Right." Then I said those fateful words: "I think I made a mistake." I hated myself in that moment. Two years after Yvonne, six months after Amy, nothing had changed. I was beyond remedy. I was ashamed.

"I see," she said again, but coldly this time. There was a very long silence. "Are you going to make dinner or should I tell the kids they need to wash themselves?"

"It's okay for you to be confused," I said defensively, "but not me."

"I'm *married*," she said.

"Well, I'm fucked up. It's just as strong a commitment, trust me."

We laughed at that, a little. Then I got it. "You told me to come even though the counselors hadn't decided. Or decided against it. You didn't tell them I was coming. That's why they're weird. That's

why I don't have a bed." I had been told I would have to continue
sleeping in a tent somewhere on campus while everyone else slept
in a dorm room.

She examined the floor. "I have a hard time being direct sometimes. I really wanted you to come."

I laughed mirthlessly. "You can see it through their eyes, though,
right? It's nuts. Desperate. Two crazy, desperate people."

"I guess you've found somebody as hungry as you are," she said.
She took out her phone, and I listened to her book me a room at the
nice hotel in town. She hung up. "You're not the only one who can
do romantic grand gestures."

"That was—really generous," I said. "I'll make dinner, yes—of
course."

"I'll go wash dirt out of ears," she said, smiled mournfully, and
disappeared.

I was grateful to have to cook. I could count on my head going
still for as long as it took. Maybe not still enough, though. Forty-five
minutes later, the roasters in the oven and little bodies with wet
hair beginning to fill the hallway outside the kitchen, it occurred
to me that the high temp should have by now filled the room with
a smoky haze. Overcome by a feeling I did not wish to be having,
I checked the heat. I exhaled—the dial was at 450. But when I ran
my hand near the oven door, which should have been conducting a
wall of heat, I felt . . . nothing. Carefully, I opened the door. It was
probably about 250 inside.

I tried the front right stove burner. Nothing. The rear right.
Nothing. The front left. Nothing. I was saying "no" over and over
when the rear left clicked, clicked, clicked, and sputtered on. Fifteen minutes before the time I said dinner would be ready, I had six
raw chickens, an oven that seemed to go no higher than 250, and
one functioning burner.

I waved Jessica down in the hallway. "Can you bring me a frying pan from the van?"

"What's the matter?" she said.

"Nothing!"

She looked at me with an expression that made clear she didn't believe me and vanished.

Several minutes later, the kitchen door opened and a frying pan was flung at me—showers were a particular nightmare this evening, which I, for one, was thrilled to hear. I maxed out the heat on the functioning burner. Then I wedged two roasters into the pan. The kitchen was like a home without beds—there wasn't even a fork in the utensil drawers; as soon as the sizzle sounded like too much, I turned the roasters with my hands. I had to get the first two chickens 70 percent done. Then I would put them back in the oven to ploddingly finish. The next two I would fry to 80 percent done. The last two almost all the way. While they were finishing in the oven, I would boil water for the egg noodles. Somehow, all this would be ready at roughly the same time and before the group of heads starting to peer through the kitchen window reached critical mass.

At some point, Jessica materialized at my elbow. Then she left and returned with two spatulas, for more awkward but less painful chicken turning. The number of heads at the window grew. The frying was going too slowly. I had an idea. When it was time to fry the next pair, I took the chickens out of the oven, set the tray on the prep table, closed my eyes, and butterflied them open with my hands. A cloudful of steam burst out, and I nearly wailed in pain. The two butterflied halves didn't quite fit on the pan, but after I weighed them down with a precarious pot full of water, I had something approximating my grandmother's chicken-under-a-brick.

She had died just after I met Alana, about whom my grandmother had had only one question: "Does she cook?" I said she was a very talented person, but she was in a hard business, so she worked a lot and—well, not often. My grandmother frowned and said something not very nice. As Alana's schedule let up, she did cook more, and well, but it was too late to tell my grandmother. When I visited her at the cemetery, I mentioned it anyway. I never believed in cemeteries or silent monologues for the dead—a person gone is a person gone, and post-death rituals always felt like only a measure of their goneness. But I visited my grandmother for more years than I thought I would. For some reason, I'd decided that, even though others in the family didn't understand, she did. Perhaps only because, when she was alive, when the matter concerned me, she was on board no matter what. So I imagined that, down there in the ground, she understood why my ex and I had held on for so long, how I could have ended up in the situation I had with Amy, why I was at a dysfunctional stove at the South Dakota School of Mines and Technology, roasting and frying chicken for forty. In truth, if my grandmother were alive, on board or not, probably she'd have understood no better than my grandfather or my parents. Her death had allowed me to imagine a kinship we might not have had in real life.

By the time the water went on for the noodles, it was an hour past the scheduled dinnertime. The kitchen was hot, the door was open, and they were hungry out there.

"So, like, what are you?" one of the popular girls, tall and thin, yelled at Loretta, half her height. "Are you a boy or a girl?"

"What do you care?" Loretta said in an even voice.

"Leave her alone," a boy said.

"I want to do what boys do," Loretta said.

The fallout from this gave us twenty minutes, but the noodle water remained still as death.

"Wait," Jessica said. She ditched the noodle water and came back a minute later with water so hot that steam was coming off of it—the kitchen faucet let out tepid water, but the bathroom had scalding. I was so elated I kissed her, which sent a loud, hooting jeer up from the hallway. As I piled in the noodles, she set out the

Black Forest cakes—the promise of these would buy another couple of minutes.

There weren't proper cutting utensils, so I ripped the chicken into pieces with my hands, and Jessica served using the spatula-tongs, adding noodles after she swished them around in chicken fat. The kids were skeptical of the chicken, but the promise of Black Forest cake afterward did its job. No one said thank you, though some did come for seconds. Earlier, I'd tried only bits of food to make sure it was done, and now I had a proper meal of the detritus. It wasn't bad. It was quite all right, actually, all things considered. Or maybe the hunger that arrives after you're done with something like that is large and indiscriminate. My restaurant work had nothing on it, though probably I would've melted down even more without that experience. I was melted down pretty good all the same—my hands were burned as red as if I'd laid them in a frying pan, which essentially I had. I sank to the floor and ran my finger along what was left on the trays of Black Forest cake. (These had come in for seconds and thirds.) Jessica slid down next to me. It was silent—the young ones had gorged and departed for bed.

"You saved it," I said. "That was like a firefight. Trench warfare."

"I don't remember the last time I cooked," she said.

"You don't like to?" I said. Somehow, in seven nights of talking seven hours a night, we hadn't discussed this. It was as if all that talk had happened to other people.

"No, I love to. Loved to. My husband has a sensitive stomach. It's usually just noodles, or take-out broth." She looked up. "Sorry to talk about him."

"It's okay. He's your husband."

Another long silence followed, but it was serene. Finally, I said, "Have you ever been with someone who's—who's—" I had never said the words out loud. The analyst had said them. The psychopharmacologist had said them. They threw around those poisonous words as if they weren't poison at all. I got them out. "Depression. Clinically."

She thought about it. "It scares me. But I'd be willing to try."

I nodded and felt for the back of her neck. She leaned into my hand. The room ticked faintly around us. It was near midnight, and a mountain of dishes.

"How about, for dinner tomorrow, things that don't need cooking?" she said. I laughed slightly. She looked up at me. "But I don't know if you're going to be here for dinner tomorrow."

I said I would be.

I stayed till the end. We took the slow route back to Denver. In Hot Springs, we stayed with the lawyer who'd written me about my first novel. As she smoked long cigarettes on her flagstone patio, she set Jessica straight on some things about divorce. When we got to Laramie, where I had another friend—it's the best thing about book touring, as good as having your books bought by strangers: you connect to people all over, a different kind of American map, and if you do it enough, it becomes so that you never have to drive very far before getting to a home where they know you—we went to the public computers at the university library, on which she wrote a final letter to her husband. Then she, my friend, and I took a long, hot walk to Kinko's, where none of the clerks could understand why Jessica wanted so much damn insurance and guarantee of delivery on a one-page letter.

Along the way south, she told me about Loretta. Loretta was always scrambling up rocks or wrestling somebody or climbing around a tree. She was suited for survival. Loretta felt like a boy, not a girl—that was why she'd gone into the boys' bathroom. Her mom had asked for that when she brought her to camp. The boys didn't care. It was the girls who gave her a hard time.

Then Jessica told me about a pair of camp boys who had gone

to rent a canoe at Custer State Park. The clerk told them the rental station was closed. On the way back, they saw a white family go up—for them, the rental station was open. Half the rangers were racist assholes, so the kids couldn't make a fuss. The older kids pretended they didn't care, but the younger kids—that was why Jessica was hugging them all the time. All they wanted was to melt in your arms.

She told me about the girl who wore long sleeves because her arms were covered with cuts. Her thighs were covered as well. The counselors had taken her penknife, but she must have had more. Many girls had cuts. Many of them had been raped, some by family members. Jessica had seen cuts on a girl as young as six, cigarette burns on the arms of a boy. Some had tried to commit suicide. There was no help for someone like that on the reservation, so they were sent to a special hospital in Rapid City, but it was like an asylum. The prospect of going there was sometimes the one thing that kept them from trying to kill themselves—or the thing that made them try extra hard. Jessica said this last part through tears. She was going to lose the science fiction bookshop in the divorce; she'd decided to apply for a master's in social work so she could try to establish a mental health counseling center on the reservation.

The kids hardly ever got away from the rez. For all their trouble there, they felt an intense sense of belonging. The border-town whites, some of whom were viciously racist, did nothing to make it easier to imagine that good things awaited outside. Meanwhile, many parents, knowing too well what their kids could run into, on or off the rez, didn't let them go anywhere on their own. They didn't even want them to go to camp, and called every day.

For that—for a sense of belonging so fierce it withstood *all of that*—I envied them. As a teenager, I'd taken on a false name, ignored my native language, run from my family, pretended in the hope it would bring native feeling. The irony was that the native feeling began to show up only when I tried to retrieve what I'd been ignoring. That had seemed like the end of the story, but it turned out that, after accepting that which would always be Russian in me, I had to figure out what would be American, those early pretenses being wishful. New York is no less America than Pine Ridge. But at Pine Ridge, there were parents so worried that what had happened to them might happen to their children that they never let the children out of their sight. No matter where I went, I found my way to people whom trauma had made berserk about safety. I felt at home among them.

Jessica met my grandfather before she met my parents, because we drove to the hospital directly from the airport. Blood had appeared in his urine, and while we were flying home, an ambulance took him away. At the hospital, he muttered incoherently, then took my hand and smiled, half guileless love, half vacant searching. But no delirium could compete with his feeling for beauty, and when Jessica went to the bathroom, he lifted up a weak thumb and curled up his lips in a way that meant he was impressed.

I had sublet my apartment, and Jessica's was occupied by her husband, so after the other classic stress tests of connection— cooking together and hours of alone time in a car—suddenly we ended up living together, too, at a friend's place that was empty. (God bless these friends, without whose musical-chair largesse New York life wouldn't be possible.) After my grandfather, more or less returned to his faculties, was discharged, I invited my parents to meet Jessica, at a café in Brooklyn. When they appeared, their brows were so knitted, they looked like one terrified line over their eyes. This turned to outright panic when they saw Jessica: a Viking, and given to the kind of close embrace, even with strangers, that makes a Russian person check his billfold. I

wanted to tell them that it was our poisonous birthright to wish
so badly for familiarity, for the security of stable information,
that when it came to something new, we preferred rushing to the
worst assumptions to having to manage inconclusiveness, with
its possibility of kinder revelations. (Few utterances disoriented
them more than "Let's wait and see.") My grandmother had gotten a cold welcome from my grandfather's family, then passed it
on to my father as he tried to join hers. How long would we keep
doing to others the same things done to us? I could say all that,
and perhaps they'd nod in a kind of understanding, or out of politeness, but none of it was durable enough to withstand the sense
of things that would surge back as soon as I went away. I knew
not to bother.

We were all so nervous that we drank a bottle of wine and forgot
to order food. But we never really forget food. Self-conscious about
meeting a new person or not, my parents had brought a care pack-
age. Some people don't leave home without umbrellas or condoms;
mine, without food. When I was in my early twenties, they brought
care packages like this all the time, until I threatened hell if they
didn't leave me to my independence, but lately they were chancing
it again because lately I was accepting again, and because sometimes my father couldn't resist showing off his Caesar salad with
"home mad mayonesse" or his "mushrooms with feeling" (filling).
Just now, the bag they withdrew as we said goodbye—you can't let
a loved one return from a trip to an empty fridge—was the most
welcome thing I could imagine.

Jessica and I started unpacking our picnic right on the steps of
a fancy brownstone near the café. There was a chicken stew, and
syrniki, the patties of farmer cheese, dotted with raisins and spiked
with vanilla, fried to a light crisp on both sides. Once, when I was
little, my mother had cooked a batch while my father was, once
again, repainting some part of our apartment at her behest. In my

six-year-old brain, they became "housepainter *syrniki*," and that is what I call them to this day.

After my parents retrieved their car—parking in the city gives them as much palpitation as the drive to the city itself—they pulled up by the brownstone for one more goodbye and saw their son sitting next to a woman who was tucking into their chicken stew and *syrniki* with all the abandon of a native. *Their* native. If the boy's grandmother were around, she would have nodded approvingly, with the authority that only the once hungry among us possess. Two people eating in famished, silent synchrony—what more did you need?

"HOUSEPAINTER" *SYRNIKI* (SEER-NEE-KEE) (V)

Time: 30–45 minutes   Serves: 4

Syr *is "cheese" in Russian, but the cheese in question here is farmer cheese—the densest and least watery you can find. These sweet little pucks will be good cold or hot, at midnight or noon, but there's nothing like them fresh out of the pan for breakfast.*

1 pound farmer cheese	2–3 tablespoons sugar
2 eggs	Raisins, to taste
4–6 tablespoons flour, plus	2 teaspoons vanilla extract
additional for dusting	Sunflower oil

1. Mix the farmer cheese with the eggs, 4 tablespoons of the flour, 2 tablespoons of the sugar, the raisins, and the vanilla. If the mix could use a little thickening, add up to 2 tablespoons more flour. If you like a sweeter taste, add the additional tablespoon of sugar.

2. Dust a cutting board or kitchen counter with flour. With your fingers, scoop up some of the cheese mixture and ball it in the palm of your hand into a sphere the size of a golf ball. Drop it into the flour and pat it down so that it starts to resemble a small hockey puck. Lift it gently and flip so the other side can get floured. Shake off excess flour, if any, and set aside. Repeat for the remaining cheese mixture. You should get 16 pucks.

3. Now do the flouring again. Ball each puck back up—it should be easier now, as it's covered with flour—and re-flour in the way described in step 2.

4. Set a nonstick pan—or two nonstick pans, if you want to save time—
over medium-low heat. Place a generous amount of sunflower oil in the
pan (the pucks should be able to slide around in it) and, once it's had a
minute or two to warm up, place the pucks in carefully. Ideally, your pans
will each fit 8. Brown for about 6 minutes on each side. Keep an eye on the
oil—the pucks will burn quickly if there isn't enough.

*Let cool and serve on their own, or with a dollop of your favorite jam, yogurt, or
even sour cream.*

✦

EPILOGUE

In the fall of 2016, I went to Latvia, in the Baltics, on a cultural mission for the State Department. I asked to be taken to Madona, in central Latvia, where my grandfather's brother, my great-uncle Aaron, was supposed to have been buried in a "brothers' grave" of Red Army soldiers killed on the 3rd Baltic Front. The burial ground was up a little hill. It felt equally tended and unkempt, memorialized and forgotten. Things get tangled up in places like Latvia. The Latvians were forcibly conscripted into the USSR in 1940; some of them welcomed the Germans, and helped them. In the same place, hundreds or thousands of non-Latvian boys and men had died trying to keep Latvia for the Soviet Union. How to commemorate this? "Where was your family during the war?" I asked the caretaker, an old woman in rain boots, through an interpreter. She said she didn't know. In Latvia, that means they were with the Germans. As I walked past the engraved names, I thought about what it was like to be someone whose family had aided the Germans and who now made her living by looking after a memorial to the soldiers who died to defeat them.

My grandfather was about to turn ninety, and I wanted to bring him a photo of a plate bearing the family surname and Aaron's initial. But I couldn't find it. The caretaker had said that, "for some reason," the original, more comprehensive plates had come down, replaced with these, a partial record. Despairingly, I scanned the Os (the first letter of my grandfather's surname) again and again. No Aaron. Appealing to the Ns in the hope of finding a misplaced O there, like a misshelved book in the library, my eyes fell on a soldier named Novikov. That was the name I had invented for myself to ward off the Jew-beating boys back in Minsk. What kind of man had this Novikov been? If he'd stayed alive, and was strolling past on the day those boys finally came, would he have interfered to defend me? I did with this discovery the only thing that I could: When we went to the middle school in town where I was giving a talk about art and identity, I told the students about Novikov and Aaron and my grandfather, and how these things could add up to a story. Otherwise baffled, to this part they listened.

To my grandfather, I pretended that Aaron's name was among those listed. I'd taken pictures, yes—they were getting developed. He was old and removed enough from reality not to know that nobody really developed pictures anymore. This was how we spoke now. The time for truth "into the forehead"—expressed directly and without mercy—was over. He had aged out. I'd stopped trying to explain, to get him to understand. I visited, I answered the same questions several times, and we settled down to watch the Russian news programs whose (anti-American) propaganda makes Fox News seem like *60 Minutes*.

By then he was already using a cane. He kept calling himself "the Last of the Mohicans": His neighbor Yasha, the Fitness Fanatic, had passed. So had Ilya, the Intellectual in the wheelchair. The friend who used to catch contraband beef over the fence had lost his wife to a car accident. He and my grandfather were the last ones standing. Sitting. My last visit before I went to Latvia was the first time my grandfather didn't accompany me out to the stairwell and try to stuff a wad of cash into my hand by way of goodbye.

In 2015, my parents returned to Vienna for the first time since 1988. This time, they bought themselves bratwursts. Thirty years after arriving in America, we have a lot more money and feel a lot less security. Or maybe statelessness is blessed by oblivion—you don't know what you don't know. By accident, you might feel good about something.

Now we know. Now, even my father, who tries to avoid doctors as sedulously as his father did, succumbs to the American way of taking care of yourself, the constant checkups that leave you with the impression you're half-dead though you are relatively healthy. "There are no healthy people," he says of the American medical system. "Only the undiagnosed." Now he wishes he had agreed to have his age revised up on his immigration documents before we left Minsk. When he was on his honeymoon, in that shed in Crimea, he wondered if he would ever get to stay in a real hotel. Now, his American earnings having made many hotel stays possible, he tries to rent places that resemble that shed.

He does all the cooking. Now it's grilled eggplant and baked fish, about as delicious as cooking so sinless can manage to be. Sometimes his talents exceed even these limitations, like a certain oatmeal cake with raspberry filling. The *syrniki* remain my mother's to make, and on special occasions she will make my grandmother's potato latkes. Special because you have to use all that oil. It's my father who resists it; after decades of chasteness, she's started making her omelets with butter, like we used to back home. "Butter's not the problem," she says. "Look at the French. It's the quality of the butter. We ate shitty Russian food for the first time in America."

In 2017, my grandfather was diagnosed with Stage III bladder cancer. Stage III was good—it wasn't in the bone. But there was a tumor the size of a soccer ball pressing on his prostate, making it impossible for him to relieve himself. After an agonizing interlude involving three hospitals and a catheter, radiation and low-dose chemo destroyed the tumor. He "felt like a human being again." Cancer is supposed to spread slowly through an old body, so we cautiously hoped for a reprieve. But his next checkup had revealed the opposite.

His hemoglobin was shredded, but, remembering what had happened to my grandmother during her gallbladder operation, he refused to hear of a transfusion. We tricked him into it: He was told he was getting my mother's blood. (With the doctor's collusion, she made a show of having it drawn.) We lied to him about everything having to do with the illness: He didn't know he had cancer. Knowing would have activated a fatalism that would have made his usual hypochondria seem like enthusiasm. Not knowing made it possible for him, beached like a big baby in the doctor's examining chair, to say, as if he was haggling at the open-air market in Minsk, "What's he saying? Think I can squeeze out another tenner?"

When he fell ill, I experienced the desire, in the time he had left, to offer him nothing but love on his terms. In doing so, I knew, I was resolving to lie better. I'd lost, but it didn't matter, because he was about to lose something much bigger.

With each visit, some new part of him fell away. His fabled hair went brittle and dry—he stared vacantly at the television while I ran my hands through it anyway. He began seeing a man in a fedora and a long coat at the side of his bed. At night, he screamed to be let out, let go.

He could no longer shave himself, an even grimmer milestone in his case, because he'd spent half a century giving shaves. I did it for him. Even in his impairment—I would tell him to stick out his chin, and he would, but then his face would collapse from the effort—it was clear he thought I was doing a shit job. But as I scraped the razor down his soapy cheek, cradling his face like a lover's, sometimes he smiled like a boy without cares. That's how it is with our people—reflexive disapproval, then begrudging acknowledgment that it had turned out all right.

Doing this reminded me of a dark evening during the catheter time. There was a blockage, perhaps caked blood around the meatus. This was too much even for Oksana, so my father and I went into my grandfather's bedroom. Then, using gauze and peroxide, I cleaned the tip of my grandfather's penis. It was one of the most painful, intimate things I'd ever done, the old man squirming and squalling like a toddler no matter how gently I went. After I was done, he wept again, now in gratitude.

Not everything about his decline was grim. His eyelashes became as long and lustrous as Jessica's. And the things that floated up from the mud barrel of his cracked psyche now obeyed an unreachable but magical logic. Once, as I was bending down to kiss him goodbye, he took my forearm with his mottled hand and said, his breath like rustling paper, "Sometimes you've got this egg in your hands, and you have to carry it such a long way. Kilometers. So careful the whole time. And then you're just a meter or two from the threshold, and poof. It's gone." It was nonsense the way poetry was nonsense, and enchanted the same way. As he lost his cognition—as he fell free of the self he'd hewn from his unkind lot—he sounded like the child whose youth had been stolen by the war, a child who had sat in him, waiting, for three-quarters of a century.

I couldn't stop thinking about that hand, gone mottled seemingly overnight. Even at ninety, his nails were clean and square. Though I'd never watched his hands purposefully, I realized I knew their habitual gestures better than my own: the way the shelf of his pinkie moved crumbs around on the tablecloth while he spoke on the phone; the way he kept his palm on his forehead as he slept, occasionally opening it as if reasoning with someone, or calculating the make on a deal; the way he spat on his fingertips when he was counting money. Sometimes he dismissed things by pushing the air away with four fingers, as if they weren't worth the trouble of an impassioned rejection. Sometimes by smacking the air left to right with the back of his hand. And sometimes, he ridged his hand as if he was about to shake someone else's but then rotated it and opened the fingers slightly in a Yiddish-like gesture that meant *Just look at that asshole.*

Oddly, our phone conversations, never long, grew longer, perhaps because it was no longer necessary to speak. Once, driving somewhere while speaking to him, I became lost in my thoughts.

When I came back, he was humming an old song as if I weren't there. He kept humming, softly and dreamily, and I just listened, even after I'd gotten to where I was going and parked, like when Oksana sometimes didn't hang up the landline properly and I stayed on, listening to the distant sounds of his life without me there to spoil it.

Things started happening to me, too. My left eyelid started twitching. I lost my sense of space and broke three cups in two days. Once, standing in the shower, I became entranced by the tile and burst into tears. I nearly punched a bus driver and crashed the car a half dozen times. He was in the world before Stalin had control of the Soviet Union. Before anyone knew the name Hitler. He had lived almost a century.

Once, as in a fairy tale, the illness receded enough for him not only to regain sense but to perform a miraculous feat. Oksana had pulled him out of his wheelchair to do leg calisthenics. My mother put on an old Soviet waltz and, little by little, he and Oksana started . . . twirling, just as they had before tango all those years ago. He was, of course, more or less swaying in place, but there he was, dancing on the doorstep of death. Later, as I was leaving, I leaned into the living room for a final look. He winked at me. I winked back.

That was our final communication. Shortly afterward, he stopped speaking, though once, Oksana pleading with him through a wall of tears to tell her who was that boy standing next to his bed, the last of him collected into enough of a gust for my name to come out. Not my Russian name, but Berele, a diminutive in the Yiddish that was his childhood language.

When we were clearing out his home, among the only things I kept was one of his clowns. There was a set—Oksana took one, my parents took one, and I did. The reason he gave for collecting them—he didn't want to offend the owner of the bric-a-brac store who'd pressed them on him—surely was only part of the story, the rest of which he probably didn't know himself. But they were the only things he owned for no purpose other than pleasure.

The clown reminds me that in two decades of weekly visits, a vast part of this man remained off-access to me, perhaps because it was off-access to him, too. I have never, at once, felt such intimacy and distance with someone, and I suspect I never will. He gave me the gift of an extraordinarily rare human experience, and it feels symbolic that it was not at all the gift he meant to give.

Jessica and I are still together. We make that roast chicken—Salvation Chicken, we call it—a lot. I got her to see Ireland in a new way. And she got me to change my mind about hipsters. For a while I made my life among them, in Williamsburg, Brooklyn, in her apartment, a future that once seemed about as likely as making my life with someone like her. You get what you wanted, just not what you planned. My hunger has been good for my work, and a near calamity for everything else. At least I know not to rely on it.

I eat more moderately now. For a while, I was even gluten- and dairy-free. I brew my own kombucha. Sometimes I even leave food on the plate. But I still go the extra mile—in New York, that takes an hour—because that place charges a dollar less for goat milk, and I still pack lots of tinfoil for the airplane. At least eight sandwiches—after all—if the haul is long, and even ten, if you want to be extra-sure. I don't care who sees.

I call Oksana and tell her about the sandwiches, and she laughs. And then the laughter gives way as we remember my grandfather. He has finally claimed his half of the burial plot he bought after my grandmother's death. He no longer has to figure out how to survive.

© Max Avdeev

Please see www.borisfishman.com for more photos
from Brooklyn and Ukraine.

AUTHOR'S NOTE

In the author's note to her memoir *Tender at the Bone*, Ruth Reichl mentions an improbable family memory, then writes that by the time she was old enough to dispute it, her "father was no longer available for questions, but I am sure that if he had been he would have insisted that the story was true. For him it was."

She goes on: "This book is absolutely in the family tradition. Everything here is true, but it may not be entirely factual. In some cases I have compressed events; in others I have made two people into one. I have occasionally embroidered. I learned early that the most important thing in life is a good story."

The novelist in me agrees, but the journalist and former fact-checker starts to feel a bit of an itch. Of course, the idea that even fully "factual" memoirs carry some whole truth is wishful; memory is slippery even for those trying to recollect it without self-serving bias, a matter complicated by the fact that we're sure it's not slippery at all. Once a recollection sets in, it seems to hold on without any interest in doubt. Especially if you keep sharing the story, which reinforces the idea that it happened *exactly this way.*

In the preceding pages, I've had to imagine more than embroider; I've compressed events and presented them out of order for clarity's sake, but only when it didn't violate the spirit of what happened. As to what, indeed, happened, what you've read is an earnest effort to get as close as our imperfect toolbox allows.

I wanted to write this book—have been dreaming of it since my first years as a writer, when I was a journalist—because its genre's potential for complexity, beauty, and meaning often feels peerless: a true story, with the immediacy and urgency of fact, told with the style and transport present more often in novels. In asking what could be proven, literary nonfiction proves a great deal, and insists especially on one of these truths: The facts rarely live at the extremes, and almost nothing can be so true that another possibility has no value. As such, this genre seems to me to have a great deal to say in our difficult times.

ACKNOWLEDGMENTS

The adolescent cries out: "I didn't ask to be born!" The grown writer takes his revenge: "I'm writing a memoir!" I come from private stock (not the Biggie kind), so my first thanks is to my family for allowing me to tell our story as I saw it. By now, that family has in it only my perplexed, weariless parents. But I am doing my best to enlarge it.

My grandfather Arkady. He was a survivor whose resourcefulness I carry within me but won't ever match.

Writing literary fiction and nonfiction means the best calves in the business, seeing as you can never drop from your toes. My agent, Henry Dunow; my editor, Terry Karten; and my publisher, Jonathan Burnham, have chosen, heroically, to serve as my spotters in this dark, frosty gym, for which I feel both great gratitude and admiration.

It's even darker without your early readers: Jessica Cole, Alana Newhouse, Alex Halberstadt, Cyd Oppenheimer.

In 2012, CEC ArtsLink, an arts organization that facilitates exchange between artists in the United States and Eastern Europe, gave me a grant to follow Oksana to her hometown. That support was as meaningful because of the funding as because of the vote of confidence. Thank you especially to Fritzie Brown, Zhenia Stadnik, and Maxim Tumenev. Apologies for being a bit late with my final report. A special thanks to Max Avdeev, who photographed that journey, as well as Oksana's kitchen in Brooklyn. No one so young should be so phenomenally talented.

Massive thanks to certain friends and supporters whose friendship and support have risen to the Russian standard (not the vodka, but that, too): Joel Berkowitz, Gary Ashman, Ellen Sussman and

Neal Rothman, Peter Godwin, Jonathan and Zach Plutzik, Asher Milbauer, Dina Nayeri, Neel Mukherjee, Karen Goldstein, the Wise Bauer family, the Kan family, Vance Serchuk, Rob Liguori and Nicole DiBella, Alana Kinarsky and Gabe Rosenhouse, and the generous and indefatigable Carolyn Hessel of the Jewish Book Council. Thanks as well to Sunil Amin for medical fact-checking. Elena Lappin gave me some invaluable counsel, in a difficult moment, on how to keep going.

This book unofficially began its gestation on May 4, 2013, when a dozen or so intrepid souls took on the handful of recipes I had by then transcribed from Oksana, and we made a party of it in my old apartment on the Lower East Side. A big thanks to them all.

The biggest is to the person with whom I share my new apartment, in addition to so much else. Jessica, I adore and admire you beyond what I can express.

My last thanks are to you, dear reader, for remaining interested in complex work—by which I mean stories without clear answers or foregone conclusions; stories in which people want contradictory things, express their wishes in garbled ways, and exhibit both nobility and weakness as they do their best to make sense of uneasy lives—during times that have often seemed hostile to such books. You're keeping alive an indispensable flame.

WORKS REFERENCED

I received a superbly conveyed education about Soviet refuseniks, the American effort to free Soviet Jewry, and the political context of the time from Gal Beckerman's *When They Come for Us, We'll Be Gone: The Epic Struggle to Save Soviet Jewry.*

Nadezhda Mandelstam's *Hope Against Hope: A Memoir* (translated by Max Hayward) was only tangentially related to my research about what my grandfather experienced before and during the war, but I couldn't stop thinking of it—with horror, but also something more exalted, because of the testimonial she created. It is among the truest, most penetrating records of what the Stalin Terror was like.

The three poems I reference by her husband, Osip Mandelstam, have no titles other than their first lines (translations mine):

"We live not feeling the ground beneath us . . ."
"The apartment is as silent as paper . . ."
"A cold spring. Timid, hungry Crimea . . ."

A version of the story, in chapter 6, about the Pepsi cans I returned for the bottle deposit appeared in an essay in the *New York Times Magazine* entitled "My Secret Pepsi Plot" (July 27, 2014). A portion of the story about my time in the kitchen at Moscow57 appeared in somewhat different form in the *Guardian*, in an essay called "Russian Soup for the Soul" (July 9, 2016). A part of the story about my grandfather's decline originally appeared in *Tablet* magazine, under the title "The Last Thing He Taught Me and the First Thing I Learned" (June 25, 2018).

The translation from *Russian Cooking in Exile* at the top of chapter 10 is mine. (The book is available in English as *Russian Cuisine in Exile.*) Robert Irwin's quote at the head of chapter 11 comes from Lawrence Weschler's *Seeing Is Forgetting the Name of the Thing One Sees: A Life of Contemporary Artist Robert Irwin.*

Anna Reid's *Borderland: A Journey Through the History of Ukraine* is not only informative but wickedly well written.

The help offered by Rebecca Manley's *To the Tashkent Station: Evacuation and Survival in the Soviet Union at War* is self-explanatory.

Someone should really translate Alexander Genis's *Kolobok and Other Culinary Adventures* into English. Genis venerates William Pokhlebkin, the dean of Russian food writing (whose *Russian Delight: A Cookbook of the Soviet Peoples* was also of use), but Genis is my Pokhlebkin. *Kolobok*—a small round loaf of bread—is a collection of food essays as knowledgeable as they are opinionated and entertaining.

As discussed in Part III, Andrew Solomon's *The Noonday Demon* and Graham Greene's novels, especially *The Heart of the Matter* and *The Comedians*, were not merely useful but the difference between hard times and much harder.

Anyone wanting a beautiful look, in a more traditional cookbook format, at what ex-Soviet food can do should consult *Kachka: A Return to Russian Cooking*, by Bonnie Frumkin Morales, the chef and owner of the eponymous restaurant in Portland, Oregon, and *Mamushka: Recipes from Ukraine and Eastern Europe*, by Ukrainian-British chef Olia Hercules.

A WORD ABOUT THE
RECIPES IN THIS BOOK AND AN
INDEX OF DISHES

The recipe I got to redevelop and test most often for this book was humble pie. I bow low before those who write and test them for a living. It goes without saying that Oksana heads my list of stove magicians, but my thanks to her go far beyond recipes. I won't repeat here what I've taken a book to say, as it goes without saying that the responsibility for any errors and infelicities in the recipes rests only with me. (Though I do thank Karen Rush for saving me from the same in my phrasing, as well as Bonnie Frumkin Morales for her counsel.)

There's a false idea out there of ex-Soviet food as bland and heavy. It all depends on how you make it, but part of what I hoped to achieve with these recipes was to alert readers, and cooks, to items like pickled watermelon, marinated peppers, and pumpkin preserves; delicate soups, vegetarian stews, and seafood and lean-meat braises; and so much more that refuses the stereotype. This is village food, but it's rough only in the circumstances from which it must do its conjuring, which make the outcomes feel that much more miraculous.

Villagers figure out how to make a lot from a little, and one of the things that humbles me about the cooking profiled in this book is just how much flavor the women (always the women) responsible for it coax from nothing richer than water, though the Ukrainians sometimes braise in dairy; how versatile a set of dishes they create from the same stable of ingredients (I must have driven up the worldwide prices of garlic, onion, and dill while testing these recipes); their ability to "cover" a table in an hour. This resourcefulness, always unfussy and self-deprecating, makes me weak in the knees in a way to which the cooking of no contemporary celebrity chef can come close. The latter, to be sure, labors under some formidable restrictions herself, but the reasons for those restrictions—the nature of our commerce—are considerably less inspiring.

This is a cuisine more of pots than pans, of time rather than flavor-bomb spices, of ingenuity rather than flash. I hardly amounted to more than a well-meaning student in the five years I spent around it for this project, but it was enough to turn me into one more voice urging us to rethink how we eat, cook, and live.

INDEX OF DISHES

ABOUT THE AUTHOR

BORIS FISHMAN was born in Minsk, Belarus, and emigrated to the United States in 1988. His work has appeared in the *New Yorker*, the *New York Times Magazine*, the *New York Times Book Review*, *Travel + Leisure*, the *London Review of Books*, *New York* magazine, the *Wall Street Journal*, and the *Guardian*, among other publications. He is the author of the novels *A Replacement Life*, which was a *New York Times* Notable Book of the Year and won the VCU Cabell First Novelist Award and the American Library Association's Sophie Brody Medal, and *Don't Let My Baby Do Rodeo*, which was also a *New York Times* Notable Book of the Year. He teaches in Princeton University's Creative Writing Program and lives in New York City.